BUCKINGHAMS
PUL

Gene

DR EILEEN SCA

VOL. XXXI

RECOLLECTIONS OF
NINETEENTH-CENTURY BUCKINGHAMSHIRE

RECOLLECTIONS
OF
NINETEENTH-CENTURY
BUCKINGHAMSHIRE

Edited by
IAN TOPLIS
GEORGE CLARKE
IAN BECKETT
HUGH HANLEY

BUCKINGHAMSHIRE RECORD SOCIETY

No. 31

MCMXCVIII

British Library Cataloguing in Publication.
A catalogue record for this book is available from the British Library

Typeset by
Denham House, Yapton, West Sussex
and printed in Great Britain by
Progressive Printing (UK) Limited, Leigh-on-Sea, Essex

CONTENTS

LIST OF ILLUSTRATIONS

ACKNOWLEDGEMENTS

In preparing this volume I have incurred many debts of gratitude. My first is to the four editors who have given so generously of their time and scholarship. The second is to the owners and custodians of the documents printed and reproduced: the RIBA British Architectural Library, Manuscripts and Archives Collection (Sir George Gilbert Scott papers: Sc GGS/3); Cherry Hollingworth and Prue Winter, for the copy journal of Elizabeth George; Anthony Wethered, for the memoirs of Owen Peel Wethered; and the Buckinghamshire Record Office, for Oscar Blount's notebook. I wish also to offer my thanks to Mr. Roy Stephens, F.S.A., of the Leopard's Head Press, for his advice and assistance with the volume, as with so many other of the Society's publications.

E.S.

The Council of the Buckinghamshire Record Society wishes to express its gratitude to the Council of Management of the Marc Fitch Fund for its generous grant in aid of printing costs.

SIR GILBERT SCOTT'S
RECOLLECTIONS
OF
BUCKINGHAMSHIRE

SIR GILBERT SCOTT'S WORK IN BUCKINGHAMSHIRE

AKELEY — Rectory (now private house) 1840–41
AMERSHAM — Union Workhouse (now hospital) 1838–41
ASTON SANDFORD — The Manor (addition) 1867
        Manor Cottage c.1867
AYLESBURY — St. Mary's Church (restorations) 1849–51 and 1866–69
BLEDLOW — Holy Trinity Church (restoration) 1876–77
BUCKINGHAM — St. Peter and St. Paul's Church (restoration) 1862–84
        Chantry Chapel of St. John (restoration) 1875
        Union Workhouse (demolished 1970) 1836
        Old Gaol (extension) 1839
        Castle House (alterations) c.1837
CHESHAM — St. Mary's Church (restoration) 1868–69
        16 High Street 1833–34
DINTON — Vicarage (now private house) 1836–37
EAST CLAYDON — St. Mary's Church (restoration) 1871–72
EDGCOTT — St. Michael's Church (restoration) 1871–75
FLEET MARSTON — St. Mary's Church (restoration) 1868–69
GAWCOTT — Holy Trinity Church (restoration not executed)
GRANBOROUGH — St. John the Baptist's Church (restoration) 1880–81*
GREAT HORWOOD — St. James's Church (restoration) 1873–74
HILLESDEN — All Saints' Church (restoration) 1873–75
        Vicarage (now private house) 1870–71
IVER — St. Peter's Church (restoration) 1846–48
LATIMER — St. Mary Magdalene's Church (extension) 1867
MARLOW — Holy Trinity Church (now offices) 1852
MIDDLE CLAYDON — All Saints' Church (restoration) 1870
        Claydon House (alterations) 1871
OLNEY — St. Peter and St. Paul's Church (restoration) 1874–77
NEWPORT PAGNELL — Union Workhouse (unexecuted competition design) 18
PADBURY — The Church of the Nativity (restoration) 1882*
SAUNDERTON — Wycombe Union Workhouse (largely demolished) 1841–42
SHALSTONE — St. Edward's Church (restoration) 1861–62
STEEPLE CLAYDON — St. Michael's Church (restoration) 1875
STONY STRATFORD — St. Mary's Church (now community centre) 1864 and
        Vicarage (attached to the community centre) 1864
TAPLOW — St. Nicholas's Church (extended, since rebuilt) 1865
WESTON TURVILLE — Rectory (now private house) 1838
WING — All Saints' Church (restoration) 1850
WINSLOW — Union Workhouse (partly demolished) 1835–36

    * Designed by Scott but executed after his death.

SIR GILBERT SCOTT'S RECOLLECTIONS
OF
A BUCKINGHAMSHIRE BOYHOOD

Introduction

George Gilbert Scott (1811–78)[1] started to write his Recollections on 22 January 1864, when he was at the height of his powers and probably held in the greatest public esteem. At the age of 52 he had had an amazingly successful career, having risen from humble beginnings to become one of the most respected architects in mid-Victorian Britain. He had built nearly two hundred buildings and was engaged upon, or had completed, almost as many church restorations, including thirteen of the great medieval cathedrals of England. In 1860 he had been elected a Royal Academician, but the high point of his career came eight months before he embarked on his Recollections, when his design was selected for the Albert Memorial,[2] although work was not to start until a year later,[3] and, following years of frustration and anguish, his largest and most important building, the Foreign Office, was at last beginning to rise slowly above the ground.[4] After such furious activity, it seems that he could now allow himself the luxury of a pause to express his version of his achievements and disappointments, but in spite of such an impressive array of accomplishments, he was not a happy man. He had suddenly realized that this professional success had been achieved at high personal cost.

Every winter he was separated from his wife and younger children for several months, when they departed from their wind-swept old house at the top of Hampstead Heath,[5] to winter in the milder climate

---

1 *DNB.* Scott was knighted on 9 August 1872, and styled 'Sir Gilbert Scott'.

2 Stephen Bayley, *The Albert Memorial, the monument in its social and architectural context*, London, 1981, p.51.

3 The Greater London Council, Survey of London, xxviii. *The Museums Area of South Kensington and Westminster*, London, 1975, p.154.

4 Ian Toplis, *The Foreign Office, an architectural history*, London, 1987, p.[148].

5 Scott lived at The Grove, Hampstead, between 1856 and 1864 (R.I.B.A. Drawings Collection Catalogue, *The Scott Family*, Amersham, 1981, p.15). The house has since been renamed The Admiral's House and is in Admiral's Walk.

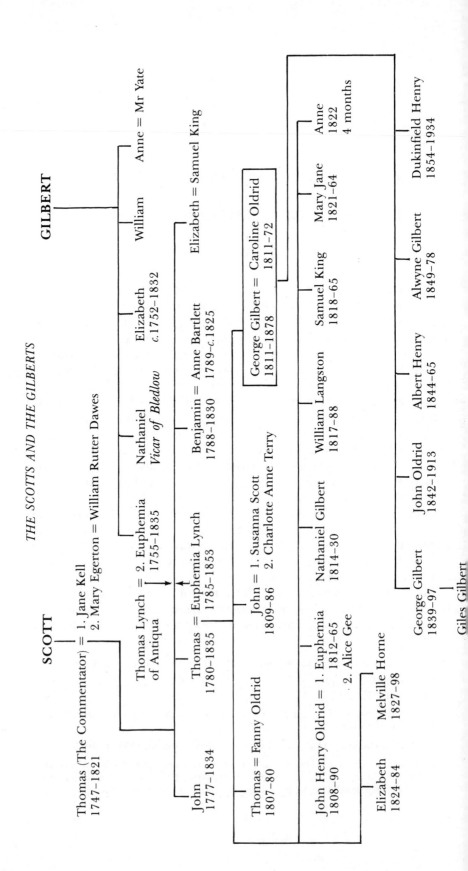

THE SCOTTS AND THE GILBERTS

BARTLETT

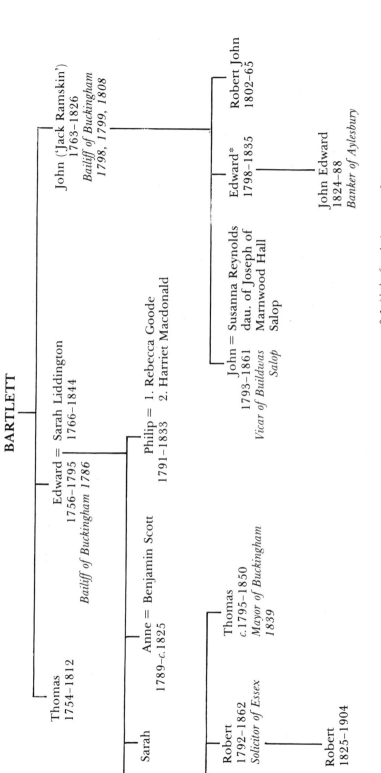

Thomas
1754–1812

Edward = Sarah Liddington
1756–1795   1766–1844
Bailiff of Buckingham 1786

John ('Jack Ramskin')
1763–1826
*Bailiff of Buckingham
1798, 1799, 1808*

Sarah
1789–c.1825

Anne = Benjamin Scott
1789–c.1825

Philip = 1. Rebecca Goode
1791–1833   2. Harriet Macdonald

John = Susanna Reynolds
1793–1861   dau. of Joseph of
Vicar of Buildwas   Marnwood Hall
Salop   Salop

Robert John
1802–65

Robert
1792–1862
Solicitor of Essex

Thomas
c.1795–1850
*Mayor of Buckingham
1839*

Edward*
1798–1835

Robert
1825–1904

John Edward
1824–88
Banker of Aylesbury

* Laid the foundation stone of Gawcott Church, January 1827

of St. Leonards,[6] enabling Scott to continue his hectic professional career in London uninterrupted by the family's activities. However, it was the death of his forty-two-year-old younger sister, Mary Jane Scott (1821–64), which made him realize the extent to which his practice had overwhelmed his personal life.

He had never been to see her since their mother died in 1853, and it was only in January 1864 when she was on her death-bed at Brighton, where she was being cared for by their physician brother, Samuel King Scott (1818–65), that Scott managed to find time to visit Mary. But it was all too late. She was hardly able to speak to him, and died on 22 January, before he could see her again. Scott was overcome with 'the most poignant grief' which led him to wonder 'where I have been & what I have been doing'.[7] His remorse was so great on the day of his sister's death, that he started, while travelling, to write down his memories of childhood and family, in an effort to console himself.[8]

Scott continued writing during the days following his sister's death, and by 20 March 1864 he had produced nearly 700 pages of close-packed pencil manuscript in two leather-bound notebooks. A year later he started again,[9] and continued into a third notebook. He then 'neglected this little chronicle now for nearly seven years',[10] re-starting on 10 March 1872, and carried on adding passages at irregular intervals until January 1878, only weeks before his death on 27 March 1878.

At the outset Scott states that his motives for setting down his Recollections are to communicate with his children, and 'to prevent misapprehension',[11] but it soon became clear to him that they should be published after his death. He was still smarting from his enforced climb-down over the style of the Foreign Office building, and it was essential for him to give his own version of the events which led to his humiliation at the hands of Lord Palmerston, and he concludes his account of that affair with the caveat that 'I must however privately warn my sons against publishing what may get them into ill odour with authorities'.[12]

---

6 III, p.93. (The location of quotations from the Recollections MS is indicated by the notebook number in Roman numerals, followed by the page number).

7 II, pp.318–[318a].

8 I, pp.74–6 (see page 26), II, pp.323–9.

9 II, p.329.

10 III, p.59.

11 I, p.2.

12 II, p.241.

Scott had four surviving sons at the time of his death, and it was the oldest, also George Gilbert Scott (1839–91),[13] who in a great act of filial duty, took up the task of editing and publishing the six hand-written notebooks which eventually comprised his father's Recollections. The younger Gilbert Scott was a busy architect in his own right, but he carried out his task with astonishing rapidity, as it was in the year after his father's death that Sampson Low published *Personal and Professional Recollections by the late Sir George Gilbert Scott, R.A. Edited by his Son, G. Gilbert Scott, F.S.A., Sometime Fellow of Jesus College, Cambridge.*[14]

The young Scott had very different ideas about religion and architecture to those of his father. He entered the Roman Catholic Church in 1880, and under the terms of his father's will he allowed the immense practice that had been built up, to go to his younger brother John Oldrid Scott (1841–1913),[15] who was more sympathetic to their father's form of architecture. Nevertheless, Gilbert junior loyally ensured that his father would appear in the best possible light in the published *Recollections*. He dutifully concealed the names of a well-known professor of architecture and a Member of Parliament, about whom his father was critical, he removed much repetitious material from his father's cathedral accounts, and omitted some emotional descriptions of family bereavements, as well as carrying out numerous minor alterations and omissions, with the intention of improving the work.

The six original manuscript notebooks have been deposited in the British Architectural Library, at the Royal Institute of British Architects, by Sir Gilbert Scott's great-grandson, the architect Richard Gilbert Scott, so it is now possible to compare the manuscript[16] with the published work and discover the extent of the revisions carried out by Scott's son. The omissions, which are restored in the following extract, include long passages about his native village, Gawcott, near Buckingham. However, Scott concedes that his memory of the sequence of more recent events is often defective, and certainly other evidence tends to confirm that the *Recollections* contain many factual inaccuracies, but when it comes to episodes in his childhood, he seems to be able to recall these with a convincing lucidity.

13 R.I.B.A., 1981, p.117.

14 A facsimile reproduction, with additional material (Introduction, Biographical Notes, and an Appendix of the main unpublished portions from the MS by Gavin Stamp, and an Index), has been published by Paul Watkins, Stamford, 1995.

15 R.I.B.A., 1981, p.88.

16 In R.I.B.A. MS Collection, Scott Family Papers Sc GGS/3.

Looking back over the forty years since his childhood, which saw some of the greatest changes over the face of Britain, he can be accused of indulging in the then popular yearning for the old days before industrialization altered the country for ever. He suggests an almost different world, where the old customs, dress and way of life, which had survived from time immemorial, were soon to be swept away. In fact, Scott would have known in 1864 that the industrial revolution had by-passed Gawcott, and even in Buckingham, apart from the coming of the railway in 1850,[17] there was little industrialization and agriculture remained the dominant activity in the area.

The following extract from Scott's Recollections finishes when he effectively departed from the rural delights of Gawcott in March 1827. It was then that his father took him to be articled to a London architect, James Edmeston (1791–1867),[18] whose office was off Bishopsgate Street. He lived with the Edmeston family at Homerton, and only returned to Gawcott for his longer holidays. From then on his professional career was centred on London. Scott's success owes much to the fact that his father decided to send him to London, where he was presented with opportunities which would have been denied to him had his father placed him with a provincial architect.

However, it was during his return visits to Gawcott that he acquired his interest in Gothic architecture, by studying the medieval churches in the area. Edmeston had no interest in this type of architecture, and, as Scott tells us at the end of the extract, thought that Scott was wasting his holidays in such studies. In the late 1820s hardly any architects built in the Gothic style, and Scott himself, as his early designs suggest, must have thought that the study of these old buildings was little more than a pleasurable pursuit.

It was also because of family connections in the Gawcott area that Scott obtained the first architectural commissions which formed the basis of his enormous practice. In 1833 his father was appointed Rector of Wappenham, just over the border in Northamptonshire, and had to build a new Rectory. Scott completed his articles in 1831, and the Wappenham Rectory became his first commission,[19] closely followed by a new house in Chesham High Street for his friend Henry Rumsey[20]

17 Julian Hunt, *Buckingham a Pictorial History*, Chichester, 1994, p.xv.

18 Howard Colvin, *A Biographical Dictionary of British Architects 1600–1840*, 3rd edn., London, 1995, p.331.

19 Nikolaus Pevsner, *Northamptonshire* in *The Buildings of England*, 2nd edn., Harmondsworth, 1973, p.442.

20 Nikolaus Pevsner and Elizabeth Williamson, *Buckinghamshire* in *The Buildings of England*, 2nd edn., London, 1994, p.242.

who had succeeded to his father's medical practice in 1833. Both houses are in the classical style of the day.

On 24 February 1835 Scott's father suddenly died,[21] which meant that his mother had to move out of her new Rectory, and he felt, perhaps without much justification,[22] that as the oldest unmarried son, it was incumbent upon him to support her and his five brothers and sisters all under the age of 17. At the time he was assisting an architect friend, Sampson Kempthorne (1809-73),[23] in his office in Regent Street to produce the drawings required for the massive union workhouse building programme needed to implement the Poor Law Amendment Act of 1834. He immediately wrote a circular 'to every influential friend of my fathers I could think of informing them that I had commenced practice & begging their patronage'.[24] He was soon rewarded for his enterprise by being appointed architect for Towcester, Brackley and Winslow Union houses in 1835, and for Northampton and Buckingham in 1836.

Scott's elder brother, John (1809-86)[25] had trained as a physician and had entered into partnership with William Stowe of Trolley Hall,[26] in Castle Street, Buckingham. Stowe had also taken on their brother, Samuel, as an apprentice at the time of their father's death, and although their oldest sister was still living at Gawcott, having married a cousin, John Henry Oldrid (1808-98)[27] (who became Curate of Gawcott after their father moved to Wappenham), Scott preferred to stay with his brothers in the grand Georgian house in Buckingham, while his workhouses were being built. He tells us that he has a 'lively recollection of the delight I used to feel' in Samuel's company.

> I used to arrive by Mail Cart at 7 in the morning just when he was getting up & sometimes on a cold morning turned into his bed to suppliment my night's rest which had been divided between — the top of the mail to Aylesbury a short bout of bed at a public-house there & what one could get balanced on the mail cart between there & Buckingham. These little visits were peculiarly

21 *DNB*.

22 Thomas Scott, ed., *The Chronicles of Eight Men* [an unpublished family history of the Thomas Scotts, in Buckinghamshire Local Studies Library, Aylesbury], *c*.1992, p.73.

23 Colvin, 1995, p.577.

24 I, pp.271-2.

25 *Alumni Cantabrigienses*, v, p.44.

26 Information from Mr Julian Hunt.

27 *Alumni Oxonienses 1715-1886*, p.1040.

delightful to me Sam was so jolley & cheery & his Master Mr Stowe so kind & took such an interest in my pursuits as well as in my favourite study at the time — geology — & afterwards my brother John & his wife Susan added to the pleasure of these little pop,[?] visits — so that they are quite among the bright spots of my memory.[28]

John Scott's wife died in 1840,[29] and soon after that he decided to give up medicine and enter the church. He graduated with distinction from Gonville and Caius College, Cambridge in 1846, and spent the rest of his life as a clergyman in the diocese of Ely, becoming an Honorary Canon of the cathedral in 1870. Samuel moved to London, where he was 'walking the Hospitals' in 1839, and in 1844 Oldrid left Gawcott for his home town of Boston, Lincolnshire, where he been appointed the Lecturer of St. Botolph's. So by the mid-1840s Scott's family connections with Buckinghamshire had disappeared.

He even failed to keep in touch with his aunt and uncle King, who lived at Latimer,[30] and with whom he stayed before he entered Edmeston's office. Perhaps the reason for this was partly because of the new church that he built at Flaunden for his uncle. The thirteenth-century church of Flaunden stood on the banks of the river Chess close to Latimer, but the village had grown up on a hill-top site a mile and a half to the north. Samuel King was the Chaplain of Latimer and also the Curate of Flaunden; so in 1838 having decided that it was necessary to provide a more convenient place of worship for the villagers of Flaunden, he commissioned his nephew to design his first church. This took the form of a single-cell building in brick and flint and is very typical of its date.[31] But as Scott's ideas on church architecture developed he became so embarrassed with its lack of sophistication that he took pains to avoid it, and he dismisses it as a 'poor barn' in his Recollections.[32] The Kings moved to Dartmouth,[33] where his uncle 'sustained severe pecuniary losses for his property'[34] and in 1852 they went to Jersey, where Samuel King died four years later.

28 III, pp.43–4.

29 Buried in Gawcott Churchyard. The headstone is inscribed: 'Susanna beloved wife of John Scott of Buckingham (Surgeon) and daughter of the late Rev. John Scott of Hull. She died October 1 1840 aged 27 years'.

30 See the genealogy of the Scott and Gilbert families.

31 Nikolaus Pevsner, *Hertfordshire* in *The Buildings of England*, 2nd edn., Harmondsworth, 1977, p.143.

32 I, p.296.

33 Thomas Scott, p.86.

34 II, p.319.

However, in the 1840s Scott was acquiring a reputation well beyond that of his native Buckinghamshire. He had won competitions for the Martyrs' Memorial at Oxford and a large orphanage at Wanstead in 1841, and in 1842 for the reconstruction of the important south London church of St. Giles, Camberwell, and Reading Gaol. In 1845 he capped these achievements by winning an international competition for the reconstruction of St. Nicholas's Church at Hamburg. This was one of largest churches in that city, and its construction continued throughout most of Scott's career. He had also carried out major church restorations at Stafford, Chesterfield and Boston.

But even as late as 1848 it was probably still Buckinghamshire which contained the greatest concentration of his less spectacular works. Here he had built four workhouses, at least four houses, extended Buckingham Gaol, and enlarged and refitted Iver Church. He had also inspected the tower of Aylesbury Church before 27 July 1848, when, 'being a native of Buckinghamshire', he was requested 'to attend the first annual meeting of the Architectural and Archaeological Society for that county, and to read a paper'.[35] This was on church restoration, and Scott later used it as the main part of his first book: *A Plea for the Faithful Restoration of our Ancient Churches*.

The direct outcome of the lecture was that Scott seems to have secured the commission to restore St. Mary's, Aylesbury. After sufficient funds were raised considerable structural improvements were carried out between 1849 and 1851, followed by another restoration campaign between 1866 and 1869.[36] As a probable indirect result of his lecture and his work on Aylesbury Church, Scott carried out eighteen further restorations in the county, of which the largest, the church of St. Peter and St. Paul at Buckingham, was not completed until after his death. He also built two new churches in Buckinghamshire during this period.

When he started his Recollections just after the death of his sister in January 1864, Scott clearly wanted to set down his fond memories of their native county. But he also acknowledges that the old churches of Buckinghamshire first awakened his interest in medieval architecture, which was to become his great passion, and that his first architectural opportunities, which led to his fame and fortune, came from his friends and contacts in the county.

35 George Gilbert Scott, *A Plea for the Faithful Restoration of our Ancient Churches*, London, 1850, p.[i].

36 Geoff Brandwood, ' "A Disgrace to the Town": Aylesbury Church and its Restoration by Gilbert Scott', *Records of Buckinghamshire*, xxxiv, 1992, pp.1–10.

Textual Note

I am very grateful to the RIBA British Architectural Library for allowing me to quote the following extract from the first of Scott's Recollections notebooks in its possession (Manuscripts and Archives Collection: Sir George Gilbert Scott Papers (Sc GGS/3)). The extract has been transcribed directly from the original manuscript, interfering minimally with the capitalization and punctuation, and including the errors of the original manuscript. It covers his life up to 1827 when he went to London to become an architect. The first 6,500 words (to page 26), were written on the day that his sister died, and he continued to write at the rate of more than 1,000 words a day, for the next seven weeks, until he had completed more than two thirds of the finished work. The quality of the writing, even before editing, and the speed with which he produced the narrative, in the midst of his professional commitments, are a clear demonstration of Scott's exceptional energy and his ability to express himself rapidly in a clear and ordered manner. His handwriting varies considerably, presumably indicating whether he was writing at a desk or when travelling, and some words appear to have been subsequently overwritten in an attempt to make them more legible.

The oblique strokes and numbers in the margin in this edition indicate the start of pages in the manuscript.

Ian Toplis

NOTEBOOK I[1]

Personal & Professional Recollections

My motive in jotting down the following miscellaneous recollections is this: that a man's Children have no means whatever of getting at the particulars of his life up to the time when their own observation & memory begins to avail them, and that are peculiarly apt to receive mistaken impressions and that it is consequently, as it appears to me, the duty of every one who has appeared much before the public to supply this defect from his own memory & thus / prevent misapprehension.   2

Birth family &c

I was born at the Parsonage House[2] at Gawcott near Buckingham on July 13th. 1811. Though My father, however like myself was born in Bucks,[3] I hardly feel that I have in reality any very direct connection with that County, clergymen being so much birds of passage that the place of their children's birth seems little more than a matter of chance.

My Grandfather, the Revd Thos. Scott[4] so well known by his commentary on the Bible & other works, was / a native of Lincolnshire   3 where his father was a considerable agriculturist. I have not been able to ascertain whether the latter was a native of that county, but as I learn that his eldest son took some pains to disclaim connexion with a family of the same name in his neighbourhood, I believe such was not the case. He (the father of My Grandfather) was born in the time of K William III and was connected I find by marriage with the Kelsalls of

---

1 RIBA: British Architectural Library: Manuscripts and Archives Collection: Sir George Gilbert Scott Papers (Sc GGS/3).

2 Scott's birthplace was demolished *c*.1950. It stood to the west of the church on the site of the existing former rectory.

3 Scott's father, Thomas Scott (1780–1835), was born at Weston Underwood (*DNB*).

4 *The Commentator* (1747–1821) between 1788 and 1792 produced a six-volume Commentary on the Bible in weekly numbers (*DNB*). On 5 December 1774, at Gayhurst, he married his first wife and Scott's grandmother, Jane Kell (Gayhurst Parish Register). She had been the housekeeper to the Wrighte family at Gayhurst (John Scott, *The Life of the Rev. Thomas Scott*, 3rd edn., London, 1822, p.67).

Kelsall in Cheshire the representative of which family was at that time Vicar of Boston (see Gwillims heraldry[5]) & also with the Wayets a very

4   respectable county family. / From the arms however made use of by My Grandfathers family I gather that they must have sprung from the Scotts of Scotts Hall in Kent who left Scotland I think in the 13th Century.

[Rest of page blank]

5   .   *[Blank page]*

6   My Mothers family were West Indian. Of the family of her father Dr. Lynch of the Island of Antigua, I know but little but her maternal grandfather was the possessor of an at that time a valuable estate known as "Gilberts Estate".

This family settled at a very early date in Antigua, previous to which they had resided in Devonshire one of their representatives being Sir Humprey Gilbert half Brother & companion in arms of Sir Walter Rayligh /

7   My Great Grandfather, Nathaniel Gilbert, appears to have been a most excellent man. Living in a century of extreme deadness in religious matters, he was roused to a sense of the shortcomings of his age in this respect either by the preaching or by the writings of Wesley and consequently joined the Wesleyians at a time when they were not considered as severed from the Church of England. At his request Wesley sent over (I believe) to Antigua some ministers of his society to instruct the negroes &c — but though the whole family joined the new society it is clear that Mr. Gilbert did not consider himself otherwise

8   than a Member of the Church / of England for he brought up his eldest son as a clergyman. Nor do I recollect even a hint of those members of the family who were living during My Childhood (including My Grandmother and a Great Aunt Miss Elizabeth Gilbert) being other than church people though the last-named, especially, treasured up most affectionately her personal recollections of John Wesley himself and retained through life a strong sympathy with his followers.

9   This family were indirectly connected with several / Good families in England

Give here the pedigee by which they are connected with Lord Northampton Sir — Abdy — The Gordons of Stocks & several other families of position. (Sir Edward Colebrook

5 John Guillim (1565–1621(*DNB*)) published *A Display of Heraldrie* in 1611. It was probably one of the later editions, such as that of 1726, to which Scott was referring.

told me that he was connected with the Gilberts & that Sir —
Le Marchant was — as also Lady Seymour (Revd. Sir J.
Seymours lady)
In some way also Sir George Grey

[*Rest of page blank*]

My Father, The Revd Thomas Scott, was the second Son of the well 10
known commentator. He was born at Weston Underwood in Bucks
during the short period of My Grandfathers residence as curate of that
village, about 1780. He about that time served several churches in that
district & the next year removed to that of Olney, the former curate
John Newton was his intimate friend & where he was brought a good
deal in contact with and the poet Cowper who was his next door
neighbour. I well recollect an old man occasionally calling on us at
Gawcott who had known my grandfather at that early period of his
clerical life. /

My Native Village   11

The following notice of My native village and of some of its
inhabitants, its customs &c I give merely as a memento of times in
which, though not long passed, there remained much more of old
customs & manners than has, probably, survived to the present
day.
Gawcott is a Hamlet of & 1½ mile from Buckingham. It had had a
chapel in former times, as is proved by a field retaining the name of
"Chapel Close" and shewing marks of ancient Building. How long
this had ceased to exist I do not know, probably for some / centuries.   12
The absence of a church had its natural consequence of producing a
partly heathenish & partly dissenting population. The former of these
evils, and perhaps partially the latter, was so much felt by one of its
inhabitants, that he determined on founding a church in his native
village. This excellent person, one John West,[6] was a man of the
humblest origin who had made what to him was a considerable fortune
by the trade of a "Lace buyer", that is to say by acting as Middle man
between the poor Lace maker & the / trader. The difficulties he met   13
with in carrying out his generous project were considerable & I have
often heard My father say that after the Church was built he had the
greatest difficulty in getting it consecrated & that he at last sent a
message to the Bishop (Tomline of Lincoln)[7] in these words "tell the

6 West's memorial tablet was re-erected in the new church.

7 Sir George Pretyman Tomline (1750–1827), Bishop of Lincoln and Dean of St.
Paul's 1787, Bishop of Winchester 1820 (*DNB*).

Bishop that if he won't consecrate it I'll give it to the dissenters" — a message which had the desired effect. This church or chapel, erected 14 during the first / years of the present century, was perhaps as absurdly unecclesiastical a structure as could be conceived. Enclosed between four walls forming a short wide oblong, it had a roof sloping all ways crowned by a belfry such as one sees over the stables of a country home. The pulpit occupied the middle of the south side the pews facing it from the North the East & the West and a gallery occupying the north side, in the centre of which were perched the singers and the band of 15 Clarinets Bass Viols &c. / by which their performances were accompanied.

The font I well recollect was a washhand stand with a white basin!

The Advowson was placed in the hands of five trustees being incumbents of parishes in the neighbourhood and belonging to the then very scarce, Evangelical party & My father was the first "Perpetual Curate". At first there was no parsonage & he lived for a time in the Vicarage at Buckingham, the vicar being non resident & there My two 16 eldest Brothers (& one who died in infancy) were born. / He soon, however, raised funds for the erection of a parsonage home which, as he had a fancy for planning, he designed himself & I must not find fault with My native house. The house was close to the church.

My earliest recollections of the Church, bear upon the digging of the vault for the founder and My sitting in the gallery at his funeral & seeing it pass the opposite windows. This was in 1814 so that it is a pretty 17 youthful remin / iscence yet, though it is My earliest, it does not come to me otherwise than any other & does not seem by any means like a *beginning* shewing that, though we forget what happened in my early childhood we nevertheless have no feeling of being *incapable* of observing & remembering it. As, for instance I can recollect who dug the vault & who took me to church & have a full sense of being conscious of who they said Mr West was & the house he had lived in — though I was but 3 years old. /

18   The inhabitants of Gawcott were a very quaint race. I recollect My father saying that when he first went there to reconnoitre he found the road to it rendered impassable by a large hole dug across it in which the inhabitants were engaged in baiting a badger; a promising prelude to an Evangelical Ministry among them! However he succeeded in bringing the place in due time into a more seemly state as to externals 19 though the old leaven remained / and a certain amount of poaching & other forms of rural blackguardism, though there grew up amongst all this a good proportion of really excellent people, some of whom had at one time belonged to the previously more normal type.

The neighbourhood of Buckingham is by no means picturesque. It is situated geologically about the junction of the Oxford clay with the lower oolite — and though in other districts the latter rises into high and picturesque hills, such is not the case with this portion of its / course. It is a plain slightly undulated agricultural country, partly arable **20** but mainly devoted to dairy farming, butter being the only produce for which it is famous. It is (or rather *was*) here & there well wooded with oak — is everywhere enclosed[8] — with a good deal of hedgerow timber sadly disfigured by lopping and usually some more ornamental timber around the villages. The latter usually retained some traces of the old "Great-house" the residence of the old proprietor who had generally succumbed / to the all-absorbing influence of a single **21** family, orginally one of their own — the Squire-race, but then the Marquis's & subsequently the Dukes of Buckingham who lorded it over the county from their semi-regal seat of Stowe, some four miles from My own humble Village.

An unpicturesque country denuded of its natural aristocracy is no doubt very dull and unattractive, yet it possesses some interest in the natural & quaint character of its inhabitants, and in its retentiveness of old customs. I have never met with so many / odd, eccentric characters **22** as in my native village, nor do I suppose that old customs were even then better kept up in many other districts; whether they are so still I know not.

The cottages were usually of the old thatched type of rough stone or timber & plaster. The one sitting-room, known as *"the house"* had the old-fashioned chimney corner in the sides of which the Master & Mistress of the family sat with the wood fire placed upon bars & bricks on the floor between them. In the ample chimney over their heads hung the bacon for the benefit of the smoke & below it all sorts of utensils /for **23** which dryness was to be desired & high over head as they sat there the occupants could see the sky through the vertical smoke shaft. The room was paved with unshapen slabs of stone from the neighbouring quarry or "stone-pit" and the oaken floor timbers shewed over head though hardly sufficiently & for a tall man to feel his head to be safe. From these timbers to the floor there was (where babies were to be found) a vertical post which revolved on its central point & from which projected an arm of wood with a circular ring or hoop at its end so contrived / as to open & shut and by passing round the babys body the **24** little thing could run round & round while its Mother was busied at household work or at the lace-pillow. The bedroom arrangements I

8 Prebend End with Gawcott Enclosure Act of 1801 (J. Hunt, *Buckingham*, pp.xiv, 29).

do not recollect but I do not think they were so defective as those we now so often hear of, and the generality of cottages had a pretty ample garden.

[*in the margin*]:

In the corner of the "parlour" was usually a smart cupboard called a "bofette" (give a quotation from Cowper about it).

The farmers I believe did not live so very differently as to general forms
25 from the cottagers the difference lying chiefly in the very / substantial distinction between abundance & scantiness of fare. They usually lived in the "House" or Kitchen, though they (and indeed some of the cottagers) had "parlours" which were only used when they had company. I have heard My father say that Mr. West the founder of the Church lived in the same room with his servants all helping themselves at dinner from a common dish placed in the middle of the round table.

I will briefly enumerate a few of the old customs of the district which
26 I can / recollect, beginning with Christmas.

Besides the usual carol singers and hymn singers who went from house to house I recollect we were always visited by a *piper* a little before Xmas. This man played an instrument which few persons of the younger generation, perhaps, know. I mean "the pipe and tabour" which consisted of a small flat drum hung by a leather thong to the end of a wooden pipe, the drum being beaten with one hand while the pipe
27 was played with the other / making a rude but merry kind of music — (one may see a player on this instrument quaintly carved in sculpture of the 13th. century on the tower at Higham Ferrers) The most characteristic, however, of Christmas observations was "Mumming". The "Mummers" came from house to house after dark in quaint dresses and, if admitted, performed the old play of "Father Christmas"

I seldom happened to see this performance (perhaps but *once*) as
28 My father had no great love for them, / and certainly what I remember of it is not of an elevated kind. The characters I remember are "Father Christmas", a Turkish Knight, Prince Arthur, St George Bealzibub, and a doctor. Father Xmas enters with a besom sweeping snow, with the sage remark

"Here comes old F.C.
Welcome or welcome not
And let old F.C.
Never be forgot"

The Turkish Knights remarks are about equally intellectual
"Here come I, the Turkish Knight /
29   Come from Turkish land to fight

Prince Arthur makes his debut as follows

"Here am I, P.A. Sword in hand
and who's the man that dares
bold bid me stand?
I'll cut him up as small as flies
And send him to the cook shops to
make mince pies.
Mince pies hot mince pies cold"
&c & as usual /

St. George informs us "I slewth the dragon with great strength and   **30**
won the King of Egypt's daughter".

I do not recollect any I heard remark of Belsebub, who by the bye
wore a very sable dress and carried a blown bladder at the end of a
stick; but the doctor on his introduction to aid the fallen Knight
romantically in forms the audience

"All diseases I very well know
"particularly the Mulligubs in the great tree" /

This is all I remember and is perhaps much more than is worth   **31**
remembering of these relics of the I [?] acted mysteries of the Middle
Ages. Some further particulars, with variations may be found in Miss
Baker's Northamptonshire Glossary.[9]

St Valentines day was kept not by letter-writing but by all the Boys &
girls in the Village going together from house to house crying "Good
morrow morrow Valentine" in response to which cry they expected / a   **32**
scramble of Ginger-bread nuts.

Easter was celebrated by fiddling and in our case this was for the
most part performed by one "Jemmy" usually called "King of the
Gipseys". This specimen of the Gipsey race was a little old man almost
as black as a negro. I have seen him fiddle, dance and sing all at once
when he was upwards of 100 years old. He lived I think chiefly in
Oxfordshire in the lanes & commons about Bicester / and shared his   **33**
sovereignty with his Consort called "fair Nancy" from her not being
of Gipsey blood. I have heard that they had sons of 70 or 80 years
old.

May day was a great festival though the May pole & the Queen of the
May had become obsolete. It was observed by the girls by carrying
about garlands and by the boys by dressing one of their number in
branches of box so as to look like a bush and then chairing him astride
of two "white / wands" or peeled willow poles laid cross-wise on two   **34**
boys shoulders. The multitude surrounding him with "white wands".

9 Anne Elizabeth Baker produced a *Glossary of Northamptonshire Words and Phrases* in
   two vols. in 1854.

This boy was called the "Bumbailie" and the whole was a purely local observance in imitation of the chairing on the same day of the Baliff or Mayor of Buckingham.

But the most amusing celebration was that of Whitsuntide. This was
35   by means of the "Whitsun Morris Dancers". / I suppose that this custom is not obsolete, but as it is known now to comparitively few, I will describe it as well as I am able.

The Morris dancers were young men perhaps about a dozen in number. They were stripped of their coats & waistcoats & wore clean white shirts, white stockings & light coloured knee breeches. They were gaily decorated with bunches of long flying bright-coloured ribbons
36   on their hats & all parts of the person & to their legs / were attached large patches of coloured cloth covered all over with little brass bells. In their hands were short "white wands" & they danced to the "pipe and tabour". In the dance each two youths always faced each other & holding their wands by both hands near the middle they contrived as they danced to strike the ends of them together so as to keep time to the tune. I well remember My intense admiration of their skill. The noise /
37   of the dozen wands keeping time with the tabour and of the jingling bells also roughly following the tune added to the lively antics of the Dancers had a most merry & exhilerating effect. One character however I have not yet mentioned — I mean the "Fool". This worthy seemed to have the liberty of dressing as he liked, for, while a perfect uniformity was observed by the others, he seemed to change his costume from year to year. For the most part, however, he was dressed most
38   fantastically / in many-coloured rags and a head-dress betokening his calling. He carried a wand, suspended to the end of which by a long thong was an inflated bladder, which he kept continually bringing down with telling force upon the heads of the spectators which he joined in a ludicrous mimicry of the dance mingled with extemporized buffooneries of his own. /
39   It may readily be imagined that this shew had great attractions for children & that we heard with grim dissent the discouragements offered to the performances by My father who opposed them as productive of drunkenness.

The other great observance was the village feast. This in our own village was of no ancient date being commemorative of the consecration of old John Wests Church. Nor can I say much in its favour being
40   marked by little else / than debauchery. In this observance My Father was a deadly foe & I recollect on the Sunday night he used to perambulate the Village in person to put a stop to the preparation of the day.

One more odd custom I will mention: this is what is called, in local parlance "low-belling" or *loud bellowing* and was the conventional form of reprobation at the beating of a wife by her husband. When such a misdemean / our had taken place a "low belling" was proclaimed **41** and in the evening all the boys in the village assembled, armed with everything which would make a noise. The majority bore cows horns which they blew with almost continuous & most sonorous blasts; Others carried tin pots & kettles which they beat vehemently with sticks, others two & two carried a dripping pan which they used as a kettle drum & sometimes an old pensioner would join them with his shrill fife. This rough band walked three times / through the whole **42** length of the Village, making the most tremendous noise one can fancy, & stopping each time at the door of the offender before which they threw down a large heap of chaff, in token of his having been engaged in *threshing* — a memento of his disgrace which it took some days to obliterate.

In the midst of this funny population we lived almost as a stranger colony. My Father was by education a Londoner and My Mother had also been educated in London though a West-Indian, as also were / my **43** Grandmother and Great Aunt who resided with us, while our isolation was rather increased by My Father taking seven or eight pupils who came from all parts of the Kingdom and by our mixing very little indeed in local society, though we had numerous friends at a distance who occasionally visted us. Our few local friends lived in the neighbouring town of Buckingham and now & then a clergyman was admitted to our / acquaintance, most of them shunning us **44** evangelicals or as they were then called "Methodists". I recollect a Head of an Oxford college who had a living in our neighbourhood and who had taken under his patronage a farmers son who shewed literary talent (and who is now an Archdeacon) turning upon him and refusing to sign his testimonials for Priests orders because he had once preached for My Father. The same learned Doctor is said while being helped home to his College after too deeply imbibing to / have **45** exclaimed to his supporters "All this I do to purge the College from the stain of *Methodism*" —

[*The published work has an extract here from Notebook IV, pp.266–58 (the pagination has been reversed).*]

My Father and Mother were among the most admirable people I have ever met with, and the most affectionate of couples. Their Marriage was purely a love match, though strengthened ever by the ties of the most earnest piety. They had become acquainted shortly after My Grandfather had taken the living of Aston Sandford, near to which is the semi-romantic / village of Bledlow on the edge of the **46** Chilterns where My Mothers uncle The Revd. Nathanial Gilbert was

Rector. My Mother having lost her father at a very early age had been brought by her Mother & Aunt to England to be educated, and had been brought up cheifly in London. As also had My Father though they were not acquainted till they met at one of these neighbouring
47 Rectories in Bucks. They were married[10] in the beautiful / church of Bledlow and such was the simplicity of Manners in that county & time that "Oh tell it not in Gath!" — My father took his wife home seated behind him on a pillion & that from the house of the proprietor of a Considerable West India estate a man of no mean connexions and a Buckinghamshire Rector!

This simplicity; however, suited their Means which were very slender.

My parents were both of what may be called "well-bred" — both by /
48 nature and training "gentlefolk" I have often witnessed with admiring wonder My fathers gentleman-like address when he met those of a higher station, — so superior to what we young villagers could ever hope to attain. He was a Man of most popular & winning manner and of a remarkably commanding aspect so that, while he felt at home with
49 persons / of any rank, he could at once quell almost with his eye the most obstreporous parishioner, and even insane persons under the most violent paroxysms would yield to him without resistance.

My Mother had been beautiful in her youth and when I first remember her was a very noble & commanding person. Somewhat taller than My father with an aquiline nose, piercing though soft dark,
50 hazel eyes and black hair. She was a most commanding / person. & though of an intensely affectionate disposition, devoted to her husband her family & the parish.

Were it not for such parents, & to our having been kept aloof from the rough society of the place and brought in contact with strangers from My father taking pupils I cannot conceive of what degree of rusticity we should have reached! As it was, we all came out into the world, certainly
51 somewhat ungarnished, / but rather *plain* than *rustic*. Our parents always tried to impress upon us the *feelings* of Gentlemen in a degree only second to their endeavours to train us up religiously.

Our village, as I have already said, was full of odd quaint characters. I will describe a few of them. To begin with the Farmers. Our great farmer was Mr Law. He cultivated two large farms one which he rented & the
52 other his own freehold. / We held him, and I believe rightly, to be very rich he was nephew & executor to the founder of the church & from him my father received the scanty endowment. He was a short burly man of no great talent but a very worthy good natured person — he

10 Scott's parents were married on 25 March 1806 (Bledlow Parish Register).

was perpetual church warden & always lined the plate he held at the church doors after charity sermons with a one pound note with which now obsolete form of money (which / has been called from its greasiness **53** "*filthy lucre*") his breeches pockets were always well filled. Then there was old Zachary Meads, a sulky obtuse old giant who was never seen at church or ever expected to do anything good. Next there was Benjamin Warr a splendid old yeoman who with his sturdy wife and a family of 20 children (most of the sons 6 ft high)/ made a fair show in one of our **54** square pews — Then, again, John Walker (of Lenborough, an allied hamlet)[11] a downright thoroughly excellent specimen of an English Farmer; a man of sterling sense honour and excellence in every way — by the bye he is but just dead (Janry 1864) & I saw his Mourning card but yesterday) he has since our day / been (I think more than once) **55** Mayor of Buckingham. He was our best singer our best Yeomanry Cavalier, our best dairy man; our most strong-headed & right-minded parishioner & withall a really christian man. The other farmers had nothing very marked which merits notice. The farmers used to dress much more in the true John Bull style than they do now Their dress was a long frock coat a very long waist / coat divided at the bottom **56** below the buttons & reaching over the hips, corderoy knee breeches &, when not top-booted, they wore shoes with large buckles. They usually carried a gun & were accompanied by a sporting dog.

Among the labourers we had many very excellent men men of real piety & worth though I need not describe them individually. I may mention that, so far as I can recollect, these men were all decently educated though how this came about / I do not know; indeed, oddly **57** enough, it seems to me that inability to read was less frequent 40 years ago among these rustic labourers than it is now in the immediate neighbourhood of London. In our time we had sunday Schools and there was a village Schoolmaster who kept school on his own account, but no parish school excepting a national School at Buckingham. The females were all employed in lace-making which was commenced so early as to leave little / time for schooling, yet I fancy they could very **58** generally read. and were by no means ignorant of bible history & of general religious knowledge.

Among the more eccentric inhabitants I may mention a man of the name of Walker surnamed "Tom O' Gawcott" a superannuated prize fighter whose great boast was that he would never "darken the doors of Jack West's church," but in his old age he relented and died / a truly **59** religious character. One of our village characters was a Mrs. Warr who

11 John Walker was born in Gawcott, farmed 187 acres and employed 10 labourers (Census 1851). He was Mayor of Buckingham in 1851 (D. J. Elliott, *Buckingham, the Loyal and Ancient Borough*, Chichester, 1975, p.244).

kept a shop for "coffee tea tobacco & snuff" opposite our churchyard. As in our childish days we were not allowed to go into the village alone "Mother Warr" as We called her carried on a great trade with us in lollypops, &c. by answering our call across the road from the church

60   yard. A brook ran through the village street and she / or her old husband had placed stepping stones to aid her passage to & fro. It was quite a picture to see her in her quaint old-fashioned dress rise at our call from her lace pillow, & step nimbly across the brook with her sweet wares. She wore a high cap, with her hair brushed-vertically from her

61   forehead, her stay-laces showing in front & her gown / divided at the waist & gathered up in a bundle behind, shewing a stiff glazed blue petticoat in front. She had short sleeves hanging loosely from the elbows & large buckles to her shoes — & on Sundays added long silk gloves a black Mantilla edged with lace & a bonnet of antique cut.

62   While personally she was tall and dignified as became her costume / & in mind as strong as you please and by no means disposed to be trifled with, though otherwise condescending & benignant. Her husband surnamed "Old Baccy" was equally antique though by no means her equal in other ways.

Under the same roof with this pristine couple lived two old women — sisters respectively to Mrs & Mr Warr. The former "Molly Adams". I think I never saw, though of this I am uncertain for she was "bedridden"

63   & had been so for years yet I seem to have known her perhaps for she was / the special pet of my excellent old Aunt Gilbert who was her constant and untiring visitor and religious instructor and I believe the poor woman was worthy of her care and was a truly pious person. The other old woman was called "Molly Warr", and if one "Molly" had become *unknown* through her maladies then the other amply made up for it through hers. My Village was as eccentric in its diseases as in its other conditions — two of its inhabitants, both named Warr, suffered from

64   the strangest form of madness & poor old Molly was one of them. / I have heard that She and two others, while girls, had been seized with "St Vitus' dance" and were kept shut up together in the same room where at certain hours, when St. Vitus was rampant, they commenced dancing till the room was not high enough for their capers. At this particular stage in their disorder the charming influence of the fiddle as played by a boy was prescribed which had the effect of reducing the

65   more active form of the attack but in the case of poor Molly / left matters not much the better, for ever afterwards she had two fits of raving madness in the 24 hours at noon & at Midnight. During eleven hours she was quiet and in offensive though the subject to her neighbours of a strange Mysterious Awe, and this was perhaps one of the hinderances to our venturing to the shop for our lollipops though when we did so she occasionally served us herself to our intensest horror, for our dread of

her was beyond description even during her lucid intervals of eleven hours. When, however, / the hated mendronal hour approached, **66** things assumed a more serious form. She began to walk up & down the room making a strange grunting sound at every step which constantly increased in loudness. At a certain stage in the paroxism, which she well knew, for I believe she was as concious as any body else, she went out into the garden behind the house & walked up & down; her walk gradually increasing to a run and her little groans / to the most violent **67** screaming which could be heard throughout the village; but which, after the clock struck twelve, subsided by degrees corresponding with their rise — when she returned, by day to the chimmney corner, and by night to her bed into which (I have it on the evidence of "Molly Adams" given through my aunt Gilbert) she vaulted through mid air head first & subsided to rest.

The other subject of madness was a young man of the same name — of a superior order in our village society, / — a noble person, tall, herculean, **68** & of strong intellect. he was suddenly seized with madness not like that of his poor old namesake but coming at accidental intervals when his cries, like hens, were audible through out the village — his friends built a bedroom expressly for him with a window out of reach & he of his own choice went to bed every night with a chain to ankle lest an attack should come on. During the intervals, / which were long, he was **69** the most excellent of men, he died under one of these strange attacks, during riegn of which it took four strong men to hold him though I recollect My father who was attacked by him resisting him single handed & reducing him to quiescence. His brother is now the leading man in the village and a most excellent person.

One of the two suffers from St Vitus' dance was known amongst us was "Nanny White". / The success of the boy fiddler had in her case **70** been perfect, and she had attained a good old age not in strong health for she was, — poor old lady, — tremulous through tendency to palsy. I call her a "lady" advisedly, because she was what one may term a *peasant-lady*. She was a person of earnest piety and of admirable conduct, — an aristocrat among the peasantry. Her income was £30 a year but she lived almost *in state*. We went as / children once a year to drink tea **71** with her (which was more than we were allowed to do with any of the farmers but good John Walker). When she received us with great dignity and — dressed in her best old-fashioned clothes, the good little old lady sat smiling and shaking in her arm chair while her waiting maid handed round the tea & cake. We all sat round on old high backed chairs with twisted pillars & cane backs which, by the bye, she had bought at the sale of furniture of the / latest despoiled of the **72** neighbouring great houses (that at Hillesden which I shall mention anon). We sat on that occasion, for the nonce, in her parlour had in the

"*House*" through which it was approached was the old dresser under which was a series of copper cauldrons of gradually diminishing sizes presenting their highly polished interiors to the spectator. This good old woman some years after, when My father had to rebuild his
73   Church made out of / her savings a really handsome subscription as "a friend" no one but my father & mother knowing whence it came till after her death. I recollect she had at one time for her maid and companion a young person named "Betsy Scott" I wish I knew enough of her to sketch her Character. She was a *lusus naturae* in intellect & piety & after her death (of consumption) My father wrote a memoir of her embodying many letters & papers of her writing, some, I think in poetry. I well recollect his applying to her the quotation from Gray —

    "Full many a gem" &c /

74   Good old benignment Nanny White! how willingly would I give up any fame or advantage I have attained in subsequent life to share your blessed lot among the saints above! I wonder whether my sweet sister Mary Jane who has this day been called to her rest (Jany 22. 1864) recollects her. She too is now a blessed saint — Never did I know a character so faultless. This morning at 6 she made signs (being nearly
75   speechless) that she wanted to write and a slate being / given to her, wrote on it in a strong steady hand "Be of good cheer thy sins be forgiven thee" —

    Oh "if the religious scarcely be saved where shall the ungodly & the sinner appear?" if the most blameless of the human race feel their sins such a burden what must those feel who live of carelessness?

    Oh Lord Jesus Christ make us all to be numbered with thy saints in Glory Everlasting!
76   I have been cheering my self today / after the death of my dear sister while travelling by writing the above reminiscence which I know she would have enjoyed to do herself, but grief *will return* & I must stop.

A sad catastropie happened at Poor "Mother Warr's" house the latter part of my residence at Gawcott. A young man chanced to go to a fair at Warwick & in passing a funeral there, felt a strange sensation come over him with a conviction that he had caught an infectious disorder.
77   On returning to Gawcott he was seized with Smallpox and / died in a few days. My father buried him secretly by lantern light omitting the tolling of the Bell to avoid attracting spectators That night poor old crazy Molly Warr remarked "how unkid it were to hear the bell a tolling as she sat in the chimmney corner" & on being informed that the bell

had not tolled she said at once that her time was come for she heard
the bell in the chimmney stack "as plain as plain". She was taken ill at
once and poor bedridden Molly Adams too & both died without any
distinctive symtims to mark the disease. After their funerals "Mother
Warr" / began to feel queer but her pride rebelled against saying so for **78**
she had been very irate at a suggestion that the old women had died of
smallpox; a suspicion which was calculated to hurt the shop. She said
nothing and when a rash appeared on her arms she put on her long gloves
— till at last on falling down from the giddiness which accompanies
the disease her son who carried her to bed found out what was the matter,
/ but it was not made known till Mother, father & son were all laid up **79**
together and then no one could be found to nurse them — fortunately
the old man who had been a "Calf-man" and had consequently had
the Cowpox — &, being less ill than the others, he was able to help
them & they all recovered, though sadly to the disfigurement of the
Young man who had been a handsome fellow.

Two of our favourite village characters were / a half cracked man & a **80**
semi-Simpleton The one known as "Cracky Meads" & the other as
"Tailor King".

"Cracky Meads" was brother to farmer Zachary Meads already
mentioned. He had been a soldier; and on his return from campaining
had found that Old Zachary had inflicted on him a very base injury
which drove the poor fellow out of his mind. After this his great desire
was to build himself a house with his own unaided hands / on a piece of **81**
waste ground by a road side. He made many beginnings but what he built
in the day the young men of the village pulled down at night.[12] At length,
however, his perseverance and active defence of his work prevailed,
and he succeeded in completing a very tolerable batchelors cottage —
and enclosed a long piece of waste as a garden which he successfully
cultivated & with the help of his pension lived pretty comfortably. He
was when unexcited quiet sullen & inoffensive but it took only a little
skilfully / directed conversation to stir him up tremendously in different **82**
ways. his most interesting excitement was that of a warlike reminisence,
when he would tell endless tales of his personal experiences, sometimes
enacting them with a bayonet he kept under his bed with a vigour hardly
consistent with the safety of his audience. His most terrible
movements, however, were against his brother "Old Zack" against
whom his imprecations were as fearful as they were / deserved. He was **83**
popular among My fathers pupils both for these displays and for his
services in getting them eggs and boiling or frying them in his cottage
and for allowing occasionally a little indulgence in the form of a
tobacco pipe.

12 If unchallenged, dwellings were allowed to be erected on waste land.

Poor "Tailor King" was a very different but equally amusing character. He was blessed with but a scanty store of sense but had a double supply of instinct. His instincts were wholly devoted to sporting matters. He was

84 always present / on the hunting field. Knew of course where every meet would take place, and by long practice in the ways of the fox could so surely prejudge his course as by wary cuts to keep up with the hunters. The time lost to his trade by these digressions was made up for by the rewards received for occasional aid, taking home a lame dog, aiding a fallen rider or a damaged horse & so he made his hunting

85 pay. He could sometimes tell you the very hole / in the hedge through which the fox would emerge from the Wood. He was an uncouth figure, his neck all on one side from katching it in a forked bow while leaping a hedge. He hunted in a light green coat, knee breeches & low shoes. We were often sent by My Mother if she wanted a hare to Mr Law to ask if he would shoot one for her & his constant reply was "I'll

86 go and ask the Tailor" or as he pronounced it tyählor. / We went with him to the tailor's shop where he was sitting cross legged at his window — D'ye know where there's ever a hare (yähr) sittin' Tyähler? was the constant question & the tailor always told him or shewed him where to find one. His conversation was a mixture of ludicrous simplicity with instinctive cunning — & by the amusement of his talk and the general

87 character of his instincts he became a great favourite among / us boys.

Another favourite was old "Warr of the Woodhouse" a clever skilled old woodman,[13] but I am ashamed to say that we only cared for him when he was drunk, or "Market Merry" as he called it, which took place once a week on Market day. When he died, after My leaving home, poor old "Mother Warr" & her husband retired from their shop to the said Woodhouse where they ended their days. /

88 My wife saw the old woman there in her old age — & says she never saw so picturesque a figure, — tall straight and dignified — still in her last-century dress and sitting at her door in the Wood plying her spinning-wheel: this was later than I saw her myself.

These are a few specimens, but the whole place was full of character even where there are no salient points to depict. The old women

89 Dame Collet, "Dame Norman Collier", Dame Tompkins &c / seem to My recollection to belong to another age and the sturdy worthiness of many of the men with their funny old fashioned way of expressing themselves form a most agreeable contrast to the contemporary tendency to pauperism which was silently making way among the less estimable part of the population & who like spotted sheep in time infected the flock.

13 Probably at Tingewick Wood, approximately two miles from Gawcott.

Our own family was a large & rapidly increasing and My eldest Brother (now Rector of Wappenham) was a youth / of pre-eminent **90** talent and was viewed as a little God by his brothers and even by his parents. This had a bad effect on me. He was viewed as a presentive person & all efforts were concentrated upon him. His next brother John got a little attention at second hand and being a boy of steady industry & good ablity he got on, but I, the Third, was too far removed to pick up even the crumbs &, not having a natural love of books and nothing occurring to make me love them, / I came off badly. So long as **91** I was under My mother I went on pretty well but I was transferred to a very incompetent and ungenial usher — and at a later period to my eldest brother who ruled me with a rod of Iron, or rather ligum vitae for he made me say My lessons with the round ruler impending over my head ready to come down at every blunder — a way of knocking classics into ones head which was by no means a success for it made me so utter / ly detest them that I at length got to prefer the round ruler **92** to work. I was also under the disadvantage of having no boys of My own age to work with — indeed with all My faults I was forwarder than any who were at all like me in age so that at 12 or 13 I had to be classed with idle fellows of 18 or more — a desultory way of going on which was very injurious. I ought certainly to have gone to school / but this **93** was out of the question as my father was poor and himself a pupilizer but was too busy with his older pupils often men of 20 to 25 or more to give me much of his personal attention so I slipped through between wind & water. I do believe, however, that if encouraged and helped I should have done well and in Mathematics I got on fairly My great relief from this life of heedlessness and rough handling was the visit of the drawing / Master. Though I never acquired any very high powers **94** of drawing under him I can never be too grateful for his help and kind encouragement. He was a Mr Jones a native of Buckingham who had been in his youth patronized by some of the Stowe family[14] and sent to London where he was I think a Student at the Royal Academy and was much noticed by Sir Joshia Reynolds of whom he entertained an affectionate rememberance / Foolishly, however, he had returned to native town **95** and had consequently failed of reaching the eminence for which nature had fitted him. He supported himself as a drawing master and a occasional portrait painter. His visits, twice a week, were the very joy

14 Robert Jones, Drawing Master and Portrait Painter of Maids Moreton (*Pigot's Directory of Buckinghamshire*, 1831–2, p.78). He could be the Robert Jones who in the early nineteenth century probably painted the classical scenes on the ceiling and above the doors in the State Dining Room at Stowe. He may also have worked on Brighton Pavilion (N. Pevsner and E. Williamson, *Buckinghamshire*, 1994, p.669).

of My life. I remember as if it were yesterday, and almost feel again while thinking of it, My anxiety when he was a little late in coming, My frequent glances towards the path by which he reached our garden and my heartfelt joy when I saw his loose drab gaiters through the
96   bushes / Mr. Jones was a mild benignant & humble minded old man — and, though he had not attained eminence, he was thoroughly grounded in his art. His knowledge of anatomy & of perspective were perfect, as was his acquaintance with the principles of colouring whether in oil or water colour, & his powers of drawing were remarkable, yet his training had stopped short of bringing his powers to bear upon actual high class work of his own. I often wish I had some of his drawings — I am sure they must evince the elements of Genius though
97   unmatured, and, consistently enough with this, he instilled into / My mind an intense love for the subject without any matured knowledge or skill. While depreciating myself however on this & other subjects it is fair to mention that my home schooling terminated when I was only about 14½ years old.

The little I learned of French My Mother taught me and I might, had I worked hard, or learned it well as she understood it perfectly & spoke it well. My Eldest brother had also a good French master in whose instruction unhappily I did not participate. /
98   How infinitely important it is for boys to feel the duty and necessity for exertion! Though I have reason to be most thankful for My success in life the defects of my education have been like a Millstone about my neck and made me almost dread superior society. A very little extra attention would have obviated this, for if, with the same means of education, My brother carried off [*in the margin*: Bells scholarship] in his freshmans year the highest university classical scholarship, why /
99   should not I have been a fair classic? True, he had four more years of it, and was a genius, but this did not make all the difference. He unhappily did not follow up his vantage-ground but rested on his oars, or he might have been a senior wrangler & near the top in classics & would now be a Bishop I have no doubt — as it was, he was 11th
100   Wrangler high in / classics & elected Tutor of his college which however he did not accept & so became a plain country parson wasting his preminent talents "in the desert air" while I have risen in a line of my own but ever mourning My slender attainments in all else. Both of
101   these partial failures arise from not working at *the right time*, / I as school-boy, My brother as an undergraduate. I cannot recover what I lost nor can he, though had he worked intensily as a schoolboy — and has done so ever since he took his degree, make up for that one bit of lost time which blighted his magnificent propects as a man of the highest talent. It is one of the greatest wonders of My life to witness /
102   the way in which young men deliberately throw away their chances of

eminence and seem satisfied with the bare prospect of getting their living; as if man was born *but to exist* — instead of to do the very utmost in his day & generation that the talents committed to him render attainable. Old Sir Robert Peel as I was told by his son used to say that if any youth of ordinary ability made up his mind as to his object in life / and bent   **103** all his energies to its attainment he would be almost certain of success — and this led his youngest son to determine when a child that he would be Prime Minister & to persevere till he became so.[15]

Being younger than most of my fathers pupils (who in fact were many of them matured men who had determined late to read for the Church) I had very little companionship & became a solitary wanderer in woods & fields & copy old churches &c in the Neighbourhood. /

My Grandfather   **104**

I have a tolerably distinct recollection of My Grandfather the author of the Commentary. We used to visit him *'en masse* about once a year. It was a time of great joy & excitement when the time came round. The Post chaise was ordered from Buckingham and usually made to carry seven. My father & mother occupied the seat 3 small children stood in front & two sat on the "Dickey" while the fat old post*boy* rode as postillion. It was some 25 miles to Aston Sandford, & I think I could find my way now by my recollections of that date. My Grandfather was when I recollect him a thin / tottering old man very grave & dignified.   **105** Being perfectly bald he wore a black velvet cap excepting when he went to church when he wore a venerable wig. He wore knee breeches with silver buckles and black silk stockings, and a regular shovel hat. His amusement was gardening but he was almost constantly at work in his study. At meals when I chiefly saw him he was rather silent owing to his deafness which rendered it difficult to him to join in general conversation. I well remember when any joke had excited laughter at the table that he would beg to be informed what it was & when brought to understand it he would only deign to utter a single word:- *"Pshaw!"*. / One day as we sat at dinner a very old apple tree   **106** loaded with fruit suddenly gave way & fell to the ground to the surprise of our party & I remember my Grandfather remarking that he wished that might be his own end to be brought down in his old age by good fruit. Family prayers at Aston Rectory were formidable particularly to a child. They lasted a full hour, several persons from the village usually

15 It was the eldest son of Sir Robert Peel who became Prime Minister. As Scott was being consulted over the restoration of Worcester Cathedral at the time, this anecdote presumably came from the Dean, John Peel (1798-1875), who was a younger brother of the Prime Minister.

CHENIES MANOR HOUSE, 1826

The chimney shafts 'being decorated with varied & admirably executed pattern work in brick'.

(British Architectural Library, RIBA, London)

CHENIES, ST. MICHAEL, 1826
The 'final resting-place' of the Russells.

(British Architectural Library, RIBA, London)

107 attending. I can picture to my memory My Grandfather walking to Church in his gown & cassock & his long curled / wig & his shovel hat. He had a most venerable look and I felt a sort of dread at it. On sundays he had a constant inmate at his table — the barber to whom he was beholden for his wig. Those who are not acquainted with the evangelical party in its earlier days can hardly understand the way in which community of religious feeling was allowed to over-ride difference of worldly position. I recollect the same at Gawcott where though not allowed to associate even with our wealthiest farmer. We ever welcomed to our table a very poor brother of his who though scarcely above a labourer was a man

108 of piety & came many miles on sunday / to attend our church. It was the same with Mr. John Stratton the barber at Great Risborough — he was a pious man & he walked over every Sunday to hear My Grandfather preach and a place was kept for him at the dinner table. This John Stratton was however a very superior man — and he had the Good fortune to get his two sons into the Church. Some time after he had settled at Risborough he found that there was an old bequest for the education for the Church of any one called John Stratton[16] living at

109 Risborough — which he at / once claimed & obtained for his son. The other boy having a good voice was placed in the Choir at Magdalen Coll. Oxford when in due time he was admitted into the College & finally into the Church. I many years afterwards called on some remaining members of the family at Risborough, & found them quite superior people.

Near Aston lived My uncle the Revd Saml King. He was son of a very excellent man Geo King Esq a large wine Merchant in the city and being a pupil of My grandfather formed an attachment to his only daughter Elizabeth and married her before or during his entrance at

110 the University of / Cambridge. After they left Cambridge he took the Curacy of Hartwell near Aylesbury where the seat of Sir George Lee was at that time occupied by the Luis XVIII & the ex Royal family of France.[17] Subsequently or at the same time he was curate of Stone close by Hartwell where I first recollect visiting him, after which he removed to Haddenham, nearer to my Grandfathers so that our visits were jointly to my Grandfather & to him. My Aunt was a very talented and lovely woman and at that time she used to aid My Grandfather in the correction of a new edition of his Commentary as also did a talented

111 young man / who then resided with him Mr. W. R. Dawse since known as an astronomer and who has recently returned in his old age & built

16 There was a bequest from Richard Stratton, but there is no mention of one from John Stratton, in *The Report of the Charity Commissioners*, 1819–37.

17 The French court occupied Hartwell House between 1807 and 1814, but Samuel King only became Curate of Hartwell in 1813.

himself a residence at Haddenham.[18] I well recollect my puzzlement at hearing that certain printed sheets which came every morning by post and seemed to be viewed with great consideration were "*proofs of the Bible*". I connected them with the idea of evidences of Xtianity". The whole household of My Grandfather seemed imbued with religious sentiment. Old "Betty" the Cook & Lizzy the waiting-maid and Old Betty Moulder an infirm inmate taken in on account of her excellence and helplessness were all patterns / of goodness and **112** even poor "John Brangwin the serving Man partook of the general effect of the atmosphere of the Rectory. Poor old fellow I visited him last spring with three of My sons at an almshouse at Cheynies — when he poured forth his recollections of My Grandfather &c for half an hour together. It was Sunday & we found him reading in the copy of the Commentary wh My Grandfather had left him in his will & he told us he just had a cold dinner — "he never had anything cooked o'sabbath day — Muster Scott never had anything cooked o'sabbath days" a precept he / had followed for more than 40 years. I regret that my recollections **113** of My Grandfather himself are so very scanty while My memory of the place and of its less important inhabitants & of trifling incidents is as perfect as if it were last year. Some five miles beyond Aston Sandford run the range of the Chiltern Hills — the "delectable Mountains" of My youth always forming our horizon though very rarely reached. They divided the county into two parts as different as possible in their character the northern where we lived homely & unpicturesque the southern Hilly & delightful. Once only in these early days I saw this beautiful / part of my county when I went to visit an aunt Widow of the **114** Revd N. Gilbert) at Woburn near Wycombe & I with be reminds My [*sic*] the pleasure I experienced I remember our all walking up Stokenchurch hill and a coach-load of passengers form, in long procession before us.

My Uncle & Aunt King

After my Grandfathers death my Uncle King was presented to the living of Latimers[19] in this Southern division of Bucks our visits to which place were the brightest spots in my early life.

18 Scott means William Rutter Dawes (1799-1868), who was a distinguised amateur astronomer. He was also a medical practitioner at Haddenham, where, in 1824 he married the Commentator's second wife, Mary, after the Commentator's death (Haddenham Parish Register). In 1857 he built Hopefield House at Haddenham (*DNB*).

19 King was appointed Chaplain of Latimer in 1821.

LATIMER VILLAGE, 1826

A 'glorious old elm tree of towering height on the little green'.

(British Architectural Library, RIBA, London)

LATIMER, ST. MARY MAGDALENE, 1826
Was 'modern & vile'.

(British Architectural Library, RIBA, London)

115　　　My uncle was a most lively & / amusing man who having no children of his own devoted himself when thrown in their way very extensively to their amusement. He was a man of multifarious resources, an excellent astronomer, perhaps the best amateur ornamental turner in the Kingdom. He was a glass painter a brass-founder — a devotee to natural science in very many forms. My Aunt was a literary person she had received the same education with her brothers instead of learning

116　　　feminine accomplishments. She was one of those / "ladies of talent" one occasionally meets with whose company is courted on account of their superior knowledge & conversational talents. I have every reason for gratitude to them both as I shall afterwards shew.

[rest of page blank]

117

My Grandmother Lynch &
My Aunt Gilbert

My Maternal Grandmother & her sister (as before mentioned) lived with us at Gawcott. The former was a very excellent quiet unobtrusive little woman. I rarely heard anything of her husband Dr. Lynch. He died early leaving her with a young family and I fancy but slenderly provided for for the only thing I ever heard of him was that he impoverished himself by being so easy going that he could not refuse any one who asked money of him. His eldest son was during my childhood a medical man at Dunmow in Essex where he also died

118　　　early leaving a large family. / My Great aunt Gilbert had accompanied My grandmother & her family to England or possibly was here already as her English recollections reached much earlier date. This must have been about 1790 as nearly as I can tell My mother being at that time about 4 years old. They resided in Great Ormond Street, Queen square which then bordered upon the fields. My aunt was a person of considerable talent, of the most intense piety and of an extraordinarily affectionate disposition and withal wonderfully simplehearted and forbearing. She devoted herself to My Mother during her childhood

119　　　with an intensity / of affection exceeding probably what a child would always find agreeable. She and My Grandmother were provided for by annuities upon their father's estate — then pretty good but ever diminishing with the decline of West India property. My Mother went to a very good school (I think in London) kept by a Miss Cox. This very superior lady was afterwards married to a Mr Woodroffe a clergyman in Gloucestershire and My Mother always kept up an affectionate /

correspondence with & they mutually visited from time to time. I   120
recollect her well visiting us at Gawcott. She was the author of a
religious novel entitled "Shades of Character or the Little Pilgrim", (&
Michael Kemp).[20] When My mother married My aunt came I believe
at once to live with her (My grandmother living for a time near her son
at Dunmow). When I made My appearance on the *tapis* My aunt
pitched upon my unworthy person as her pet and ever afterwards
followed Me up with an assiduity of affection which it is impossible to
exaggerate. / This was probably enhanced (though My conduct was   121
not calculated to produce that effect) by her having the charge of me
when 5 years old for some months while I made a stay on account of
some casual disorder at Margate. This was in 1816 and as it was the
landmark of My childhood I will give a few reminiscences of it.

Of the Coach journey to London I have hardly a glimmer of
recollection. On our arrival however we transferred ourselves to the
house of a sort of "Gaius mine host" who dwelt hard by the coach
office where we alighted. This was a Mr. Broughton of / Swan yard   122
Holborn Bridge who kept a boarding house for travellers in general
with a preferance for the Evangelical party and a still more special preferance for Missionaries and especially those to New Zealand. This his
most powerful preferance of all was rendered manifest to the eye by
his rooms being hung with patoo-patoos[21] war-rugs and all the marvels
of a New Zealand Museum — and occasionally a tatooed Chief or two
to his intense joy took up their quarters under his roof / all this,   123
however, I gathered at subsequent visits. Mr. Broughton shewed his
special regard for the Commentator — My Grandfather by opening
his house to his descendants at all times gratuitously — indeed he
demanded their acceptance of his hospitality as a right. Swan Yard
which has perished in the extension of Farringdon street was opposite
the then Fleet market, and was a Waggon Yard, devoted to Broad
wheeled wagons and Straw, and the house was far from lively. / at the   124
time of our visit Mrs. Broughton who was enormously corpulent was
laid up with the gout and I was forthwith conducted by My aunt to the
good lady's bedroom. Here I was so terrified at the sight of her vast
person enveloped in volumes of dimity and her legs swaddled in a

---

20 Anne Cox (1766–1830) married the Revd. Nathaniel George Woodrooffe in London,
   in 1803, and spent the rest of her life at Somerford Keynes, near Cirencester (*DNB*).
   Her *History of Michael Kemp, the happy farmer's lad*, first appeared in 1819, and ran to
   nine editions by 1855. But her most important book, *Shades of Character*, which
   came out in 1824, was 'designed to promote the formation of the female character
   on the basis of Christian principle'(*DNB*). The final and seventh edition, of 1855,
   was subtitled the *Infant pilgrim*.

21 Patoo-patoos are hand clubs.

stupendous gouty stocking of white & pink lambs-wool that I at once proclaimed a mutiny & refused to stop in the house in which I so
125 resolutely persisted that My / good aunt actually yeilded to me, and transferred me to the cabin of the Margate sailing packet which was to start in the Morning. Here we met a number of Buckingham friends who were to join us in our lodgings at Margate. The most conspicious amongst whom was a family of Quakers. Our Medical Mr Southam his wife two grown up daughters & a son of 10 years old — We had also My dear old friend Mrs. Rogers with her 3 daughters. the two eldest long
126 after- / wards married to my friends Mr Stowe and Major Macdonald. Also a Mr. Goode[22] uncle to the present dean of Ripon.

My impression of the Cabin is very vivid. It was very full of passengers and I well recollect a lively & lengthened argument in which My aunt was a warm disputant as to whether in dealing with Savages — we ought to aim at civilizing before christianizing or Vice
127 Versa / a point on which the cabin was about equally divided. As the night drew on the Ladies and Children retired to the births which lined the sides while the Gentlemen retained their chairs. I well recollect peeping out from between my curtains & seeing gentlemen who had been warm in the argument sitting asleep round tables on which their heads & elbows were deposited.

Of the next day my leading recollection is the sweeping of the boom
128 across the deck as we tacked and the havoc it always / threatened amongst the crowded passengers.

Arrived at Margate we took lodgings on "the Fort" at the house of one Capn. Bourne — My aunt & I the Southams the Rogers and I think Mr Goode all living together as one family & Mrs. Rogers maid aiding My Aunt & helping her to keep me out of mischief.

There was already a steamer to Margate but it was such a new thing
129 that the visitors & inhabitants / crowded to the pier to see it come in. I well remember the excitement of seeing its approach & hearing the band.

One of My most vivid recollections of Margate was our going with the Southams to a Quakers Meeting at a place called Drapers & hearing several ladies preach. I also recollect seeing a fleet of 32 East India men pass in a row — probably under convoy as the war was but recently over. /
130 While at Margate I lost an infant Sister named Elizabeth. (Oh that I

---

22 Francis Goode maintained the family business of grocers and tallow chandlers in Buckingham (*Pigot & Co's London and New Commercial Directory*, 1823–24, p.151), while other members of the family became prominent Evangelical clergymen, particularly his brother, William (1762–1816), and his nephews Francis (1797?–1842), and William (1801–68), the Dean of Ripon (*DNB*).

had lost none since! My dearest Mary I am so grieved most deeply for your loss — but how selfish to do so for it is your infinite gain!)

After leaving Margate we visited my Uncle Lynch at Dunmow and in passing through London My aunt stayed with an old Wesleyan friend Mr Jones of Finsbury Square. I remember their shewing me from / his windows gas lights as great curiosities. We also went to see 131 another Miss Gilbert — a cousin of My aunts, we called her "Cousin Harriet". She was a wild eccentric person & while we were there went into a frightful fit of hysterics owing to having been visiting the Grave of a near relative and I confess I do not wonder that a lady being alone should not do so for this relation had been her sole companion. I have two coins still which this old / cousin gave to me that day or rather I 132 have recently given them to My Son Alwyne. I will not however increase frivolous reminiscences. It is vexatious to think of the perversity of childrens Memories — I recollect the funeral of Mr West in 1814 and this digression from my village home in 1816 as well almost as if they happened last year — Yet of the Battle of Waterloo which occurred in the intervening year I have not even the slightest recollection!

My dear Aunt Gilbert was most interesting in her recollections. John Wesley was the great / Saint of her memory I remember her telling 133 Me of his having kissed her which she esteemed a great privilege. She had been an intimate ally of Mrs. Fletcher of Madeley who after her husbands death became a sort of female evangelist "all round the Wrekin". This hill by the bye was familiar to my childish ideas from her having lived so long under its shadow. When this was I know not but it was during the days of Mrs. Fletcher and one Lady Dorothea Whitmore. Who the latter was I do not know but the family I find still resides in the neighbourhood. One of My aunts sisters / by the bye had 134 married a Mr. Yate of Madeley. Her son the Revd. George Yate is still Rector of Wrockwardine. I remember another Son a naval officer — bringing us a flag to Gawcott wh. he had taken in the American War & a daughter Anne Yate used to visit us — (by the way it was she who took me to Mr Wests funeral). She died of Consumption some few years later. "Poor Cousin Anne"!

My aunt kept up a very extensive correspondence and had done so all her life. One of her great correspond / ents was her brother William 135 who lived in America. This was a very remarkable Character. He was a barrister & a man of most acute genius and was just rising into fame when his mind gave way. His insanity took a political line — and the first rage of the French revolution being rampant at the time he went to France to ally himself with Robespierre & Co — but I fancy took fright when he got nearer and returned. He subsequently went to America as the only Country with the government of which he could

feel satisfied. He was a friend of Southey & Coleridge during their
136 early / days Southey remarks of him in his life of Wesley &c.

[rest of page blank]

137   *[blank]*

138   Another constant correspondent was a cousin a Mr Gordon of
Stocks near Tring & of, *[blank]*.
      Poor man he had corresponded to the last & then came the news
that he had shot himself. I remember one of My aunt's last letters to
him — which was evidently intended to help him out of religious despair
— for she quoted the passage "Though thy Sins be as scarlet they shall
be white as snow, &c. Let us hope that he also was insane! /
139   Another correspondent was a Lady Abdy also a cousin. My aunts
object in all these cases was a religious one this being the main subject
of her thoughts.
      My aunt was a poetess — I have none of her poetry but She wrote a
good deal & not badly. She was in great requisition for epitaphs &c. I
wish I could get some of her longer productions. I hope to append
some extracts from a sketch of her life by one more capable of depicting
her character — She was an admirable woman & in My view quite a
140 historical / person. She had a large chest filled with selected letters
from her correspondents from John Wesley downwards but *Pro
Pudor*! This most valuable collection was indiscriminately destroyed
after her death which I think happened in 1832 a grievous error! She
lies buried a little South of the church of Gawcott. My Grandmother
lived a few years longer & was buried at Wappenham. both were I
think 80 or upwards at their death. /

141   Buckingham Friends

      Our local friends were cheifly inhabitants of Buckingm. Who most of
took to My father on his first arrival and became many of them constant
attendants at his ch. Among the latter, the Bartlett family were the
cheif. The Heads of this family John & Edward[23] Bartlett were I think
partners in a multifarious business. The latter died before my time but
the former in my day united the businesses of Tanning to Banking
while sons of the latter were great wool staplers. They were the leading
142 people at Buckingham. Our great / friend and Ally was old Mrs. Bartlett
the widow of Edward. a thoroughly excellent person in every way &

---

23 See the genealogy of the Bartlett family.

GAWCOTT, HOLY TRINITY, August 1827
Of which 'I cannot say much about either design or execution'.

(British Architectural Library, RIBA, London)

My Mothers cheif local friend. She had 3 sons & two daughters — Of the former one (Robert) was a solicitor in large practice at Chelmsford & Clerk of the Peace of the Coy. of Essex (whose Son is now a excellent clergyman in the East of London) Philip & Thomas were the woolstaplers. The former a talented hearty — jovial fellow & the latter a very worthy man. The Daughters were very ladylike persons & were

143   married respec / tively to Major Macdonald and to My youngest uncle Revd. Benjn. Scott.

All of this generation are now dead.

Old John Bartlett (profanly known as "Jack Ramskin) was a sort of little King in Buckm. A rough morose money-making man who took the command[24] at everything. I think his family are also dead — His eldest Son was a most pious & excellent Clergyman Vicar of Bildwas in Shropshire[25] a perfect contrast to his father, gentle & polished in the extreme /

144   The Bartlett family came over every Sunday en masse to Gawcott church as did others from Buckm. who held with Evangelical views & Mrs. B used usualy to dine with us.

Our medical man in early days was a sturdy old Quaker (already mentioned) Mr Southam — but he took his Doctors degree & removed to Coventry shortly after we took in his place Mr Stowe a very talented and excellent man who at that time was one of our most valued friends. He married the eldest daughter of our friend Mrs.

145   Rogers / whose second daughter became long afterwards the second wife of Major Macdonald. Mr Stowe died quite recently. I would mention that his eldest son[26] was on the staff of *The Times* & was sent to the Crimea to administer the fund raised by the Times for the relief of the Soldiers when he unfortunately died of feaver. He was a most promising man.

Another of our great friends though not of our immigrant church comers was Mr Hearn[27] the private solicitor & the Banker of Buckm. A truely estimable man & still living to a great age.

24 John Bartlett was Bailiff of Buckingham 1798, 1799, 1808, and is known for his opposition to the Marquess of Buckingham.

25 The Revd. John Bartlett married Susanna Reynolds, the daughter of an ironmaster of Coalbrookdale, and built Marnwood Hall, on land that she had inherited. Scott and his wife stayed there in 1845, and he describes the house, on the southern slopes of The Wrekin, as 'in a most exquisite position cut out of a hanging wood' (III, p.139).

26 William Henry Stowe (1825–55) (*DNB*).

27 Thomas Hearn purchased Castle House, West Street, Buckingham, in 1837 and consulted Scott on its alterations (Elliott, p.61). He was the Parliamentary Agent of the Verneys, and a partner in Bartlett's Bank after 1830 (A. Dell, *May the voters . . . a biographical sketch of William Rickford, M.P. (1768–1854)*, Aylesbury, 1986, p.15).

I have mentioned Major Macdonald & I will also / add that he was a **146** very noble person and one of the best & warmest friends besides being a sort of half brother in law of My fathers, or also of My uncles (Benjamin). He too has lately died at a very advanced age.

I enumerate these old friends merely that my sons if they read these memoranda may know better who they were.

[rest of page blank]

Stowe   147

We lived within about 4 miles of Stowe,— then in its greatest glory. The Marquis (afterwards Duke) of Buckingham was the puissant potentate of the district and Stowe was his seat of Government. It was a great advantage I think to have a great centre of art and princely splendour to refer to when we liked. It was a set off against the otherwise almost unmitigated rusticity of the neighbourhood. To Stowe we all made an annual pilgrimage. This was the great day of our year. It took place in Early June that we might enjoy the glories of Lilac & Laburnham / The **148** journey was somewhat grotesque —My father rode his old horse "Jack" or subsequently "Tripod". The older boys walked while My Mother my eldest sister & the children performed the journey in the Bakers cart,— a tilted but unsprung vehicle furnished with chairs for the occasion and further furnished with a large basket filled with provisions which were conveyed by our serving man William to the "Temple of Concord and Victory"[28] which was our traditional lunching place. I well recollect the gratification afforded by the hard boiled eggs / &c eaten beneath the unwonted shade of a Classic Temple. **149**

Stowe was really a very fine place though gimcrack. It was most extensive & well wooded indeed the park with its woods merged gradually off into the Forest of Whittlebury. It was approached from Buckingham by a perfectly straight road of some 3 miles long and bordered by a wide grass road and an avenue on either side — & leading to a triumphal arch — known as "the Corinthian Arch".[29] From

---

28 The Temple of Concord and Victory is one of the grandest of the Stowe temples. It stands near to the house and was originally built in 1747, but altered in 1762 to celebrate victory in the Seven Years' War. In 1927 it was altered again, when some columns were removed and built into the new school chapel (N. Pevsner and E. Williamson, *Buckinghamshire*, 1994, pp.684, 686). The temple has recently been restored by the National Trust, and the missing columns replaced.

29 The Corinthian Arch was designed by the amateur architect, Thomas Pitt, 1st Lord Camelford, between 1765 and 1767 (N. Pevsner and E. Williamson, *Buckinghamshire*, 1994, p.674). Pitt (1737-93), was a nephew of the 1st Earl of Chatham, the brother-in-law of Earl Temple (Colvin, 1995, p.758).

several other directions it was somewhat similarly approached. So that
150 from the / Buckingham lodges to those in the direction of Towcester
could hardly be less than 8 miles. The house had (and has) a frontage
of nearly 1000 feet though it is fair to mention that its extreme wings
hardly form a part of its Architecture — It is entered properly speaking
from behind where it assumes the form of a convex semicircle. To us
however the approach was from the garden front which is the great
architectural facade & looks south — Here the entrance is by an octastyle
151 corinthian portico[30] approached / by a lofty flight of steps rising the
height of a basement storey I well remember the kind of awe with
which this stately approach inspired Me and how vast it appeared to
My young imagination. We were welcomed under the Portico by an
almost equally stately Groom of the Chambers Mr. Broadway a man
of portentous aspect and intense dignity of demeanour. He paid special
attention to us from his respect for My father and devoted much pains
to shewing and explaining the pictures &c. I can fancy I hear now his
152 dignified and measured words in which he introduced the / pictures
to our youthful inspection. "The Burgomeister Six, by Rembrandt"
"The Portrait of the Elder by the Younger Rembrandt" &c.[31] His tone
gave us a reverence for the old masters beyond what our discrimination
would have alone inspired. It was really a very fine collection and
being the only one I had seen I feel thankful to think that I had the
opportunity through it of seeing noble art so early. The Sculpture was
153 also fine containing a great number of antiques / which were mostly
ranged round a large elliptical Saloon entered directly from the garden
portico. My veneration was greatly enhanced by the fact of one vast
room being wholly devoted to the collection of engravings classified in
an infinite number of portfolios, & another to similarly arranged
music and the library being so extensive as to demand the services of a
man of learning and position (a dignified Roman Catholic priest Dr

30 The south front of Stowe has a hexastyle portico, with six columns, not eight, as
Scott states.

31 It is unfortunate that recent scholarship has has raised considerable doubt over the
authenticity of the two paintings that Scott specifically mentions at Stowe, although
the collection contained a few genuine Rembrandts at the time. The Stowe
Guidebook of 1827 mentions a portrait of 'A Burgomaster' and later editions describe,
presumably, the same portrait as that of 'Burgomaster Six'. This has since been
identified as *Eleazar Swalmius*, demoted to the 'School of Rembrandt', and is now
in the Koninklijk museum at Antwerp. The *Guidebook* of 1827 also mentions a portrait
of Rembrandt's father in the Duchess's Dressing Room. This has not been identified,
and had disappeared by 1848. It may have been the *Portrait of an Old Man with a
White Beard . . . etc.*, which was sold at Christies in 1839, along with other unimportant
paintings. I am particularly grateful to Mr Colin Anson for supplying me with the
information contained in this note.

O'Connor)[32] as the librarian. One modern picture the destruction of Herculaneum by Martin used to fill us with wonder as did a magnificent / astronomical clock, giving the true motions & positions of the planets **154** & only wound up once in four years i e on the 29th of February.

The house was in point of fact a sort of "Palace of delights" a wilderness of art, vertu & magnificence, of which I have not seen an equal on the whole — & it is beyond measure aggravating to think of its glorious contents having been dispersed through the folly of its possessor!

The Duke of My day was / Grandfather to the present one   **155**

He was a man of considerable ability & attainments and of portentous ambition & pride. I believe that the downfall of the family was fully as much owing to him as to his son. He literally came under the woe pronounced upon those who "add field to field till there is no place that they may be left alone in the earth", for he nearly ruined the family by purchasing estates with borrowed money the interest on which exceeded the rental. /

By the bye we made two annual peregrinations there for we went   **156** over to the review of the Yeomanry Cavalry of which the Marquis of Chandos — (The late Duke) was Lt Colonel. It makes me feel very antique to remember that I was present at the festivities which celebrated the Baptism of the present Duke, and very magnificent they were.[33] The fireworks were I suppose as fine as that day could produce — I recollect on that day, while /

[*In the published work this paragraph is placed after the next.*]   **157**

Of the architecture of Stowe I cannot say much from memory nor is it necessary as it remains I believe intact.

sitting on a bench so placed as to overlook a very large piece of water surrounded by beech plantations hearing the remarks of two old women — "Lawk how unkid" said one, "you can see nothin but water!" — "Oh bless you" replied her more knowing companion "Why, the sea's *twice* as big as that".

As Stowe was My introduction to classic architecture and high art / so was my liking for Gothic architecture due to the old churches in My   **158**

---

32 Charles O'Conor (1764-1828) (*DNB*), was a scholar of Irish manscripts who arranged for his father's manuscript collection to be transferred to the Gothic Library at Stowe (John Beckett, *The Rise and Fall of the Grenvilles*, Manchester, 1994, pp.74, 76, 120).

33 The christening festivities for the son of the Marquess of Chandos lasted a whole week in June 1824 (Beckett, p.145).

neighbourhood. The district is not famed for its old churches, yet it possessed several of considerable merit Our own village was utterly devoid of early remains though I venerated the old "chapel close" where its ancient church or chapel had once stood. In the same way Buckingham had lost its old Church a very fine edifice which fell in

159 17[*space*].[34] My drawing master Mr. Jones remembered its / fall and told me that it had an Ailse called the Gawcott Aisle. The old church yard remains though the church now stands on the Castle Hill & a very ungainly edifice it is. There is only one really ancient building in Buckm. The chapel of St. Thomas of Canterbury now a grammar school.[35]

The Building which directed My attention to Gothic architecture was the church of Hillesden. 2 miles to the south of Gawcott. This is a church of late date but of remarkable beauty. It was our great lion, & every

160 new comer was / taken to see it on the earliest possible opportunity and was appraised by Me in proportion to his appreciation of its beauties. I always looked upon Hillesden with the most romantic feelings. It was a beautiful spot as compared with our neighbourhood in general, was situated on a considerable elevation and surrounded by fine old plantations and avenues of lofty trees conspicuous throughout the district. Near the Church stood the "Great house" a

161 deserted mansion of the / time I believe of Charles II. The Place had from early in the 16th. century belonged to the family of *Denton*. They were stanch Royal Royalists and suffered severely during the great rebellion. We used to be told that Sir Alexander Denton the then proprietor after a vigorous defence of his mansion was taken and after being conducted for some distance from his home was made to turn back to see his residence in flames. He was imprisoned died a prisoner.[36] The family in the direct line had become extinct & its last member having married

162 Mr Coke of Holkham became the / Mother of the celebrated Mr Coke afterwards Earl of Leicester. He was the proprietor of Hillesden in My early days & I recollect going to the home of a farmer whose wife boasted

34 It was in 1776 that the tower of Buckingham Church fell. In 1777 Robert Bartlett, then Bailiff, laid the foundation stone for the new church on a new site on the top of Castle Hill donated by the Verney family (Hunt, p.xviii). The architect was possibly Francis Hiorne of Warwick (Colvin, 1995, p.496).

35 The chapel was built in the 12th century, and in the 13th century was dedicated to St. John the Baptist and St. Thomas of Canterbury. It became the Royal Latin School, and in 1857 Scott produced a design for a new bell turret (Elliott, pp.177–8). He restored the whole building in 1875, and in 1907 the school moved out (N. Pevsner and E. Williamson, *Buckinghamshire*, 1994, pp.195–6).

36 A less dramatic account of Sir Alexander Denton's departure from Hillesden is in Margaret M. Verney, *Bucks Biographies*, Oxford, 1912, p.116.

HILLESDEN, ALL SAINTS, 1826
'Mr Jones used to meet Me there to teach me to sketch.'
(Courtesy of the Churchwardens and P.C.C. of Hillesden)

that they had been playfellows when children. The House had been much reduced in size but what remained though uninhabited retained its old furniture. I particularly remember the bedrooms. The beds placed in odd recesses between two closets partitioned off on either side &

[sketch of layout]

163 through which you would have to go & get into bed / by doors in their sides. The grounds still retained their form — with terraces & a large fish pond — There were also stables of *earlier* date probably of Edward VI's time — and a rather elegant octagonal Dove-cote of brick. Mr. Coke had repeatedly refused to sell the Hillesden estate to the Duke of Buckm but at length it was purchased by Mr Farquhar of Font Hill who immediately afterwards sold it to the Duke.[37]

164   This was a sorrowful event to me, as the / Duke was in My eyes the great enemy of local history. He soon destroyed the old house — & carried off the curious old watch box in the form of a brick gate pier to Stowe[38] — while timber began to disappear & keepers destroyed the liberty of the woods & the little glory which had remained departed.

    The church however was there after all & to it I made my frequent pilgrimages & a little later dear old Mr. Jones used to meet Me there to

165 teach me to sketch / These were perhaps the happiest occasions of My youth & I look back upon them now with a glow of delight.[39]

    Hillesden Church is of late date The Tower is humbler in its pretentions than the rest of the church and is of rather early simple "perpendicular" work The Church itself was begun in 1493 I believe by the Monks of

37 Coke sold Hillesden in spring 1824 to John Farquarson to whom he 'expressed in the strongest terms' that it should not get into the hands of the Duke of Buckingham. However, Buckingham offered Farquarson £20,000 more than he had paid for it, and in the following September the land was conveyed to Buckingham (Beckett, p.144).

38 This could have been the so-called Chackmore Fountain, which stood on the eastern side of the Grand Avenue, near to Chackmore. It was 'a small brick structure like a sentry-box, with apsidal sides and a central doorway surrounded by dressed stone'. It was vandalised, declared unsafe and demolished 'many decades ago' (Michael Bevington, *Templa Quam Dilecta, Number 1, The Grand Avenue, The Corinthian Arch & the Entrance Drives*, Buckingham, 1989, p.13).

39 Scott wrote in 1873 that the church was particularly dear to him, the delight of his youth, and its study 'led me to devote my life to the Art of which it is so charming an example. Some of the happiest of my early recollections are of the days I spent there, either with my Drawing Master making sketches of it, or locked up there whole days measuring its details'. (Sir George Gilbert Scott, R.A., *Proposed Restoration of All Saints' Church, Hillesden, Bucks.*, London, 1873, p.[3], reprinted in *Records of Buckinghamshire*, iv, pp.309–18).

Nutley to whom the Rectorial tythes belonged. It is a very exquisite specimen of this latest phase of Gothic architecture and possess all the refine / ment of its best specimens such as the Royal Chapels at Westminster & Windsor indeed I have seen no detail of that period to surpass these at this church. **166**

[A line plan of Hillesden Church is here]

In plan it consists of a nave with aisles and quasi transepts a large chancel with North Aisle — a sacristry of two stories at the North East angle of the chancel aisle the upper story of which is approached by a very large / newel stair at the extreme North Eastern angle. **167** This Stair turret is a very exquisite & striking feature being finished with a sort of crown of flying buttresses & pinnacles of which I have seen no other instance indeed it is one of the most beautifully designed features I know.

The upper sacristry has a series of radiating loop holes looking into the church. The walls of the Chancel are covered with Stone / panelling. **168** The ceilings throughout had panels of plaster, with wood mouldings I have since seen some which had unhappily been taken down & found the plaster to be in thick & very hard slabs on which were set out curious geometric figures drawn with the compasses as if to form the guides for painted decorations.

The rood screen was perfect and of exquisite beauty.[40] The fittings were nearly all of the orginal date and very good / though of course of a **169** very late character. The chief exception was the great square pew of the Dentons a somewhat dignified work of Charles IIs reign furnished with great high backed chairs.

The Monuments of the Dentons were of course of very varied date from Edward VI time or there about downwards. There is by the way a fine monument to one of the earliest of the family (after Hillesden came into their hands in Hereford Cathedral which I have lately had the pleasure of reinstating after lying in pieces for / 20 years. The north **170** porch is a very charming structure of exquisite design & finish. The church yard Cross appears to be of the 14th. century I hope greatly to have a hand in the restoration of the church to which I owe so much as my initiator into Gothic architecture.[41] I fear it is in a very damaged

---

40 Scott surveyed the screen and presented the drawing to the Architectural Society in January 1835.

41 Nine years after Scott wrote this he was eventually commissioned to carry out the restoration of Hillesden. The contractor was Franklin of Deddington and the work cost £2,200. Scott gave all his services free of charge, and donated the fan-vaulting and the pinnacles to the porch. The church was re-opened in June 1875 (*Records of Buckinghamshire*, iv, pp.318–25).

state — I should have mentioned the remains of painted glass which it contains. They are beautiful fragments of the style of those in Kings
171 College Chapel / though more delicate in finish. The principal remains illustrate the life of the patron Saint, St Nicholas. In other windows where most of the glass is gone fragments remain in the heads containing charming representations of Mediaeval Cities such as one sees in the background of Van Eyke's pictures.

172 I recollect My father writing to the Duke of / Buckm. to urge his repairing this church — The result was his whitewashing the exterior of the Tower!

Maids Morton Church the second in rank in our district is also of "perpendicular" date but earlier. its Tower is of admirable & unique design. It at that time retained its old seats with fleur de lis poppy
173 heads also / a beautiful stoup at the Door which have since been ruthlessly destroyed.

Tingewick Church was the nearest of our Medieval Structures to Gawcott. It was a good church, containing Norman arcade & a few fragments on the South wall of the same date the rest I think all perpendicular — The tower was attributed to William of Wikeham. It
174 has since undergone strange transmogrifi / cations — The south wall has been rebuilt I think *twice* & much good & interesting old work destroyed.

My father, at different times took the curacies of Hillesden & Tingewick in combination with Gawcott.

The only other church I will mention as connected with My youthful days is Chetwood. I was never more astonished than when I first saw this church never having before seen or heard of "Early English" Architecture. It is a fragment of a small Monastic Church and its east
175 window consists of five noble lancets / with externally plain but bold detail — On either side are fine triplets. Never having before seen such windows I was greatly perplexed at them and failing to get the key & being reduced to peeping through the keyhole of the west door. I was astonished and perplexed to find the east windows to have shafts with foliated capitals a thing I had never seen & could not understand /
176 I remember continuing all day in a state of morbid excitement on the subject & having no access to architectural books it was very long ere I solved the mystery.

My taking in this way to old churches led My father first to think of My becoming an architect after consulting with My Uncle King on
177 the subject it became a fixed arrangement. I was / then about 14 years old and shortly afterwards My Uncle very kindly offered to take me under his own charge and to superintend me in studies having a tendency in that direction. I accordingly took up My residence at Latimers, in 1826. I had two years before made a trip to London where

My eyes were opened to much which I had never thought of before. Westminster Abbey I need not say I was charmed with — it was the only gothic minster / I had seen nor did I see any other excepting **178** St.Albans & Ely till after My articles had expired in 1830! I recollect when I saw Westminster Abbey in 1824 they were putting up the present reredos or rather "restoring" in artificial stone the old one.[42]

My Uncles instruction was mainly in Mathematics in which he carried me on through trigonometry & mechanics in which I took great pleasure. He also gave me direct instruction in / architecture of which **179** he possessed a very fair knowledge. I was by him initiated into Classic Architecture both Greek & Roman and a friend of his (The Rev. H. Foyster) who had been once intended for our profession having lent me a copy of Sir William Chambers[43] and some one else a portion of Stewarts Athens[44] I was able to follow up Architectural drawing as then taught pretty systematically. And by the time I was articled / had **180** already been put through My facings to a certain reasonable extent. I think I also had access to Rickman[45] as I certainly got to know the ordinary facts as to the different periods of Mediaeval Architecture. The only treatise I had before seen on this subject had been an article in the Edinburgh Encyclopaedia. Of which I remember little but the illustrations — & especially a West elevation of Rheims cathedral in which I took, when quite / a child the greatest delight. I suppose I **181** stayed with My Uncle about a twelve month on & off. Though a somewhat solitary life it was one of very great pleasure & enjoyment. The country there is particularly charming and so wholly different from My own home as to be like a new world. My love of woodland was here transferred from oak woods choked up with hazel & blackthorn to beech-woods through which you may wander without obstruction. The / very wild flowers & wild fruits were different while the search for **182** Chalcedonies & fossils among the flints with which the woods were bestrewed afforded amusement to my solitary wanderings & pleasure

42 The altar screen of Westminster Abbey was carried out by Francis Bernasconi to the designs of Benjamin Dean Wyatt. Scott was to replace the artificial stone with genuine stone and modify the design between 1863 and 1867 (T. Cocke, *900 Years: The Restorations of Westminster Abbey*, London, 1995, pp.63, 83–4).

43 Sir William Chambers' *Treatise on the Decorative Part of Civil Architecture* first appeared in 1759. It has been republished several times and it was probably the 1825 edition by Joseph Gwilt which Scott saw.

44 *The Antiquities of Athens* by James Stuart and Nicholas Revitt was published in five volumes between 1825 and 1830.

45 Thomas Rickman's *An Attempt to Discriminate the Styles of English Architecture* first appeared in 1817, but it was probably the second edition of 1820 which Scott saw.

MIDDLE CLAYDON, ALL SAINTS, June 1831
'In my summer holidays I devoted most of My time to measuring & sketching' in the area.
(British Architectural Library, RIBA, London)

STEWKLEY, ST. MICHAEL, August 1827

Showing on the left how 'I thoroughly taught myself perspective'.

(British Architectural Library, RIBA, London)

in shewing what I had found on my return. My uncle too was a man of infinite resources — Turning carried to a perfection probably never

183 surpassed. Mechanical pursuits of other kinds practical astronomy / & other branches of science occupied his leisure hours while his conversation was always lively & instructive. My Aunt too was a person of great talent & attainments & they had occasionally at their table persons of extensive information while they themselves visited at the aristocratic houses of the neighbourhood. Where their company was rather

184 sought as of persons / of talent & varied information.

The twin villages of Isenhampstead Latimers and Isenhampstead Cheynies (Commonly called Latimers & Cheynies) are situated within a mile of one another, and are rivals in beauty of situation they both overlook the charming valley of the little Chiltern trout-stream the "Chess" which rises 5 miles off at Chesham, and falls into the Colne near Watford. This little valley is not much known to the world at large

185 though of / exquisite beauty and now or formerly containing the dwelling places of some noble families — Cheynies was the old residence of the family of Cheyney and later of the Russells whose original seat there remains though but a farm house and whose mortal remains are still brought there from the more lordly Abbey of Woburn and deposited there in their final resting-place. Latimers (now by the dictum of its proprietor called Latimer) is one of the residences of the Cavendish family. It belonged at the time I am speaking of to Old Lord George Cavendish afterwards created Earl of /

186 Burlington. He was brother to a former Duke of Devonshire — uncle to the then duke and Grandfather of the present Duke. He was a noted patron of "the Turf" and had another seat at Holkar in Furness. His eldest son the father of the present Duke was dead & his next son Mr.Charles Cavendish (late Lord Chesham) was the expectant heir of Latimers.

The two "great houses" were both probably of the age of Henry VIIth or VIII (perhaps Latimers was a little later) and both were cheifly

187 famous for their / chimneys. Latimers was spoiled in the Strawberry Hill style with the exception of its beautiful stacks of tall octagonal chimney shafts in charming proportions & profile but all alike. Cheynies had been so dismantled that its cheif glory was also in these its upper regions — but unlike those at Latimers they are nearly all different the shafts being decorated with varied & admirably executed pattern work in brick both still remain though those at Cheynies have their

188 Caps reconstructed & spoiled. The House at Latimers / has been rebuilt by Blore all but its chimnies Latimers is charmingly situated and I think My Uncles Rectory was even better placed than the Great house. The church was modern & vile — but the village which was in two parts one on the hill & the other below was very picturesque with

old timber houses & a glorious old elm tree of towering height on the
little green. The upper village is now destroyed and the whole merged
into the *grounds* — perhaps to the increase of the beauty but certainly
to the dimin / ution of the *interest* of the place. Latimers is a sort of   **189**
hamlet of the little town of Chesham 5 miles up the valley where My
brother John (now Rector of Tyd St Giles in Cambridgeshire) was at
the time articled to a Medical Man, Mr Rumsey. This was an increase
to My happiness as I could occasionally walk over & see him. My
recollection of the whole district is as of a little Paradise. The Hills,
valley, river, trees flowers, fruits fossils &c all seem inveloped in a kind
of imaginary halo. I fancy I never saw such wild-flowers, or ate such /
cherries or such trout as there. There I terminated my childhood &   **190**
thence I emerged into the wide world in the prosaic turmoil of which I
have ever since been immersed.

Here then let me bid good-bye to my childish years — strange half
mythic days — full of quaint rough interest — full of faults of regrets
— yet of pleasure of thankfulness & of affection. Oh that I had availed
my self of / the many privileges of these My early days of its religious   **191**
opportunities & of its means of intellectual improvement. But regrets
are unavailing. Let me rather thank God for my pious and excellent
parents and for the many blessings of My life and crave His forgiveness
for my negligences & shortcomings.

Before quitting these early times I must however enumerate My
brothers & sisters & a few relations I have more or less omitted to
mention. /

My brothers & sisters were & are possessed of age as follows   **192**
 Thomas — b.— Feb 1807 I think
 Nathaniel Gilbert died in infancy
 John b Novr. 1809
 (Myself July 13th 1811)
 Euphemia 1813
 Nathaniel Gilbert 1814
 Elizabeth died in infancy
 William Langstone 1817
 Anne died in infancy
 Samuel King — 1819 or 20
 Mary Jane 1821
 Elizabeth do not recollects[46]
 Melville Horne 1827 /

My fathers brothers were The Revd. John Scott vicar of St. Marys   **193**
Hull & North Ferriby & The Rev Benjamin Scott of Bidford & Salford

---

46 Elizabeth Scott was born in 1824 (Gawcott Parish Register).

Warwickshire his sister (Elizabeth) Mrs. King My fathers first Cousin
Revd. Thos. Webster Vicar of Oakington Cambridgeshire &c & many
others one of whom was My dear Mother in law Mrs. Oldrid daughter
of my grandfathers eldest brother John William ?

My Mother's Brothers Mr. John Lynch formerly of Dunmow died
perhaps about 1819 or so several of whose family are living &
194 Nathaniel who died young. She had a half sister. Her / fathers
daughter by a prior marriage — a Mrs. Watson who died before my
time. Her most representative relation was her first Cousin The Revd
Nathaniel Gilbert Son of the beforementioned Rector of Bledlow of
the same name & proprietor of the Antigua Estate. He died a few years
back but his widow who still holds the estate is living at Leamington —
She also was a cousin a daughter of the Revd Melville Horne. /

195 My fathers brothers & sister visited us (unless my father & Mother
visited *them*) every year at least & it was a great occasion for they usually
had several of our cousins with them which we much enjoyed.

My Uncle John of Hull was a most dignified man & fully as much so
as any modern Archbishop. He was a man of great ability and
excellence. My Uncle Benjamin was a great Mechanician and a man of
Science. He lost his wife I suppose about 1825. after which he married
again & his widow is living. /

196   [*blank*]

197 While I was under the direction and tuition of My uncle King he and
his father Thomas King Esq of London, were on the look out for an
architect to whom to article me. It was a *sine qua non* that he should be a
religious man and it was necessary that his terms should be moderate.
They happened to enquire of Charles Dudley Esqr. travelling agent to
the Bible Society who after telling them that there was scarcely a
religious Architect in London recommended Mr. Edmeston, better
198 known as a poet than as an Architect[47] & it was finally settled / that I
was to go to him on or about Lady Day, 1827.

About this time I may mention, by the way, that old John Wests
church had shewn signs of falling to pieces and My Father after the first
perplexity was over set vigorously to work to raise subscriptions for
rebuilding it. He was wonderfully supported by religious friends in all
parts of the Country, and raised I think £1400 or £1500.

Among the large subscribers I recollect Mr Broadley Wilson, Mr

---

47 James Edmeston (1791–1867) wrote the words of over 2,000 hymns, including the
   popular *Lead us Heavenly Father, lead us* (John Julian, *A Dictionary of Hymnology*, New
   York, 1957, I, pp.321–2).

Joseph Wilson & Mr Deacon all men of note in the city also Mrs. Lawrence of Studley Park Yorkshire. / It was unluckly that the rebuilding of the church should have been necessary at perhaps the darkest period or nearly so of church architecture (though not quite so bad as that of old Mr. West to be sure). My Father was again his own Architect, made his own working drawings & contracted with his builder at Buckingham Mr. Wilmore. I cannot say much about either design or execution but these were days to be winked at as no one knew anything whatever of the subject. It did however exceed the old church in having a western tower and an eastern apse! and is a more reasonable in arrange / ment though not much more ecclesiastical. **199** **200**

[*Sketch of church 'No 1' and church 'No 2'*]

I often wish we now had it to build.

I recollect one day when its foundations were being put in Our friend Mr Thomas Bartlett coming to see the work and My Father telling him that he was about to place me with an Architect. Mr. Bartlett congratulated me upon it and added "I have no doubt you will rise to the head of your profession"[48] when My father at once replied "Oh no /his abilities are not sufficient for that" I hardly knew which to believe. It would be conceited to hold with the one but I would not quite knock under to the other! **201**

The new church was commenced I fancy when I was living at Latimers but I saw a little of the work at intervals. My first initiation into practical building though the lessons learned were not of the best as Mr Willmore was far from being a good builder. It was built of the rough bluish limestone of our Gawcott pits with dressings of a freestone from Cosgrove near Stoney Stratford. /

During my stay at home before leaving for London My dear brother Melville was born — just 20 years after the birth of my oldest brother who was then at Cambridge. **202**

My father took me to London & placed me with Mr. Edmeston with whom I lived at his house at Homerton, his office being at Salvador House,[49] in Bishopsgate Street. The first remark of My new master which I recollect was to the effect that the cost of Gothic architecture

48 Thomas Bartlett, as Mayor of Buckingham in 1837, signed the contract to extend the gaol, which nominated Scott as the architect (Buckingham Borough Records 4/42/1–2, in the Buckinghamshire County Record Office).

49 Edmeston's office was in White Hart Court (Robson's *Classification of Trades etc . . . for London*, 1829). The inn has since been rebuilt, and is immediately south of Liverpool Street Station.

HILLESDEN, ALL SAINTS, 1826
Showing the churchyard cross, which 'appears to be of the 14th. century'.
(British Architectural Library, RIBA, London)

CHETWODE, ST. NICHOLAS AND ST. MARY, 1830
'I was astonished and perplexed to find the east windows to have shafts with foliated capitals.'
(British Architectural Library, RIBA, London)

203 was so great as to be almost prohibitory; that he had tried it once at a dissenting / chapel he had built at Leytonstone & that the very cementing of the exterior had amounted to a sum which he named with evident dismay!

I had no idea beforehand of the line practice followed by My future initiator into the mysteries of My profession. I went to him with a mythic veneration of his supposed skill and for his imaginary works though without an idea of what they might be. The morning after my being deposited at his house he invited me to walk out and see some of his works — when — Oh, horrors! the bubble burst, and the fond **204** theme of My youthful imagination was / realized in the form of a few second rate brick houses with cemented porticoes of two ungainly columns each! I shall never forget the sudden letting down of My aspirations! A somewhat romantic youth, assigned to follow the noble art of Architecture for the love he had formed for it from the Ancient Churches of his neighbourhood & then condemned to indulge his taste by building houses at Hackney in the debased style of 1827!

I am not sure, however, that I was any very serious loser from this. **205** Mr. Edmestons / practice was a mere blank sheet as to matters of taste and left me quite open to indulge in private my old preferences or to choose in future what course I liked. I learned too in his office a great deal which I might have missed in a better one. I learned all the common routine of building specifying &c so far as practised by him and had a good deal of time for reading and drawing on my own account. Still, however, I confess it had a lowering and deadening effect and failed to inspire me with that high artistic sentiment which ought to be impressed upon the mind of every young architect. /

206 Mr & Mrs. Edmeston were very kind persons and as they had a good library which was in my evening sitting room I had excellent opportunities of that kind for self-improvement and I think I took very fair advantage of them. I read much & drew much made myself acquainted with classic architecture from books such as Stewarts Athens the Works of the Dilettante Society[50] Desgodetz[51] Vitruvius[52] &c and with Gothic so far as the scanty means went. I thoroughly

---

50 The Dilettante Society published Stuart's work, as well as commissioning other travellers to go to Greece and Turkey to study ancient Greek architecture and publishing their discoveries.

51 Antonine Desgodetz published *Les Edifices Antiques de Rome* in 1682 and an English edition appeared in 1771.

52 Marcus Vitruvius Pollio (usually referred to as Vitruvius), is the only known ancient writer on architecture. His treatise in ten books, *De Architectura*, was dedicated to the Emperor Augustus. Scott probably saw the 1826 translation by Joseph Gwilt.

taught myself perspective in one fortnight from Joshua Kirby[53] so much so that I have never had to look at a book on / it again indeed I **207** used to set myself the most difficult problems & invent new ways of solving them. I had liberal holidays at Midsummer and Christmas when I went home to my intense delight. In my summer holidays I devoted most of My time to measuring & sketching at Hillesden, Maid's Morton &c and on my return I devoted my evenings for a long time to drawing out what I had measured and most elaborately tinting them in indian ink sponged nearly out twice according to the custom of the day. I remember indulging My rural yearnings, by designing a Farm Yard & its buildings / in true rustic style. I think it was on this **208** occasion that Mr. Edmeston wrote seriously to My father warning him that I was employing My leisure hours on matters which could never by any possibility be of any practical use to me!

53 John Joshua Kirby published *Dr. Brooke Taylor's Method of Perspective* in 1754 (Colvin, 1995, p.588).

THE JOURNAL OF
ELIZABETH GEORGE
OF DADFORD

The arrival of Queen Victoria at the Corinthian Arch, Stowe, on January 15th, 1845

THE JOURNAL OF
ELIZABETH GEORGE OF DADFORD

Introduction

Elizabeth George's journal is not at all what one would expect from a farmer's daughter in north Buckinghamshire at the start of Victoria's reign. Instead of recording the annual farming round, interspersed with visits to neighbours and gossip about the local gentry, most of the events she describes concern a very different layer of society: a grandee from Wales is put up in the spare bedroom, a royal duke changes his stockings in front of the sitting-room fire, and the great house on the hill is visited by no less a person than the Queen herself. For the great house in question, the centre of Elizabeth's world, was Stowe, the seat of the Temple-Grenville family, whose head in the 1840s was the second Duke of Buckingham and Chandos; and the farm at Dadford, where Elizabeth lived, was less than a mile away in the valley below.

Nor is it strictly accurate to call her memoir a 'journal'. She made no attempt to keep a daily diary, but selected four occasions which she judged especially important and memorable for the society to which she belonged: the visit of the royal shooting party in 1840, the funeral of her uncle in 1843, the coming of age of the Marquess of Chandos in 1844, and the visit of Queen Victoria in 1845. Each of these is described in detail, and though other events linked to them are briefly mentioned in passing, the journal consists essentially of these four set pieces, written up at the time and worked over during the following years. Shortly before her death in 1872 she added a brief epilogue, a factual and, at the last, poignant commentary on the outcome of the events described twenty-five years earlier.

The date of Elizabeth's birth was 19 November 1803. She was the fourth of five children, four girls and a boy, born to Aaron and Penelope George between 1798 and 1805. The first two sisters, Hester and Mary, were the only ones who were married, Hester to a farmer at Lillingstone Dayrell, some three miles away, and Mary to another farmer, who was also tenant of the New Inn, next to the Corinthian Arch, the triumphal gateway on the Buckingham side of the Stowe estate. Both these sisters had several children. Anne, the third sister, like Elizabeth herself, never married, nor did Aaron, the youngest of the family and the only son, until his old age. A year after he was born their mother Penelope died, so that the youngest three children can hardly have had any memory of their mother, and perhaps for this reason there was an unusually close bond between them. In 1840, when Elizabeth began her journal, she was keeping house for her two bachelor uncles, Thomas and Benjamin, at the Dadford Farm; Aaron and Anne were then living at Brick Kiln Farm, only a few hundred yards down the valley, close enough for visits to be paid or messages passed two or three times a day. There they looked after their father in his declining years. Aaron was tenant of the farm, as his father, also Aaron, had been before him.

On her father's side Elizabeth was descended from a line of farmers. She believed, probably correctly, that the Georges had been farming Dadford Farm and Brick Kiln (formerly Hog Hole) Farm in unbroken succession since at least 1604, when — so the Duke told her — one John George had sold the farms to Sir Thomas Temple, becoming tenant of the land he had previously owned. She was proud of the long history of the Georges, which stretched back to a time before records existed, and this made her all the more conscious that her bachelor brother Aaron, the last of the male line, was unlikely to marry and father a son, with the result that the succession of Georges at Dadford would come to an end with him. This is indeed what happened. Generations of Georges lie buried close to the tower of the little church hidden in the trees by Stowe House, and there is an area of Stowe deer park which is still known as 'George's Piece', but these are the only relics, apart from this journal, of the family which was for centuries the principal tenant, first of the Temples and then of the Grenvilles. Elizabeth was aware that she was chronicling the end of the Georges.

What she could not realize, but what a modern reader is conscious of, is that she was also chronicling the effective end of the Grenvilles, and this gives her journal an added historical importance. Two of the events she recorded were the celebrations at the coming of age of the Duke's only son and the visit of Queen Victoria. Her feelings about these occasions were by no means uncritical, but her comments were muted, since she regarded both events as natural and appropriate for a noble family like the Grenvilles. There were underlying and sinister motives, however, of which she was ignorant. As John Beckett has shown in *The Rise and Fall of the Grenvilles*, the Duke of Buckingham, whose folly had brought him to the edge of bankruptcy, arranged and exploited these festivities to manoeuvre his son into signing away his inheritance and so stave off the creditors a little longer. Elizabeth would not have believed him capable of such crafty and cynical scheming. She would have agreed that he might sometimes behave in an arbitrary or misguided way, but never that he could be underhand. In any case he was always to be forgiven, for she regarded him with an almost feudal devotion. The respect was mutual, and the Duke is said to have felt more at home among his tenants and to have behaved more generously towards them than towards any of his other associates. By the time Elizabeth wrote the epilogue to her journal the Duke was dead, and the disastrous results of his mismanagement were obvious to all, including Elizabeth, and to her in a particularly cruel way, for her ancestral home had been sold and she had been forced to move. Even so, the feeling she conveys in the epilogue is not blame, but pity.

The most influential person on her mother's side was her grandfather, John Mander, a master carpenter who came to Stowe in 1772 during the rebuilding of the house. Construction had hardly started when his predecessor went for a swim in the lake and was drowned. So Mander arrived in a crisis. But he took charge of the huge joiners' and carpenters' programme, saw the building work through to completion and stayed on at Stowe for almost fifty years, serving three owners — Earl Temple, the Marquess of Buckingham and the first Duke — and finally becoming a respected clerk of works. For much of that time he lived in the Boycott Pavilion, the garden building usually given to the senior employee on the maintenance staff. Elizabeth was to live there herself with her 'good brother Aaron George the 3rd' from 1858, after they had left their old farm at Dadford, until her death fourteen years later. She thought of it as her second home, 'having spent so much time there in childhood, with my Grandfather and Grandmother Mander who resided in the house nearly 40 years'. This strongly suggests that after her mother's death Elizabeth was looked after by the Manders, and it may not be fanciful to imagine the little girl, wide-eyed and observant, accompanying her grandfather when his duties took him through the state rooms of Stowe. Later on she joined him or the housekeeper when visitors were being shown round, and this makes it less surprising that a local farmer's daughter should have had such intimate and detailed familiarity with the interior of Stowe House over two generations.

But although this may account for Elizabeth's exceptional knowledge, it does not explain the quality of her journal. In the end, of course, this is inexplicable, as with any creative writing, but her uniqueness owes a good deal to the fact that she was an invalid. In a note on her family she wrote of herself that she had 'suffered from very ill health the whole of her life after she was 13 years of age never being quite well for one day'. The exact nature of her illness is not known, but there is evidence that at least twice in later life she had a prolonged mental breakdown, and several times in her journal she recorded her hesitation to commit herself to any activity which she feared might be beyond her strength. On the other hand it is obvious that she ran her uncles' household with strict efficiency, and the way she coped with the crisis of the royal shooting party showed a remarkable degree of stamina. It is tempting to describe her as a 'professional' invalid, in the sense that, like other more famous women in the nineteenth century, she adopted the role to strengthen her position in society. As a detached observer she could watch and listen from the sidelines, and comment with impunity. She had an excellent ear for dialogue, and her insight into human pretension, especially male pretension, coupled with her keen sense of the ridiculous, provide the reader with scenes of rich social comedy.

Her detachment also gave her a special advantage when she came to describe the grand occasions at Stowe. We know well enough from several eyewitnesses the details of the Marquess's coming of age and the Queen's visit — the order of events, who was there, who had precedence and so on — but only Elizabeth's journal gives us an oblique view of the festivities which places them in original and telling perspective. It is rather like the famous chapters in *Vanity Fair*, where Thackeray describes the battle of Waterloo as seen through the eyes of the non-combatants and camp-followers in Brussels. We sit waiting with Elizabeth at the farm in Dadford, until the distant firing of a cannon alerts us that the Queen has entered the park; later, as darkness falls, we can just see the coloured lights illuminating the house and hear the 'dull, dead roar like thunder from the multitude up at Stowe'; and from time to time messengers and friends come back to Dadford with reports on the action going forward up on the hill. Only once did Elizabeth take part herself. Aaron and Anne persuaded her to go with them to the tenants' ball given in honour of the Marquess of Chandos, and for a couple of hours she sat gossiping in the marquee and watching the dancers. But by the time supper was announced she had had enough and asked Aaron to take her home.

During Queen Victoria's visit Elizabeth never left Dadford, but a few days after the Queen's departure the Duke brought his shooting party to lunch at the farm, and as a special favour to the George family he said that Anne and Elizabeth could take a few friends to view the suite of rooms which had been specially prepared for the Queen's use. Many other people had applied, he said, but all had been refused. So the next day the little party of seven spent two hours on a unique conducted tour of the royal apartments. What the other six thought is not known, but fortunately Elizabeth wrote a detailed account of the afternoon in her journal. It is the most perceptive and evocative description of the interior of Stowe House in its heyday which is ever likely to be discovered.

The Text

After Elizabeth George's death the journal passed to the Bennett family, into which her sister Mary had married, and has been handed down as a treasured possession to the present generation. One of her great-nieces, Helen Bennett, a kindergarten teacher, made a copy for her cousin, Annie Scott Clarke, in 1932, but for some reason this copy remained in the Bennett family. This was fortunate, since the original has disappeared, probably being lost when Helen's stored possessions were destroyed in the 1939–45 War. The copy journal then passed to her cousin Philip Bartlett, who first showed it to me, and it is with the kind permission and encouragement of his daughters, Cherry Hollingworth and Prue Winter, that the full journal is now published. My thanks are also due to another cousin, Robert Bennett, for help in hunting down additional facts of the family history.

The present text, therefore, is taken from Helen's copy journal, which raises the editorial problem of deciding how accurate a transcript the copy is. Paragraphing and spelling are variable, punctuation consists mostly of dashes, and when inverted commas are used, they are often misleading. Is this what Elizabeth wrote, or did Helen change things in copying? Only one other example of Elizabeth's writing has survived (apart from a list of Aaron's shirts, twice updated, pasted on the back of a cupboard door), and that is a collection of notes she wrote on the fly leaves and margins of a seventeenth-century book, entitled *The Mystery of Selfe Deceiving*, which served the George family for the purpose usually fulfilled by a family bible. Simple entries of births and deaths had been started by her grandfather, 'Aaron George (the Elder)', and these were continued in extended notes of family history by Elizabeth, valuable information which has been used and quoted above in the Introduction. The style and punctuation of these family notes are similar to the journal, and the use of dashes is typical of writing style in Elizabeth's generation. So it has seemed that the only reasonable course is to rely on Helen Bennett's as an accurate copy and to keep editorial interference to a minimum.

The text, which runs on for 228 continuous pages in the copy, has been presented in five separate sections — four episodes and an epilogue. Some abbreviations have been silently expanded; occasional capital letters, full stops, commas and question marks have been added where the sense would be awkward to follow without them; and a few obvious spelling errors have been corrected. Only the inverted commas have been rationalized throughout. Otherwise the text has been left as it is. It has been the experience of several generations that Elizabeth George's skill as a writer carries the reader through anomalies of grammar and punctuation without serious difficulty. An over-zealous editor is an unnecessary obstacle.

George Clarke

I

January 30th 1840

Memorable as the day on which we had the honour to entertain two Royal Personages, together with his grace the Duke of Buckingham and Chandos, several other noblemen and a large party of untitled gentlemen all 30 people.

The Duke of Buckingham had for some years made a practice of coming to luncheon with my uncle several times during each shooting season — in fact our house appeared to be quite a favourite rendezvous with his Grace and not without good cause — I will venture to say. In the first place our family had been Tenants of the same farm in regular succession from Father to son, for 240 years, ever since the land had been purchased by Sir Thomas Temple and the present Duke has told us, that he finds from old title deeds, our farm and some other lands adjoining, belong'd to a John George, before it became the property of the Temples of Stowe. It is therefore very probable that the farm had been *occupied* by our fore-fathers long before they ceased to be the owners.

Notwithstanding this, my Uncle never presumed the least on the influence such a position might be expected to give him over his Landlord — He was always the most upright and straightforward of Tenants, with an independent spirit that would have scorn'd to seek for favours in any underhand way, altho' he had for 20 years suffered grievously from Game depredation (to such an extent that we did not get the seed again on the ploughed land, and had never had compensation for the loss) yet he had (altho' a plain Farmer) such a nice sense of what was handsome and honourable, that he would never make the least complaint or ask for any redress when the Duke came to see us — he said it would be taking an unfair advantage as the Duke could not very well refuse when seated at our table and being gratuitously entertained with all the Gentlemen of his party. It was not therefore surprising that he should say he never felt so comfortable or so much at home as when sitting with Uncle his 'good Old Tenant' — I think myself Uncle carried his delicacy rather too far some times, he certainly did a great injustice to himself, and it served to encourage the Duke in his unfair and wasteful preservation of Game. However let that pass — no matter how great cause we might have to complain, his Grace was always so exceedingly kind and affable in his behaviour and of so noble and distinguish'd a presence that he possessed a sort of fascination that made most people forget everything at the time, except the pleasure of being in his company.

For my own part, I always felt quite at my ease when conversing with him and was pleased to afford him the best accommodation in my power. Our house being large and generally pretty well provisioned made it less trouble to us, though it would have been to some others and his Grace used to laugh and say he liked to bring a large party, because Uncle was 'an old Batchelor so he would have no pity upon him and would give him a good benefit'.

He had been here twice before during the present winter — and we heard that it was expected the Queen's Uncle and cousin (The Duke of Cambridge and Prince George) would come to stay a few days at Stowe before the shooting season was over. On the evening that the firing of cannon and the bells announced the arrival of the Royal Visitors I said to Uncle 'Suppose the Duke should bring them here to lunch some day when they are out shooting' — My supposition was held to be a great improbability — for Uncle said 'O he wont think of coming here when they are with him.' So I felt in a manner free from anxiety on that point and was thankful to be so, for I had taken a cold, which caused severe inflammation of my chest and lungs, insomuch that I could not even *whisper* a single word, and my doctor enjoined perfect quiet, desiring that I would keep in bed a few days.

We had been compelled to dismiss our Dairymaid, and her successor only arrived two days before, the other girl was comparatively a stranger, coming the last Michaelmas, and did not know where to find any things that were not in common use —

I knew the Duke had pass'd though the village accompanied by his Royal Visitors and a large party and I understood they were shooting on our farm, but felt little concern about their movements thinking I should have nothing to do in it — therefore I was sadly startled and almost shudder'd in my bed after hearing a thundering rap at the front door — the Girl answered it, and I recognized the head keeper's voice and distinctly heard him say 'the Duke desires his compliments to Mr George and if quite agreeable will come and take Lunch with him and I was to say, "the party would be 30 in number" ' — This message was repeated to Uncle and the answer he returned was 'Tell his Grace I shall be pleased to accommodate himself and friends in the best way I can.'

In a few minutes both the maids rush'd upstairs to tell me, not thinking that I had overheard the message — I took my slate and chalk being obliged to write every word I had to say — They held up their hands exclaiming 'Whatever shall we do?' — Ill as I felt I saw that I must get up, tho' I knew what additional suffering it would cause me, and it was impossible I could dress and write directions to them at one and the same time — So I desired they would go light fires in the Parlour and sitting room — also get a good fire made in the kitchen and plenty of boiling water — I knew, a rump of beef had been boiled for dinner, there was also part of a roast sparib and some raised pork pies — mince pies etc. but the beef was of course neither hot nor cold then — so I ordered it to be set out at the cellar window on the snow, and I knew what we had ready cooked in the house was not sufficient to set out a table for 30 persons — I told the Girls to ask Uncle to come up to me; when he came he seemed inclined to take the matter very easily and begged I would not hurry or flurry myself — I said 'Uncle it is no use preparation must be made directly, there is but little time before us, they will be here in less than 2 hours. There are two couples of Fowls put up to feed — they must be killed directly and prepar'd for roasting, we shall also require a large dish of frizzled ham — gravy and egg sauce and plenty of hot mesh'd potatoes' — he said it could *not* be done. I said, 'it must be done it would never do to accede to the Duke's proposal and not prepare what was sufficient' (all this I had to write) and I wrote 'now pray dont ask more questions than you can help, but please do as I ask you without questioning me, for I shall never get thro' it if I have to hinder all the time to write' — I said, 'have the fowls killed, put them into a pan and tell the Girl to cover them with boiling water and let them lie a few minutes; the feathers will then strip off quickly — there is no time to pluck them, then if she draws them and gets a good fire, I will be with her to make gravy and sauce if I am able to stand' — and I asked him to have the pony saddled and get a large flag basket ready while I wrote a hasty note to each of my two sisters who lived near, requesting them to send all the butter they could spare, also any ready cooked meat — adding 'I will repay you in kind next week.' The boy was to go to Anne at Brick Kiln farm first, then on to Mrs Bennett at New Inn —

When I got downstairs, so many things had to be look'd out, and so much to do, I really hardly knew however I should get all done, had I been only tolerably well and able to speak, I should not have minded it a bit, but it was so distressing to me for I could not move my arms without paining my chest and there was nothing I could quite leave to the Girls, not even to get the mesh'd potatoes done, and I had to be present and help set the tables as well as to help cook. Our dining table when set out full length in the large parlour, would not, I knew, seat more than 20 or 22 comfortably — so I set out the centre table in [the] sitting room for eight — taking care to have a large cheerful fire in each — there was also a large fire in the front kitchen, as well as in the back where we work'd.

I had 3 wash stands with plenty of napkins in [the] front kitchen, also a lot of Uncle's stockings airing before the fire — in case any wet footed Gentleman should require a change of dry, and had a sofa set along before that fire and my couch in front of the sitting room fire.

When the rooms were ready I felt so ill and exhausted that I should have been glad to creep any where to lie down, but that could not be, I had got the sauce to make and to see to the fowls and the boiled ham and before it was quite ready, the whole company came flocking in, glad to get out of the snow — it was half an hour before the appointed time.

The Duke was as usual very kind — Uncle told him I could not speak, but he little thought how ill I was — he said 'I will see that every one well cleans his shoes' — and set the example himself, the royal Duke and the prince also following his example, very energetically scraping and brushing their boots before they came in. I was introduced to them by the Duke, who very considerately spoke for me for the Duke of Cambridge like his father George the Third is remarkable for asking a multitude of unnecessary frivolous questions. He was thoroughly soaked about the feet, and took his place on the couch in front of the fire ordering his own tall Game Keeper might be sent in to act as Valet — so, in stalked a gigantic keeper and kneeling down on the hearthrug he drew off his royal Master's wet boots and stockings and exchang'd them for others that he had got ready in his pocket.

The Duke meantime turning his head round to stare at me, when I was obliged to go in for some thing that I wanted, I should have drawn back when I saw how the two were occupied, but he said 'O come in, never mind an old gentleman like me, What is your name and how long have you kept your Uncle's house?' — I could not speak to answer, so made a curtsey and escaped out of the room as speedily as I could.

All the others had washed their hands and gone into the large parlour. I soon found some of them would be willing to come back into the sitting room to take their lunch at the table I had set there.

It was impossible all could sit at the same table as the Duke's and other grandees, but they were determined to remain in the same room so three or four Captains and the Mayor of Buckingham drew a side table in front of the large sofa and wedged themselves in to it some way without any table cloth, merely asking the Girl who waited to fetch them some knives and forks with the cruets out of the other room. Our Duke insisted that Uncle should take the head of the table, which he would rather not have done, but his Grace said 'Nobody shall sit at the head of your table but yourself' and 'you must carve for his Royal Highness who will sit at your right hand.'

Accordingly, they were placed so, the Duke of Cambridge on one side, and Prince George on the other, then the Duke of Buckingham, Lord De L'isle and Dudley, Lords Holland and Hotham, Sir Wm. Clayton, George Simon Harcourt M.P. for Bucks and others of less note, Colonel Hall, Captains Johnson, Neville, Carrington and Dewes.

I thought when I looked round the room, how immeasurably inferior all the rest were to the Duke of Buckingham, in person and deportment — as for the Duke of Cambridge so far as manners went I should have considered he was a vulgar old man even had he been a Farmer — his son, Prince George was much more decorous, and evidently felt greatly annoyed by the vicious and frivolous discourse of his Papa — The young Prince has a fine, tall lithe figure and not bad features, but a blotchy, bad complexion.

I only went into the room now and then, the poor girl who waited, said, directly I disappeared, the Duke of Cambridge talk'd to her in such a way that she would have left them to wait upon themselves had it not been for 'Master' and the Duke of Buckingham. She said she hardly knew how to be thankful enough to Uncle when he spoke up so fearlessly to vindicate her character. She said, the Queen's Uncle must have led a loose, bad life himself or he would not have been so suspicious of other people.

His Royal Highness did not indulge in that kind of language when I was present, but I thought what I heard him say, was very frivolous and ridiculous, among other speeches (he talked incessantly) he said to Uncle — 'I say do you know that you are kin to me?' What answer could Uncle give to such a question, he simply said 'No'. His Royal Highness ask'd if he was not the 'Son of Farmer George'. Uncle said 'Yes' — 'Well then,' replied the Duke, 'I am also the son of "Farmer George" so we must be kin I think.' He had seen our draining machine standing in the Dairy Ground — wanted to know if that was the ruin of a favourite old tree and if Uncle had not put the frame and chain round it to preserve it, and then, casting his eyes up suddenly to the ceiling he said 'What is up over here? bedrooms I suppose, how many bedrooms have you etc, etc' and many more questions equally trifling. His Royal Highness certainly was very affable, showed no hauteur, but one naturally expects some kind of dignity in a Prince of the Royal blood, and I had always understood the Duke of Cambridge to be the best of George the 3rd's numerous sons. After partaking very heartily of our lunch, the company had wine and departed. When the Duke of Buckingham observed that His Royal Highness did not let Uncle fill his glass again after the 3rd time he said 'O my G-d, I cant drink any more I am as full now as ever I can stick.' Which I thought we should have considered rather a vulgar reply had the speaker been an old Farmer, instead of being H.R.H. the Duke of Cambridge.

Candles had been lighted two hours and it was nearly 7 o'clock before our Guests departed. The Duke of Buckingham asked if the Shooting Omnibus had arrived to convey them up to Stowe, he found it was waiting in the Yard — several Gentlemen preferred walking the Prince for one.

I heard a few days later that the Duchess was very much displeased because the Duke did not come home earlier, all the Gentlemen having of course to dress, which delayed the dinner half an hour.

The head Cook was also aggrieved, having exerted his abilities to set on a first rate Banquet.

All the Shooters had already spoiled their appetites and could not do justice to what was placed before them.

The Duke found fault with his cooks — saying he found things much more to his taste at Farm houses particularly vegetables. His Grace forgot to make allowances for the difference there must be between a keen, and a cloyed appetite — and perhaps did not know how a dinner was deteriorated in quality by remaining half an hour beyond the time specified.

Everybody seemed to think we had been highly honour'd; yet I much doubt whether any of our neighbours would have willingly incurred the trouble.

I know I was not able to get up for a week afterwards.

When Uncle went to Buckingham on Saturday, the first persons he met were Messrs Hearn and Smith the Lawyers, who jokingly enquired whether he would condescend to shake hands with them after having entertained a Royal Duke and a Prince.

The next time the Duke brought a party to Lunch was in November 1841. He said 'I saw the Duke of Cambridge the other day in London, when he enquired after "those good old Batchelors" — desired to be remember'd to you, and said if he ever came to Stowe again, he should not fail to pay you another visit.'

Her Majesty, Adelaide Queen Dowager, visited the Duke and Duchess of Buckingham in August 1840.

The weather had for some time been very hot and dry, insomuch that the herbage in the park was all scorched up and even the lawn on the Garden front was bare of grass.

Great preparation had been made for that distinguish'd Guest. Her Majesty arrived on the 12th and I believe came here from Alton Towers, [where] she had been on a visit to the Earl of Shrewsbury. She remained at Stowe 3 days and the neighbourhood was en fête all the time.

The poor of all the surrounding parishes dined in tents on the North Front the day that the Queen came.

On the second day in the afternoon the Gardens were thrown open to the Public for a Grand Promenade and Military Concert.

There was a great Concourse of people assembled and they had a good view of the Queen as she sat in the South Portico under the Orange Trees. She was accompanied by her sister Ida, Grand Duchess of Sax Weimar and of course her Host and Hostess with all the distinguish'd personages, the Arch Bishop of Canterbury being one who were staying at Stowe were in attendance upon her.

The following Evening a Grand Masquerade Ball was given in a spacious Booth or Marquee on the North Side — cost the Duke £1,000 in Erection tho' only used that night. I suppose His Grace was fearful that so large a company dancing in the house would in some way injure the splendid furniture but supper was set in the State Dining room and the whole range of apartments were lighted up — presenting a most magnificent spectacle.

II

April 27th 1843 — Half past nine o'clock in the evening — This has been a day I shall never forget!

The remains of my beloved Uncle Thomas have been consigned to the grave!

The friends, whom this sad event had gathered around us, having all left, with the exception of my dear Ann, our Home is again restored to silence and ourselves; and the overwhelming grief that oppressed me during the day, having at length subsided into a calm resignation to God's Will, I feel able to make this record before I retire to rest.

I do not expect I shall be able to rise from my bed tomorrow, and I know I shall deeply feel the absence of my dear Sister, when she has left us, but I will endeavour to bear it with composure knowing such bereavements are for our good; teaching us humility and leading us to a knowledge and conviction of our entire dependence on The Almighty's Will.

A more severe trial than the death of my good Uncle can never befall me — My best Friend, my second Father, with all a Father's care, combined with the patient disinterested affection of a Mother — he supplied the place of both Parents to me during a long period of suffering, and infirm health, and it will always cause a feeling of melancholy regret when I remember that I was not able in some measure to repay his kindness, by a constant attendance upon him during the illness that preceded his death.

I could only think and care for him, and direct others *to do*, what I would so gladly have performed myself.

Sometimes the loss I have sustained seems like a dream to me, as tho' it could not be true, that I should never in this life behold my good Uncle again; yet 'I have heard the bell toll'd on his Burial day' 'And saw the Hearse that bore him slow away.'

May 4th

A week has elapsed since I wrote the fore-going page, I will now add a few more particulars respecting the Funeral. I was awoke about 4 o'clock in the Morning by the plaintive notes of a Black-bird, which had built a nest in the shrubs directly opposite dear Uncle's windows, and during several weeks its early song had been the first sound that

80

announced the return of Day; it was never heard unnoticed by the poor Invalid, and the bird's notes were this morning so unusually low and melancholy that they seemed to me, like a sorrowful Lament for the loss of the good man whose remains were so soon to leave the House for ever, and my tears flowed freely in unison.

I saw no one till 9 o'clock, my kind sister being unwilling to disturb me earlier, and as we had made all the arrangements the evening before, I knew it was not necessary that I should give any further directions, and I had decided on having a little fire to myself in Uncle Benjamin's room, well knowing, I should require to rest quietly several times during the day, and I thought it would be very comfortable also for Uncle to air his clothes by, before I should go to it.

The day tho' fine was cold, but as there were 4 fires down stairs, I knew all the company might have been in warm rooms, without mixing the mourners and the other Visitors. Had the Parlour been reserved for the Family, there would then have been the sitting Room for the Pall-Bearers and friends, the front Kitchen for Mr King and his man, and the back Kitchen for the Bearers and servants — and, there was a good fire in each apartment and also refreshments, in each —

But Mrs Turpin so very strongly opposed such an arrangement, saying 'Mourners always sat in a room up stairs and it would look so, for any of the Family to be seen below!'

I thought the objections she made were not deserving of much consideration, but, as I did not feel disposed to enter into any argument she had her own way. A table was set out with refreshments in the cold best bed-room and all the Family sat shivering there for 2 hours — the warm sitting room below, being meantime quite unoccupied.

Mrs Turpin had reserved that, for the Lawyer, but Mr Smith would not stay there alone, for as soon as he found the rest of the company were in the Parlour he went there also, as might have been expected.

Our Mourning was not sent home till near the middle of the day, and I felt so weak and ill that I do not think I could have put it on, had not my sister been there to assist me.

As soon as we were dressed, I proposed to Ann, that we would go to the Chamber of Death, and look for the last time, at the coffin of our good Uncle.

We had never before experienced the loss of so near and dear a relative (our Mother having died during my infancy) and the sorrow we felt was deep and sincere — yet only for ourselves did we sorrow, not a doubt rested in our minds but the Friend we mourned was gone to receive the reward promised to the 'Just and Upright' — the meek and merciful Christian who had ever done unto others as he would they should do unto him, and even more —

Many were the expressions of attachment I heard uttered that day by friends who were round us, all eagerly bore testomony to the worth and amiable character of the deceased, and to the general respect and estimation in which he had always been held — of the consolations that may be obtained under such a loss as had so recently befallen us, none can equal the comfort that such considerations afford . . .

Altho' 4 o'clock was the Hour appointed for the Funeral, our friends began to arrive much earlier; Mr King having arrangements to make, was here soon after one, Uncle John, and Aunt Curtis, my Brother, Mr & Mrs Scott, Mary & William George, Mr & Mrs Bennett, Mr Thos. Flowers, and Uncle's old friend, Mr Harper of Twyford Lodge came soon after 2.

I staid downstairs till the Pall Bearers were coming and then retired with Ann to my room, where we passed the remainder of our time. I lay down on the bed, and my dear sister sat by me near the window, and gave notice of every fresh arrival, as she could see any body who came up the yard — she soon told me that Mr Marriott was come; and then in quick succession named — Mr Langton, Mr Hadland, Mr Attwood, Mr J. Bennett, Mr Salmons and Mr Smith — and shortly after, slow, and heavy footsteps up the stairs told us that the Bearers were coming to remove the Corpse.

I can scarcely describe my feelings when I heard them pass by the door again on their way down.

My sister was listening intently to every sound, and I *saw* she felt the same sensations of solemn awe; we gave no utterance to our thoughts but sat linked together in silent sorrow till she was summoned to prepare for joining the Mourners. Mrs Turpin then came to me, and set my chair near the window that I might see the Funeral procession go down the road — first walked Mr King & Mr Smith, then the 6 Pall bearers two & two, then followed the Hearse — the Bearers three on each side, wearing silk hat bands like the Pall Bearers, and after the Hearse the Mourners — my sisters and Aunt, riding — the others on foot.

I watched the slow and solemn train with streaming eyes, till I could see it no more, and *then* I felt, that poor Uncle was *indeed* gone from us; but so calm and happy had been his death, so peaceful and consolatory all the circumstances attending it, that I knew I ought rather humbly to hope we might hereafter go to *him* than wish 'to call his unbound spirit back to us & life again'

'May my last end be like his' — —

Before the return of the Funeral Party from church I had gone down into the parlour & desired Mrs Turpin to prepare tea etc. for Mr King and the Pall bearers in the sitting room, hoping we might have our Tea quietly, and spend the remainder of the day free from intrusion.

Uncle Benj. did not intend that the *will* should have been read till *after* Tea; but our Family circle was no sooner formed than the Lawyer sent to enquire if we were ready to admit him, consequently, Tea was postponed and Mr Smith came in and took his seat at the table.

I felt but very little care or anxiety about the will, being as I thought pretty well aware of the Testator's intentions, and expecting that the whole property was left for the use of Uncle Benjamin during his life, and for equal distribution among nephews and nieces at his decease, and I believe such had been the general expectation, for no anxious solicitude was exhibited by anybody present and when Mr Smith began reading the preamable 'This is the *last* Will and Testament of *me* Thomas George', I felt as tho' it had been the voice of poor Uncle himself, speaking to us from the grave, and my thoughts partook much more of sorrow that it was indeed his *last* will, than of curiousity to hear how *that* will would affect my future prospects. Aaron and Thomas Scott were appointed Executors, and the property bequeathed to Uncle Benjamin for Life then, after a long preamble about lands and conditions, which nobody appeared to attend to, I was startled to hear my own name made the subject of a separate clause, and to find that my good Uncle's Fatherly care for me had gone beyond his life-time, but I felt much more affected by such an unsuspected mark of favour, than rejoiced, and I even began to *fear*, that in case I survived Uncle B. the use of the whole was to be transferred to me, and I should not have felt comfortable had it been so; therefore it was quite a relief to me, when I heard the other names follow; and so little care did I then feel about my own portion that I could not have told anyone under what conditions it was beqeathed.

I soon found that no dissatisfaction was likely to arise from poor Uncle's distinction in my favour, indeed he had so ordered it that eventually neither of the others would have less on that account.

At the conclusion of the Will, Mr Smith made an observation which quite surprised me, and which furnished an additional proof, how little purely circumstantial evidence is to be relied on, even when coming from the most respectable witnesses, if they are not perfectly acquainted with *all* the particulars of the case —

What Mr S. said was — 'I believe that is all but I have the satisfaction to add, that I have been speaking to Mr Andrewes today, and he told me I might say, that *he* saw Mr George a few days before his death when he administered the Sacrament for the last time, and that he told him then, he had settled his affairs; and that he felt very comfortable; for he had made a Will; that it was just such a will as he intended to make, and he had done just as he always meant to do' — Now Anne and I had partaken of the Sacrament, and heard every word that passed as we stood by the bedside — Poor Uncle had taken it several times before in his illness, but when Mr Andrewes paid his last visit about two days before he died, extreme weakness had affected his mind, and at intervals he talk'd in a very incoherent way; often fancying people had been in his room conversing with him, whom he had not seen for years — any person coming in, who did not live in the house or know all about it, would really have supposed he was quite collected and sensible and that the decribed visit and conversation was a fact that had just happened — For instance the day before, when I went into his room early and enquired how he felt he said 'Oh I slept pretty well, but I have had Lepper here these two hours, and it has tired me sadly — bless the man, why cant he say at once what he will give for the cows, without so much haggling? I am sure I was very moderate in my price, for I wish'd him to have a good profit — I know he needs to be careful how he deals — for he is left with a family of little Motherless children.' The fact was, Uncle had never seen, or spoken, to Lepper for three months — yet when telling me the above he talk'd so connectedly that I could see any person who had just call'd to see him, would little have supposed it was a delusion — they would have thought he was quite sensible — On the day Mr Andrewes alluded to (when speaking to Mr Smith) after the Sacrament had been administered Mr A. remarked to Uncle — 'Well now, I hope you feel quite comfortable. I suppose you have settled your worldly affairs' — and he said 'Yes, we settled it at last, I was afraid we should have had a family quarrel but we had a Meeting at Buckingham — I met John and the other parties, and we settled it and I was glad enough when it was over' — That was exactly what poor Uncle said, he never said he had settled his affairs and that he had done what he intended to do but I daresay Mr Andrewes thought Uncle was replying to his enquiry as to having made a Will, and he did not notice his precise words or forgot how he had express'd himself — Ann said 'poor Uncle is so weak, that his mind wanders very much now.' Mr Andrewes caught her up, and said 'no not the least I am sure he is quite sensible' — And no doubt in a disputed Will case the evidence of the clergyman would have been conclusive — or at least would have had great weight and yet we may see by this how very mistaken he might be.

About the end of July 1843 Aunt Curtis died suddenly at Chackmore — she was Father's and Uncle's only sister, and had married late in life a Mr James Curtis of London (who held a situation in the customs). Mr C. was, I believe an intimate friend of Mrs Mills by whom he was introduced to Aunt during one of her visits to London — Curtis had not long been a widower, and had 4 children; only one daughter (about 16) remaining at home — I suppose he did not find his house very comfortable, and very eagerly responded to Mrs Mills' recommendation of her 'friend Miss George' poor Aunt's fortune being also without doubt a very important consideration. He only came courting once to Dadford and was then very pressing to get married. Uncles were far from approving of the match, but of course Aunt was her own mistress, therefore all they could do was to get half of her money secur'd to her — which proved a very fortunate thing as she found soon after her marriage that her husband was deeply envolved, and she, I believe paid the whole of his debts — hoping after so doing, to live in peace and quietness, but there was a worthless son who continually annoyed her. She therefore felt anxious to get away from London altogether and at length when Curtis obtained his discharge from the Customs with the superannuated salary they came first to reside at Moreton till the house at Chackmore (long occupied by Major Vapar) became vacant and was taken for Aunt by Uncle Thomas; but she had only been there about 2 years when her Death occurred. I believe Curtis did not survive her 12 months.

1844

My dear Father departed this life after having been afflicted with paralysis of the spine which quite confined him to his bed. He was so helpless and unable to move that 2 sitters up, were required every night during two years and a half — his dutiful and exemplary son taking turn every other night — there was a nurse also in the house who did nothing else but attend upon Father, but it was impossible for one person to move him, therefore my dear sister or the servant had often to run upstairs a dozen times in the day when the nurse rang for assistance — I believe Paralysis invariably affects the temper of those who are suffering from it — we were not therefore surprised when poor Father became very irritable and difficult to please having been formerly one of the most good humour'd men in the neighbourhood — I had not been able to visit him for some time before he died and as is generally the case in such long afflictions his Death came upon us very suddenly.

I went to the Funeral but did not accompany the rest to church — Mrs Jessey was with my sister to take charge of the arrangements, and Martha Mold to make the servants mourning — After poor Father's removal only Uncle Benjamin and Uncle John remained of the Family — Uncle John having left the New Inn more than 12 months, came to reside with Uncle B. & I at Dadford but had no share in the business. My brother and sister, of course, remained in the farm and house at Brick Kiln Farm — Poor Anne died to my great grief December 10th 1852. I had been staying with her a few days — She had long been failing in health and having taken cold in the Autumn, rapid consumption followed which, acting on a weaken'd constitution soon carried her off — I was long before I became reconciled to her loss — could not for some time realize that I should never see her any more — Few days used to pass without communication between us — several boys and men went from Dadford to Aaron's to work, we had therefore constant opportunity of sending to each other, and I seldom sat down to the Tea table without having a note or parcel brought in by the servant — 'from Miss Anne'.

For a long time I could not divest myself of the expectation of the accustomed daily remembrance; it had been one of the chief consolations of my own bad health — and — I knew that to me the loss would be irreparable. My dear sister had always been greatly respected, for she was as amiable in character as handsome in person. I have seen no one in this neighbourhood at all to be compared to dear Anne in personal appearance.

III

The Autumn after poor Father's death A.D. 1844 was distinguished by the coming of age of the Marquis of Chandos, only son of the Duke and Duchess of Buckingham — As would be expected great preparations had been made for the celebration of this important Event. The Duke had spoken to us about it the last time he came here to lunch (some time in February) and he said then, he supposed should nothing unforseen happen he should have a whole week's Festivity at Stowe and he expected the house to be full of company for, of course the whole of their Family connexions must be invited upon such an occasion, together with all the Gentry in the County.

We promised his Grace the use of our two spare bedrooms, in case it would be an accommodation to him: he thanked us and said he would bear our offer in mind. I remember we had a very fine autumn, and the weather was quite summerlike when the 10th of September arrived. Our Garden was splendid with all manner of rich coloured bright blossoms, and the air was so warm and balmy, that Alfresco amusements would be pursued without danger of taking cold.

Of course great preparations had been made for the celebration of Lord Chandos' birthday. We did not think of inviting any friends who would require sleeping apartments, knowing we should have none to spare; but a week before the time arrived, I received a letter from Mr Wm. Porter of Northampton, saying if it would be agreable to us, he should very much like to come and witness the festivities, and should bring a young Gentleman with him. After consulting Uncle, I sent word that they would be quite welcome, provided they were willing to share the same bed. I did not for a moment doubt but they would come. Had we been inclined to profit by the occasion, our two spare rooms would, I am convinced have let for £20 for the week. Instances came to our knowledge of tradesmen at Buckingham charging £5 for a bed for *one* night! and they found nothing else, only hot water, indeed my Brother at Brick Kiln farm, and we at Dadford were the only Tenants who accommodated the Duke's friends *gratis*, and, we boarded their servants as well.

I said to Uncle before the time came, 'Well I hope if the Duke *does* send anybody here, it will be somebody of consequence, and not half pay officers or any people of that Class.' My sister Anne said the same of the rooms they had offered to the Duke and their accommodation was first rate, for since poor Father's decease, they had newly paper'd and painted the bedrooms, and there was also a handsome new 4 post bed in the best room, making it altogether the freshest and most elegant apartment in the parish with such a delightful view up into the Park from the two windows. My sister had Miss Shepherd of Blakesley staying with her.

For several days before the 10th of September I had been very busy cooking & getting our two spare rooms in the nicest order that I could and wondering who would make use of them.

On Saturday I was uncommonly surprised to receive a message from the Duke by the Gardener, to this effect — 'The Duke desires his compliments to Mr George, and if quite agreable, he will send Sir Watkin Wynne to sleep here during the week and he may be expected on Monday afternoon.' When I repeated the message to Uncle, he laughed and (reminding me of the wish I had express'd in regard to the rank of our expected Guests) said 'I hope now you are going to have one of the very first of the Duke's relations you will be satisfied.'

Quite so, I was only surprised that the Duke liked to send such a consequential young Gentleman out to sleep, so many apartments that he had fitted up at Stowe. I knew Sir Watkin had only been of age himself about a year ago and I had read accounts in the Newspapers of the Festivities at Wynnstay on the occasion far exceeding in splendour and extent, what he came to partake of at Stowe — 14 Oxen had been roasted whole at his coming of age, and his Aunt, the Duchess of Northumberland presided as Mistress of the house, and Hostess — he having no Mother living or sister old enough.

By Monday a sort of Programme of what was to be done at Stowe was made public.

On Tuesday, the poor of 6 or 7 surrounding parishes were to dine in tents on the Park or North side of the house. Bonfires to be lighted on all the neighbouring hills at dusk — a Grand dinner party in the house, to finish with a superb display of fireworks.

Ox roasting and all manner of diversions at Buckingham —

Wednesday Morning — a Grand Battue in the preserves — with a Masquerade ball at night, for which a spacious and highly decorated booth had been erected *on the lawn* on the North front (a mistake — I should have said the booth was in the Court Yard) with covered entrances from the Colonnades.

Thusday — Addresses from the Corporation, and a Dinner for the whole of the Tenantry at which the Duke was to preside and a ball for the Tenants at night.

On Friday a Morning Concert and at night a ball for all the servants, also the servants of the Guests.

Our Northampton friends arrived early in the day on Tuesday. I had set out our large dining table the whole length of the Great Parlour the evening before — thinking I should then be ready for any comers. Fortunately I had secured the services of an old Servant from Twyford for the week, had I not done so, I do not know how I should have got thro' it. Public Holidays at Stowe always unhinge all our Domestic arrangements — Men Servants, maid servants, and Labourers, become very dissatisfied unless they can be off on the gad — and no work is done willingly — tho' their pay goes on just the same. We found it difficult even to get the cows milk'd several nights. Our two girls went up to the North front to see the people dine in the Marquees leaving the woman and I to do as well as we could.

By the middle of the day our large parlour was full. Some of my Guests I am sure I did not know; but they said they knew Mr George quite well, and I could not say to the contrary — so I served all alike. The stables were full of horses, and many tied up under the open hovel; vehicles of all kinds in the yard. Uncle and the Northampton Gents went off to Buckingham in the morning to see what was going on there. Aaron came about the middle of the day, and ask'd me if I would not go up in the evening to view the Fireworks, saying the Tenants were to be admitted to the Colonnades, which would not only secure a good view but offer'd comfortable sitting — I told him I should very much like to go, if I could get away — he said 'then I will bring the gig for you about 8 o'clock, your company will be all going after they have had tea, and you can lock up the house.'

I thought of getting a quiet hour to rest in the afternoon before I began preparing for the return of our Guests to tea — but I was soon interrupted. Between 4 and 5 o'clock a carriage and pair (with a large Imperial on the roof) drove up the yard — in addition to the Coachman there were two Servants out of Livery — I found it was Sir Watkin's equipage — he had himself alighted at Stowe, and sent the Servants down to our house with his luggage. I had to receive them — the Coachman drove away to Buckingham I suppose. The two valets had all the luggage to unpack and to carry it upstairs. I was surprised that Sir Watkin should require such a quantity of wearing apparel for a week's use; but the head valet explained to me that they had only just returned from a Tour on the Continent, and consequently had got everything that they took there — I next shewed our Rooms to Mr Jones (the Gentleman's Gentleman).

Sir Watkin was, of course, to have the large best room, and I thought the small one adjoining, would be most convenient for the Valet. The Imperial had been taken into the little room — as it contained all the luggage I thought no other receptacle would be needed; but the Valet saw there were two sets of drawers in the large room, and another set where he was to sleep. So he enquired whether they could not have the use of them, because he must unpack Sir Watkin's clothes before bedtime.

Now the best room drawers contained all my best apparel, and I could not shift my things into other drawers, because all the others were occupied — So, as the shortest way, I called the woman to help me. We spread a pair of sheets on the carpet on the floor, into which I bundled all my robes etc. then tied up the ends of the sheets, and took the bundles up into one of the attics — the corpulent, consequential serving-man looking on all the time, alternatively taking snuff and drinking drams of Brandy from a pocket Flask — pretending that it was medicine — he was very communicative and loud in the praise of Sir Watkin's Estates and large Income — thinking thereby that, no doubt, he should impress us with a sense of his own personal importance, as the confidential Servant who had lived with Sir Watkin's Father, and had much to do with the management of his young Master's affairs. He said Sir Watkin's rental was £90,000 per annum and that he was called the 'King of Wales'. I never saw such a number and variety of clothes belonging to one man, as were heaped about the room after they were unpacked; only the linen and smaller articles were put into the drawers — coats and waistcoats etc. were stack'd up on the tops. I am sure there were not fewer than 40 satin neck handkerchiefs and scarves; silk stockings and pink silk under vests in abundance.

When I went up to turn the bed down in the evening, I found a splendid dressing box and jewel case left open on the dressing table and a rich thick silk dressing gown hanging over the back of the easy chair.

I thought I should have preferred seeing all the costly jewellery lock'd up, because it was having me answerable for its safe keeping. I did not know that we had any dishonest person in the house, but I knew such things might be a temptation to a Servant Girl, who was fond of dress and ornaments.

Soon after our arrangements were completed upstairs, visitors came thronging back from Stowe to get their tea.

Mr Jones and his assistant sat in the front kitchen with our damsels. After tea, as it was getting dusk everybody retraced their steps up to Stowe in readiness for the Fireworks. I and the woman got things set away and then went and stood out in the front garden, to listen to the distant music, and to see the bonfires kindled. I do not believe there was a person besides ourselves left in the village except an old bed-ridden man.

I can hardly describe my feelings — such utter solitude in the spot where we were, with a distant, dull, dead roar like thunder from the multitude up at Stowe — then the lurid glare of the bonfires — a flickering light playing on all the trees in the Garden — I felt as though I could have wept.

At 8 o'clock I expected to have seen my Brother with his gig, and I was prepared to go — half past 8 arrived and no brother I began to wonder what had happened — the shades of evening were deepening into night, and I saw several rockets go up in the air, before Aaron appeared, and when he *did* come, it was on foot, and he seemed tired and very much annoyed — saying he had been a long way in search of the gig horse — his man thinking I suppose that he should have to get the gig ready and be detained a little, had actually taken the horse out of the stable and turn'd it loose on the Turnpike road, that it might be lost if wanted — he then took himself off up to Stowe and when Aaron went out to order the gig — behold neither man or horse *was* to be found.

I felt rather disappointed, but told my good Brother I was very sorry he had so much trouble, and I desired him not to fret about it, but to hasten to Stowe directly, or he would lose the best of the Display. I said — 'You know I should not have had long to stay for our Company will be flocking back to supper when it is over, and Sir Watkin may come first.' When Aaron was gone the woman and I set the supper out in the large parlour, and I had afterwards an hour to rest on the Sofa in the sitting room. I pictured to myself, what was passing at Stowe, and knowing so well, the splendour that was always to be seen in the house, even in ordinary times, I could imagine what it must be when the place was en Fête, and the whole range of noble reception rooms (16 in number) all thrown open and brilliantly illuminated. Then I fancied I could see the Company and remember'd that one of the most distinguished of them, would soon be here. I had formed quite a romantic picture of Sir Watkin.

I suppose from his youth, large possessions and grand family connexions — I thought of him, as of a chivalrous Welch Chieftain — and knowing that he was an Officer in the Royal Horse Guards, I naturally expected that he would appear in full uniform; with a noble person, and stately presence somewhat like our own Duke, only much younger.

About 12 o'clock we had the house full again. Many from Northampton — some of whom I did not know but they came with others that I knew well.

Then we had many Farmer relatives (tho' distant) in Northamptonshire — they of course always make our house their Home when they come to Stowe — could not very well do otherwise for there is no Inn in the Village, or even in the parish except the 'New Inn' and that lies a half mile on the other side of Stowe House.

When the company were all at supper in the large parlour, with Uncle to preside, I went and sat in the sitting room to be near at hand in case I was wanted — I was soon aroused by a thundering rap at the front door — the sitting room door leading to the passage was shut so I could not see who entered; but, I judged it was the King of Wales from the tone of his voice and the high key in which he spoke — beginning with 'Mr George' — 'Mr George' — 'Mr Benjamin'.

The Valet directly came to him from the front kitchen and it amused me to hear him say very gravely — 'Sir Watkin, Mr George is engaged, he has company in the Drawing room.' 'O,' said Sir W 'then pray dont disturb him, let me have a light and shew me to my room will you — By the bye tho' between Stowe and my bed is a confounded long staircase — Aye a mile I think — *downhill* tonight, but *uphill* in the morning; then down again to dress for dinner, back again when I am dress'd and then down again to sleep — Rather too much of that sort of thing — Eh Jones?'

Now before the gentleman arrived, I had thought I would meet him in the Passage and speak to him or at least give him an opportunity of speaking to me if he wanted anything; but after I had heard his loud authorative voice I determined to keep out of sight and thought — 'My ministrations shall be felt, but not seen.'

When Sir Watkin had got a light, I could hear that the Valet did not follow to shew him his room — so I ran across the passage to the Kitchen to tell him to go — and in so doing, caught a glimpse of the Baronet's figure, as he sprang upstairs with a ponderous step that shook the very staircase — I did not see his face, but such a broad back and heavily built frame I hardly ever saw in a young man under 23 years old. From that hasty view (had I not known his age) I should have judged him to be over 40 — So vanished my highly imaginative Illusion —

When our Company broke up, it was nearly 2 o'clock in the morning. Some of the Northampton party seemed unwilling to turn out, but it was unavoidable — tho' we had entertained we could not lodge them so they drove off to Brackley in search of beds. We were under no obligation to them, had never been in their house in our lives.

But really, that week, everything seem'd diverted from its usual course — Servants did as they *liked* and Mistresses did as they *could*. Our two girls had been absent all day, sight seeing — yet the fireworks were no sooner over than they came to Uncle at Stowe, and told him they were going to the Dancing at Buckingham with their Friends but would come home in the morning — Uncle told them to go if they liked; but added 'remember if you do go away now — you stay away for good — I will not take you in again.' So, I suppose they were not quite so fond of their beaux as to risk good places for their sake — and came home to have a good supper tho' they stayed away when most wanted — I was thankful to get up into my room, and to have quiet and silence in the house for a few hours. We had not long to rest — I believe Sir Watkin's deputy Valet was down first, and I soon heard him pumping water for his Master's bath — No doubt at Wynnstay there is a Bath room, with a plentiful supply of hot and cold water to be obtained by merely turning the taps — We had no such accommodation to offer but the pump was in our back kitchen and we have always a 20 Gallon copper of water heated every morning for the dairy work. So I thought they might make very good shift and did not feel inclined to ask if one of our men should come in to carry up the water. Mr Jones stood at Sir Watkin's door to take the buckets from the other, and just emptied them into the bath; and I daresay he was then at liberty to attend to his own toilette and prepare for the journey he had to take — an order had been sent to Buckingham the evening before for a Fly, to be ready at 8 o'clock to take Mr Jones to Wolverton and he told us he must start directly after breakfast as he was going to get some new Regimentals for Sir Watkin to appear in at the Ball the same evening — he said the cost of the uniform would be upwards of £200 and ask'd me to see that his deputy went to Buckingham in the afternoon to meet the coach from Wolverton which would bring the parcel. Mr Jones, himself, after executing this commision, would not return to Stowe, but proposed going direct to Wynnstay, where, he said his presence would be indispensable, to prepare the house for Sir Watkin, after he had been so long from home.

Our two Northampton friends said they should go and see the shooting in the morning, and then proposed stationing themselves near the Colonnades at night in the hope of being well amused by seeing the company alight from their carriages when they came to the Masquerade Ball — in addition to the large and distinguished party staying in the house, invitations had been sent to all the gentry in the county, so that it was expected no less than 1,000 Guests would be present.

Sir Watkin seemed to have a deal of letter writing and business to attend to, after he was dress'd and was busily employed in his bed room for 2 hours before he left for Stowe. The footman brought him about 30 letters and packets — many were left open on the bed — I expect he only answered a portion of the number — the bed was strewn with broken sealing wax and all manner of things — such as patterns of buttons — horse gear (Sir W. keeps a pack of Fox Hounds) and applications innumerable for his custom and patronage — some were purely begging letters — one in french, the suppliant saying he had been emboldened by Sir W's known high character for generosity, and by the remembrance of his noble Father, to apply to him for help, and he trusted not in vain — Sir Watkin's servant said it was only a repetition of the annoyance his Master had to encounter every morning of his life — one of the Penalties of Greatness and not always rewarded by a knowledge that they (the possessors) are doing good — as they often get imposed upon by worthless and idle Impostors.

About 9 o'clock Sir Watkin went to Stowe — As he passed out at the front door I heard him tell his servant, who was idling about in the Garden, to go and put all his clothes into the Drawers, and he said 'enquire if my linen cannot be wash'd in the village — you will have to go to Buckingham in the afternoon, so attend to these matters immediately.' John Thomas (or whatever his name might be) said — 'Yes, Sir Watkin' but he did not do what he had been order'd to do. I went up in the room after he was gone to Buckingham, and found nothing had been put into the drawers — nothing prepared for the Laundress; but all the soiled shirts etc. thrown into the closet — yet my Lord had fetched his own things down out of the attic, and had taken possession of the carpetted room that was at first assigned to the head valet — I soon saw, like many other Gentlemen's Servants he made very free with his Master's property and not content with *sharing* the use of his linen, kept the best for himself — The nightshirt he had laid out on his own bed, was far better and whiter than the one Sir Watkin wore (the collar being half off that). Both were marked exactly the same — viz — A crest and W,W,W (Watkin, Williams, Wynn). He had also taken 3 or 4 of the satin neck scarves that Mr Jones put into the drawer in the best room and I saw that he wore one, the Evening that he went up to the Servants' ball at Stowe.

I thought to myself such an insignificant person as I — must not be surprised that I cannot get anything well done, except I see to it personally; for I find so great a Man as Sir Watkin, has to give orders about the washing of his shirts, and then his orders are not obey'd.

About 12 o'clock on Wednesday a porter arrived from Buckingham with a Trunk and portmanteau on a truck. He said the luggage belonged to Captain Holmes, that he was to bring it here and ask Uncle to give the owner lodging till Saturday.

I directly told the man we had not a bed to spare — I said 'perhaps you have made a mistake and were to have gone to my Brother's, and I am sure he cannot take another in' — 'O no there was no mistake' he was sure he was to come to Mr Benjn. George's.

I called Uncle, reminding him that we could not accommodate Mr Holmes except we, or our Northampton Friends turned out of our rooms — The man added Captain Holmes had desired him to tell Uncle that while in the Yeomanry, he had been one of his Troop when he commanded the Guns, and he knew he would not 'refuse an old Comrade'.

This appeal, as I expected proved irresistible — the Porter was told to bring the luggage into the passage, and the woman had orders to take it up into the room at the end of the house — the room that had been occupied by Mr Porter and his Friend Mr Marsh.

Mr Holmes, the Elder (commonly known as 'Whipper in the House of Commons') had been at Stowe several days — had a bed there and I suppose shared the services of a Valet with several other Gentlemen, who, like himself, did not ordinarily keep one. The Son, Captain Thos. Knox Holmes, is 'a gay man about Town'. In early youth, I have heard he was eminently handsome, and now at 40 contrives to look under 30.

He is admitted into high circles, I suppose for the sake of his conversational powers, and being moreover a capital singer, and musician, can make himself agreeable to most parties, but I fancy he is not much respected. It was easy to see that Sir Watkin wish'd to keep him at a distance — never waited to have his company either going to, or returning from Stowe, tho' the Captain told our Girl to tell 'Watty' (as he familiarly called him) that he should like to go with him, if he knew his time.

Our Northampton Friends spent the day (Wednesday) at Aaron's in readiness to accompany Anne's party to Stowe in the evening, to see the arrival of Ladies and Gentlemen, dressed in character for the Masquerade.

Before tea time Sir Watkin's Valet returned to our house from Buckingham, with the new suit of regimentals, and was quite proud to display them in the kitchen. The Garments to fit the Wearer, were of course of large dimensions, both wide and long; but very handsome, and would no doubt set off his tall, strong figure to the best advantage — Scarlet Coatee, trimmed with gold lace, gold epaulettes and sword knot, black cloth trousers with gold stripe up the side; undress officer's cap with gold band. He came to dress while we were at tea, I kept the sitting-room door shut, and heard him run up the stairs follow'd by his lacquey — They were not long dressing, and Sir Watkin seemed in a desperate hurry to reach Stowe, when he was equipped — ask'd Uncle whether he could not lend him a vehicle of some sort, did not care what it was, had been on his legs all the morning up the Park Hill to be in readiness for the unusually (for them) early dinner.

Uncle told Sir Watkin he might have the gig — if his man would help our Carter catch the horse — this was soon accomplish'd, and he drove off like a Jehu.

No sooner gone, than Holmes came to dress, and called out very loudly for *his servant* saying he expected to have found him here, had order'd him to come on first, and get his clothes unpack'd — Now I have every reason to believe this bluster was all finesse, and that he no more expected he should have a valet to dress him than I expected to have a Lady's maid.

Our servant Kate offered to take out his clothes when she shewed him up to his room — *that* would not have suited the Gentleman —

and when she enquired if he had any boots or shoes for our boy to clean, he said — 'No', that was already done for the day, and 'My Valet will certainly be here in the Morning.'

Kate soon found out how the Boots and Shoes were to be kept in order, without letting our servant have them (who might expect some gratuity) — After Mr Holmes had been engaged in his toilette some time, the bell rang furiously, she went up, and he said — 'O can you bring me a little Oatmeal — I have cut my hand' — she glanced at his hands, saw nothing like blood or a cut, but she saw his fingers were stained with the patent blacking that he had been applying to his boots.

She came to me for Oatmeal — I said — 'there is no common oatmeal in the house, you must take him a packet of the prepared oaten flour that we use for gruel' — Kate replied 'he wants it I know, to mix with his hair oil to get the black stains from his hands, for he told me to bring a pitcher of hot water, and be quick' — After he had gone, she found his bottle of blacking and a paint brush concealed up the Chimney, on the top of the lid of the register stove. What a deal of trouble and deception it would have saved, had he been candid and manly enough to tell the Girl that he did not keep a Valet, and should not require much assistance if she would only bring him a few things that he wanted. She would not have thought *that* any discredit to him; but his prevaricating deceit made her say 'I can see he is *proud* and mean.' Those who were present at the Masquerade decribed it as a very splendid scene: half of the Guests were in character — some dresses very grand or picturesque; others very ugly.

Uncles and I did not sit up for our Gentlemen, we retired early, leaving the Char. woman and Sir Watkin's Valet in waiting. Sir W. came first, then Holmes who took possession of his room, and soon made himself snug. When Porter and Marsh arrived, the Woman told them their room was occupied, and she 'supposed they would have to return to Mr Aaron's to sleep'. I did not hear what they said; but I could judge they would not be well pleased, and I felt rather vexed, besides I knew it would put my Brother and Sister to additional trouble and inconvenience.

Then, I foresaw there was further disappointment in store for them on the following day. I had seen by their dress boots, white waistcoats and other items in their luggage that they had come prepared for, and expecting to go to the Tenants' Ball. Tickets had been sent for my Uncles and I early in the week with notice that we were to apply without delay at the Steward's Office in case we wish'd for tickets for our Friends.

I wanted Uncle to ask Mr Parrott if he would admit Mr Porter and

Mr Marsh, but he seem'd very much adverse and I did not like to apply without his sanction. I am certain tickets would have been willingly supplied. The Duke, I know would have felt annoyed had he known of the circumstance.

There were so many reasons why Uncle should be accommodated; in addition to being the Tenant who paid most rent — our house was at the time occupied in part by the Duke's Guests. I dont know the precise reason why Uncle would not apply for tickets; but I think it was from his old fashioned notion, that having offered the use of our rooms, attendance etc. gratuitously, it would be like taking compensation in another shape, if he required entertainment for our Visitors — very few stood upon such considerations — we heard that the family occupying the small farm at Sheepshear though they accommodated no lodgers had 15 tickets for themselves and their friends.

Thursday Morning Aaron came to persuade me to go to the Tenants' ball in the evening, were it only for a few hours. He said he had felt so sorry that I was disappointed in my wish with regard to the fireworks and that he and Anne had been saying I should seem to have no participation in the Festivities at all, if I stayed away from the Tenants' ball.

He was going to dine with the Duke himself at 5 o'clock; but said Druce should bring the gig up for me in the afternoon.

Our Northampton Gents had announced their intention of returning home after dinner; Aaron wanted them to stay till the following day — and told them if they came up to Stowe in the evening he would see what he could do for them — they, no doubt, knew that (except thro' Uncle) their admittance would be contrary to the regulations — and therefore begged he would not think any more about it — as they had an Invitation to attend a party at Northampton that was likely to prove very pleasant.

The Gig came for me about 4 o'clock — Uncle was just going to Stowe — when I reach'd my Brother's house I found Anne and Miss Shepherd had gone up stairs to dress. I soon joined them, and looking out at the window we saw Aaron and the old Admiral (Sir John Talbot) coming arm in arm across the Dairy Ground, apparently in a very social conversation.

Before my sister began dressing for the ball, I was well amused by her account of the manner in which she, and Miss Shepherd had passed the few preceding days, and of the numerous mistakes that had been made with regard to the Gentlemen who came there from Stowe for a bed.

In the first instance, the Duke sent to ask whether they could accommodate 'Sir John Talbot' without specifying that he was an Admiral, and an old Gentleman — then the Marquis wrote a note to Aaron asking for a bed for a College companion (Mr Murray, son to the Bishop of Rochester).

To both these applications an answer was returned in the affirmative; but from a mistake, Mr Murray's luggage, and Sir John's (arriving together) got confused, and taken to the wrong rooms — Sir John was to have had the best room — Mr Murray arrived first on Tuesday night, was taken for Sir John and shown up to the best room — but he soon rang the bell saying 'this is Sir John's luggage, not mine, is there not some mistake? I am Mr Murray.'

Explanation followed, and of course he left the apartment with his belongings and Sir John's luggage was brought in. When Anne and her party return'd from the fireworks they expected to find Sir John had arrived — such was not the case — so my sister and Miss Shepherd went to bed leaving Aaron in waiting. Five o'clock came and no Sir John — my Brother went out at the back door into the court and there saw an unusual and singular looking figure in Naval uniform sitting on a form against the pump — this proved to be Sir John Talbot an old Gentleman of 70 years — dress'd in a gold laced cock'd hat — and enveloped in a military cloak.

He seemed almost benumbed with cold and scarcely able to articulate; but he told Aaron the Duke had started him from Stowe about 2 o'clock under the guidance of a Game Keeper, who accompanied him as far as the Lodge between the boundary of the park, and my Brother's Dairy Ground, telling him if he kept straight on he would soon see the farm house — then I suppose turn'd back — the Admiral, being an old Gentleman and a perfect stranger did not readily find the way — and when he got to the house disliked the thought of applying for admittance — he said 'I supposed you might be all in bed.' Aaron lost no time in conducting the old Gentleman into the house; had a good fire made, and persuaded him to drink a cup of coffee before he went to bed.

It appeared he had a servant at Stowe, tho' not his regular Valet, having, he told Aaron been obliged to despatch the Valet to Ireland on important business. This was on Tuesday, by Wednesday evening the Admiral had got settled in his temporary lodging and expressed himself well satisfied with it, and quite grateful for the attention bestowed upon him by my Brother and Sister — he said 'I thought at first it was rather too bad of the Duke to send an old Gentleman like me, out to sleep, but I do not at all regret it now, as I know I can be made more quiet and comfortable with you, than I should have been at Stowe — The walk in the day twice, I do not mind since you are so kind as to accommodate me with your gig and servant the other times.'

My sister then told me how they had spent Wednesday — our

Northampton visitors being Aaron's Guests that day, and having, as I
before stated accompanied him to Stowe in the evening to see the
Masquerade Anne & Miss Shepherd return'd home first — and
Messrs Porter and Marsh being unaware that their bed had been
appropriated to Holmes came to Dadford, and hearing from our
Charwoman how matters stood followed her advice by going back to
Brick Kiln Farm. I suppose Aaron had not reached home when they
got there — and probably Anne and Miss Shepherd had gone to rest
— so the Girl shewed them to her Master's room and they took possession
of his bed — since he had not been in bed the night before, it was not
very comfortable to find his own bed was not at liberty; but, he thought at
any rate he would make sure of the sofa in the parlour and told the Girl
so; she said 'O Master you can't go there — there is a Gentleman from
Stowe in the parlour' and going in, he found the Marquis's Tutor —
Mr Jeffs — preparing to divest himself of his clothes — He said he had
no rest the previous night, and was not very particular; could sleep
anywhere — Aaron told him there was still a small bed unoccupied in
his room; but added 'I dare say you would not like to go there, on
account of the two young men who are in my bed' — he shrugged up
his shoulders and made a gesture of dissent.

Aaron said 'Neither do I choose to go there' but you shall have the
bed and blankets down to make the sofa comfortable — the Girl was
sent to fetch them, and Aaron helped the young Gentleman to arrange
his couch, both of them laughing at their awkwardness.

When the Tutor had got the parlour and sofa, nothing remained for
the Master of the house but uneasy slumber (without undressing) on
two chairs in the sitting room — this was not a very good preparation
for the Tenants' Ball the following night — (I saw Aarom looked very
heavy eyed when he came up to Dadford in the morning to ask, and
persuade me to go). However he had brightened up again before I
went in the afternoon, and soon dressed for the Tenants' dinner. Sir
John had also been to his room for the same purpose.

Aaron told Druce to drive the Admiral back to Stowe when he was
ready to go. We heard him talking very much to himself while dressing
— apparently rehearsing a speech that he intended to deliver after
dinner, for on this day all the Gentlemen visiting at Stowe dined with
the Tenants in company of the Duke — 'other times' Sir John said 'the
Lady Mary' (Lady Arundel) 'always keeps a chair for me next to her
own' —

When the Gentlemen had left, Anne Miss Shepherd and I had our
tea very snugly, and at 8 o'clock repaired to Stowe.

I scarcely ever knew the weather so warm and balmy in September,
had it not been for the shortness of the days we might have fancied
ourselves abroad on a fine night in July — neither had the verdure of

the grass and trees in the least begun to fade. Up the course between the Avenue, torches were placed to light the road; giving the approach to the Mansion a festive and feudal appearance — but rather objectionable as likely to frighten a timid or a restive Horse.

We went in though the stone Yard, then were admitted into the great passage, at the door near the Housekeeper's room. My brother soon came to us, and very glad we were to see him, for the passage was crowded, the greater number of the Guests being strangers to us. Anne and Miss Shepherd repaired to the dressing room — I did not intend to dance or even to remain long, so I told Aaron if he would conduct me, I would proceed directly to the ball-room.

We found a spacious booth or Pavilion circular in shape — lined and festooned with bright striped cotton, white and scarlet — and brilliantly lighted by chinese lamps — a double row of sofas in a semicircle, on a kind of raised platform afforded very comfortable sitting to those who did not choose to dance, and at the same time gave them a good view of the company.

I found my sister Mrs Bennett here and took my seat next to her — she said it was the only time she had taken any part in the Festivities — having so much to attend to, at home. Mr Bennett dined with the Duke and afterwards went back to the New Inn — George, the eldest son stayed to the Ball.

After chatting a short time with Mrs Bennett, my brother left the booth in search of Anne and Miss Shepherd. Dancing had commenced long before — the Duke having opened the ball with Mrs Roper for his partner.

Directly after my Sister Anne appear'd, I saw his Grace go and shake hands with her, at the same time asking her to dance with him. They were certainly the finest couple in the room. The Duke was, of course, in full dress, wearing the blue ribbon, diamond star, and other insignia, as a Knight of the Garter, and well did this brave apparel become his noble, stately figure.

I never saw my dear Anne look better — she was in slight mourning — her dress a handsome new black satin, very full, and the trimming a mixture of velvet and crape — plain high body — white crape collar and under sleeves — gold brooch and locket, and on her head a light half cap of white tulle, tied with gauze ribbon — just covering the ears (for she was fearful of getting an ear ache) yet leaving her fine glossy, platted black hair to be seen. My sister had often danced with the Duke before, and he had also taken her to supper on his last Birth-day.

Aaron look'd very well indeed, dressed in black, with the exception of white waistcoat and gloves.

His partner was Miss Shepherd, whose fresh, young beauty (she is only 17) and slight but pretty figure, made her very attractive — she was also very genteelly attired, in buff silk, lace bertha, and pearl ornaments. Of course, in so large a company there was a wide difference in age and appearance — many young members of the Tenantry especially the feminine portion, were as well dressed and look'd as well, as the aristocratic Ladies — some on the contrary were very homely. I was well amused by watching the dancers — listening to the conversation around me — and delighted with the fine music of the Yeomanry band — About 10 o'clock most of the Visitors staying in the house, came into the Pavilion — some of them joined the dancers but a greater number were only spectators.

Many of the Grandees were pointed out and named to me. The Duchess and Lady Anna I knew well — their dress was elegant, and as became the occasion, both appeared in high spirits.

I saw also the Chancellor, Lord Lyndhurst, with his handsome daughter — the Hon Miss Copley — The Archbishop of Canterbury, Earl Fortescue, Earl Carysford, Lord Braybrooke, Sir Stephen Glynne, Sir Watkin Wynne, Lord De Lisle, Lord Nugent — Nevilles, Probys, [Wynd]hams, Lytt[el]tons — indeed all the collateral branches of the family — but not one of the Duchess' relatives — I suppose she is not on friendly terms with the Marquis of Bread[al]bane or with her sister Lady Pringle — more pity it should be so.

When supper was announced, I told my brother I should like to go home — Uncle Benjn. offered to take me, saying he would soon return, that the gig might be ready for Sir John Talbot when Aaron's man came to fetch him.

We were soon at Dadford — I had scarcely taken off my bonnet and mantle when Sir Watkin opened the sitting room door and march'd in. I had not spoken to him before — he wanted to know why I left the ball so early. I told him I did not think it would suit my health to sit up all night, having had but little sleep during the week. Uncle informed Sir Watkin that *he* meant to return for a few more hours and ask'd him if he did not think the Duke must be very much fatigued. Sir Watkin said they all expected he would be quite knock'd up by the end of the week, for he would *do* so much *himself*, was not contented with ordering and superintending — after a few more remarks, seeing that Uncle stood with hat in hand as though he wanted to be going, the Gentleman said — 'I am detaining you I fear — you would like to rejoin your neighbours at Stowe, I will therefore go to bed.' They went out into the passage but even after Sir Watkin had gone up a few stairs, he turn'd round and stopp'd Uncle to joke with him about being an old Bachelor.

He said 'the Duke tells me you are the oldest Tenant he has and that your family or forefathers have held this farm and the one occupied by your nephew, for so many generations that he supposes you were Farmers in the Parish before the Temples came to Stowe and I understand you have no son to succeed you.'

'How old is your nephew?' Uncle said, 'above 30.' 'Why for goodness dont he get married then? why your Family will be extinct, if he follows your example and dies an old Bachelor.' When Uncle had gone back to Stowe and Sir Watkin got to bed I told our Woman I would also go to bed, and would leave her to wait for Holmes and her Master.

The next day was Friday — we heard very little of the proceedings at Stowe, but there was a ball for the servants that night. When Sir Watkin's valet was sitting with our two maids and the woman at breakfast — he said 'Are you *young ladies* invited to the Ball?' pity but our dowdy squat Dairy Maid (aged 40) should be addressed as 'a *young lady*'. Gentlemen's servants like him generally shew more civility and good manners to their own class than they do to others, who are higher in the social scale — and they shew the partiality in more substantial matters — we heard soon afterwards that the Butler and house Steward took care to provide a much better supper, and far better wines for the Servants' entertainment than they had done for the Tenants.

Sir Watkins order'd his man to pack the luggage in the Imperial before he went to the Ball — telling him that he should leave early the next Morning.

Uncle is an early riser, but he had only just got downstairs when Sir Watkin's carriage drove up the yard. The Gentleman was taking leave of Uncle when the Captain's bell rang. Kate ran up to know what he wanted he said — 'Is Wattey going without coming to bid me good bye? — haste and tell him I shall hope to see him, if only for a few minutes before he goes.' The message was deliver'd and presently the 'King of Wales' came stalking by my room door and along the passage towards Holmes' apartment — again the bell rang, and Kate had orders to bring a pitcher of hot water and two glasses — she said, on going into the room, she found the Captain sitting at the foot of the bed, in his shirt, bare legs and feet — yet he did not seem the least disconcerted by the presence of a young woman — and kept her there in attendance. Sir Watkin sat opposite in the easy chair and partook of some kind of liquor that Holmes almost forced upon him; but he did not remain long.

I heard him repass my door, and very soon afterwards the carriage drove away. His Majesty did not thank Uncle before his Departure, which can only be accounted for, by the supposition that he was under an impression — the Duke *hired* our rooms for the use of his Guests — payment we neither expected, or, if tender'd, should have taken — but, thanks were surely due, for such comfortable accommodation; his servant having been boarded, as well as lodg'd. He (the Servant) gave Kate half a sovereign to be divided between our 3 females and the boy who clean'd boots etc. whether Sir Watkin specified the sum or left it to his Valet I do not know. It was quite as much as I thought they deserved; and caused altercation enough amongst themselves with annoyance to me, but they were not satisfied and were unwilling that the char-woman who had done all the extra work should participate; she, being an humble meek kind of person would have given way, but I decided when appealed to, that *she* should share anything that was given by company during the week — and I said if there were any more words about it, I would ask Uncle to request the captain not to give anything — *that* stopped the altercation.

Holmes, I understood, gave them 5s. 'What was that' said they 'compared to what Miss Anne's Girl got?' — she sent them word that herself and Druce each clear'd 25s. by the company who had been to Brick Kiln Farm.

I could not see that our two servants deserved anything; they had neglected their regular work — and went to see all the festivities.

Saturday morning, about 2 hours after Sir Watkin had left, Holmes took leave of Uncle; where he went to, I dont know; but I suppose not up to Stowe, for his Papa came soon afterwards with a Fly, to take away his luggage and seemed surprised to find he was not there. Kate conducted the old Gentleman upstairs and she said he burst out in quite a passion on finding nothing had been put up or got ready. All the clothes lay in a heap on the floor, music, books, everything — in a chair a parcel of clean linen, that had come home from the wash — Papa pointing to it said 'Is *that paid* for?' The Girl replied — 'Mr Holmes paid the woman.' 'Did he?' said the old man 'then that's a wonder.'

'Pray, what does he mean by leaving his luggage in this manner for *me* to pack?' — Of course Kate could not tell him what he meant, but she helped to put the things into the trunk and portmanteau. I daresay the young one wish'd our maid to suppose that he expected his much talk'd of Valet, would be sent to put up the luggage.

In the course of the morning when I and the woman were engaged setting the spare rooms to rights — I opened the closet in the best room, and there found all the shirts and other linen that Sir Watkin order'd his servant to send to the Laundress — it had not been done and the disobedient negligent fellow either forgot it altogether, or would not take the trouble to open the Imperial again, after he pack'd it before going to the ball — I found a dozen shirts, 3 or 4 silk shirts, drawers, stockings, handkerchiefs — quite a heap — and I question if Sir Watkin would ever have known of his loss, had they not been restor'd — for of course the Valet would not have betrayed his own negligence.

I thought the best thing we could do, would be to make a large package of the things, and send them without delay to Sir Watkin's Town House in London, as I knew he was going there before he return'd to Wynnstay — Uncle despatch'd a man with them to meet the Wolverton coach at Buckingham, which would insure their delivery in Grafton Street the same night.

We were all day employed getting our house in order and resuming our usual way of going on. I felt quite thankful that it was all over and should have been sorry had the next week been the same thing over again — We heard afterwards that the Duke had shut up the whole suite of apartments that were prepared for the Queen and the Prince during the summer.

Her Majesty did not come to make use of them then, but I suppose his Grace had set his mind upon a Royal visit, and was unwilling that those splendid rooms should be used or even seen by any general company — had not such been the case, the whole of his visitors could have had beds in the house — some few remained at Stowe during the next week, amongst them, Sir John Talbot who told my sister at New Inn, he had discover'd that he was accommodated gratuitously by my Brother. He said 'I shall go and thank him before I leave the neighbourhood — I cannot think of offering money to such a respectable young man; but I shall well remunerate his servants for I can tell you, the young Farmer was so kind, that he placed his *carriage!* and his people at my disposal, and I could not have been better attended to, had I been staying at an expensive Hotel.' In accordance with these expressions, the old Admiral made his appearance one morning at Brick Kiln Farm — Aaron happened to be at home — He said 'I am come to bid you farewell. I have a conscience and I could not leave Stowe without thanking you for your kind accommodation' — Aaron replied 'you are quite welcome Sir John, I am always willing to oblige the Duke's friends.' The old Gentleman drew himself up, and said very proudly 'the Duke of Buckingham *is* the Duke of Buckingham and *I* am Admiral Sir John Talbot, allow me to thank you on my own account' — and he gave his address to my Brother, desiring he would remember that he would be pleased to see him again. In taking leave of Anne he left two sovereigns to be divided between the Girl, Druce and the odd job boy — this gratuity led to Anne's Girl boasting to our Servants of the profitable week she had.

My sister at the New Inn and her household were very busy, and full, all the time, so that excepting a few hours at the ball, she like me, had taken no part in the festivities — My other married sister Mrs Scott resides at Lillingstone, and not being a Tenant, had only witnessed such parts of the proceedings as were open to the public. — Well, this is a very long and circumstantial account of the coming of age of the Marquis of Chandos: it has been written in a careless piecemeal sort of way at odd times, and I know it is very badly composed and full of mistakes, but I thought I should like to leave a record of the manner in which this important Event had been celebrated, more to be read by the young people amongst our kindred who may come after us (perhaps fifty years hereafter) than for any of them who are now living — I know *I* should have been highly delighted had I ever found a book of this sort (that had been written by an Aunt or Cousin of our family) descriptive of events that had occurred at Stowe or in the neighbourhood before we were born. I have never even had the happiness of seeing a letter of my dear Mother's — I should have consider'd one quite a treasure, as I had the misfortune to lose her during my infancy, and consequently can have no personal recollection of her — a few memoranda in a pocket book is all that remains to us of her writing —

E. George
10th October 1844

IV

During the winter following 1844/45 the Duke came several times to lunch with us in the shooting season.

January 8th

We heard that *at last* the Queen was certainly coming to Stowe before the end of the month. We had heard the same so many times during the last year, that little notice was taken of it.

Everything had been kept in a constant state of preparation, so there was not anything unusual going on at Stowe, till the few days before her Majesty's arrival; all the best stock'd game preserves had been left unmolested that Prince Albert might have good sport; but there was a general regret that the Queen had not visited Stowe (a place renowned for its Gardens and pleasure grounds) during the summer — they were in the highest perfection then of course; even *now* everything that extreme order and neatness could do, to render them attractive had been done, but snow fell on the second day after her Majesty came, and made walking and driving in the grounds cheerless, and hid many beauties — The Museum and the conservatories were visited with great interest by the royal Party, but *even there summer* was wanting for perfect enjoyment — how very different is the effect of fountains playing in a hot summer day, and in the midst of winter. Queen Victoria arrived at Stowe on the 15th of January 1845, and remained 3 days.

The Buckingham Troop of Yeomanry met the Royal Party at the Wolverton station (on the North Western Railway). I believe the Newport troop joined the procession at Stratford.

In every village or available point on the line of route, between the Railway and Buckingham, arches and flags, and crowds of spectators were to be seen.

At Buckingham of course, was the most mark'd demonstration; for several days active measures had been taken for the Queen's Reception — the town was gaily decorated, and every house prepared for a general illumination in the evening.

There was the usual procession of the corporation, clergymen, and principal inhabitants, to meet the Royal Cortège. At the entrance of the Town an address read by the Mayor — School children on platforms singing and huzzaing, bell ringing, cannons firing — Public dinners and all those rejoicings that generally greet a visit from a Popular Sovereign.

Uncle went on horseback with the other tenants to meet the Procession somewhere on the road. Aaron was with the Troop. Lord Chandos (commanding) rode with other officers by the side of the Queen's Carriage.

The Duke and Duchess, of course, remained at Stowe to receive the Royal Guests — and quite a novel kind of rural guard was ranged in ranks on the north side of the Mansion.

These were 500 of the Labourers, belonging to Stowe, and the surrounding parishes; every one dress'd in a new white smock frock, and wearing green favours; to each the Duke presented a gratuity of 5s. —the Masters also gave them their usual day's pay in addition, and they were either to treat themselves with a dinner at Buckingham, or spend the money in their own families as pleased them best.

We had only two visitors staying in the house during the week; these were two sons of our cousin Mr Flowers of Turringham; but I had, for several days been very busy with much extra cooking, as I knew accommodation, both indoors and out would be required in the way of refreshments, and stabling.

On the day of the Queen's arrival, Uncle left home about 12 o'clock on horseback, very smart, in a new great coat and wearing a green ribbon round his hat inscribed in gilt letters — 'God save the Queen'. All our regular men (dressed in new smock frocks) went up to Stowe to be put in their places about 3 o'clock. I had the Dining table set out in our large parlour, all day, to be ready for any friends who came — the Dairy maid went to see the arrival, also our visitors, only the housemaid and myself remained at home. One of our young labourers stayed away tho' pretending he did not wish to go, because he thought 'somebody *ought* to remain, to take care to the yard etc.'

I soon discovered the motive, for this apparently considerate behaviour. Uncle had order'd corn to be served to the horses of *all* our personal friends, tho' owing to the game depredations, every feed of corn consumed by our own horses had to be purchased. We dont even get the seed again on our plough'd land. The young man knew this fact quite well, yet he took in every Baker's or other tradesman's cart and horse from the adjoining *near* villages of Silverstone, Syresham etc, etc, that might have been fed at home an hour before if they required it. To all these horses, he gave a feed of oats or beans.

I heard him come in and go to the Dresser drawer, in the best kitchen, and I guessed he came for the key of the granary — going to an upstairs window soon after, I saw that not only the stables and waggon hovels, but also the long open cattle-shed were filled with horses.

I put on my bonnet, and went to inspect, found them all eating corn. I at once, told the man to give me the key of the granary — and ask'd him what right he had to make so free with his Master's property. Not knowing what else to say I suppose he replied that he 'thought it was only fair to serve them all alike'

No doubt when the owners came, he told them he had fed their horses, as well as given them standing room, and they would be expected to give him at least 6*d*. each; he would almost demand it. Uncle would have known nothing of his unfaithfulness had I not gone to look after him for all the cart people had been for their vehicles before he return'd with a party to tea at 6 o'clock.

Mr & Mrs Scott with several others, had been to see the Queen's arrival at Stowe, and from them I heard a description of what took place. I knew from the firing of the Guns when the Royal Visitors had enter'd the home park. I think it was then nearly 5 o'clock — our men came home to milk the cows, and soon afterwards, every body seem'd preparing to go to Buckingham to see the Illuminations.

Quite a company went from our house with Uncle — at Aaron's was the same. My sister took our niece Annie Bennett in the gig — other vehicles accompanied them. About midnight Uncle returned with part of our Visitors — all seem'd in high glee, saying they had never seen Buckingham so gay — and the Illuminations and fireworks had pleased them very much — Our visitors had supper, then a gossip with pipes, cigars and accompaniments — it was after 1 o'clock when we retired to bed.

From my room window I could see the North front at Stowe house was brilliantly illuminated in colour'd lamps — very large letters — 'God save the Queen' — 'V & A' — on a crimson ground surrounded by green wreaths, and other devices. The 4th Regt. of Yeomanry had been commanded to act as a guard of honour day and night during the Royal visit — they had a spacious Marquee in which their meals etc. were taken.

I heard some of them laughingly say, their wives were to send their *Victuals*, so they should have to put up with cold fare for several days. The Yeomanry band was in constant attendance — a grand dinner party to be entertained in the state Dining room — not a very numerous company — for — according to Etiquette on such occasions, the Queen was consider'd Hostess, and no invitations were given except at her suggestion, or by her sanction. In addition to the royal suite — the list of visitors comprised Sir Robert Peel (prime minister), Earl of Aberdeen, Earl and Countess of Jersey, Earl and Countess Delawarr, Earl and Countess Orkney — Marquis of Breadalbane, Lord and Lady Southampton, Sir Jas. Graham, Marchioness of Douro, Lady Clementina Villiers, Lady Mary West, Hon Miss Kerr, Generals Bouverie and Wemyss, Sir Tanbrey [T. Aubrey?],

Dr Buckland, Mr & Mrs Robarts, Captain Carrington, Revd Mr Andrews, Mr Smith and several others.

The Marquis of Breadalbane, it was understood, had been invited by her Majesty, with the laudable intention of bringing about a reconciliation between the Brother and Sister — we shall see if that end is attained. The Marquis himself has always been a great favourite with the Queen and the Prince — they have several times visited him at his splendid and picturesque highland home Taymouth Castle in Perthshire. What took place in Stowe on Thursday made very little difference to us at Dadford — We heard the Prince and His Grace, accompanied by a large party would shoot the Ganza Hill and Stratford Wood preserves, in the morning. A few of the Yeomanry in plain clothes, were present to keep the ground, and to prevent the Spectators from pressing too near (Aaron and Charles were two). The slaughter of game was immense. It was slaughter, and nothing better; the game had no chance to escape, being driven by an army of beaters directly under fire.

Before the Prince had got tired of the Sport, he was hastily summon'd by an Equerry to attend the Queen, (important Despatches had arrived) and like a dutiful subject, Albert immediately gave up his gun, and went, with Sir Robert Peel and Sir J. Graham to hold a Council with her Majesty.

In the evening a large party had the honour of dining with the Queen, among others the High Sheriff, several of the neighbouring Gentry and clergy — also the Mayor of Buckingham. After dinner was a Concert.

Mrs Stowe was present and from her, my sister had a description of the Royal party and of the presentations, (for the Queen held a Court in the State Drawing room). Mrs Stowe said the Duchess was splendidly attired, wearing her Diamond Coronet, and look'd much more like a Queen than the real Queen did.

Queen Victoria was very plainly and simply dressed in black velvet, with no other ornament for her hair than a wreath of natural purple heather, brought for her, from his conservatory at Taymouth, by the Marquis of Breadalbane.

Every one seemed surprised at the extreme youthfulness of the Queen's appearance, although the mother of 4 children, and 25 years of age, it was remarked that she look'd like a girl of 18. No doubt her Majesty would give a good deal were it possible to add a few inches to her stature — a tall figure and distinguish'd air are certainly great advantages to a Sovereign either male or female; tho' we know the mental qualifications are much more important, as regards the welfare of the people over whom they are supposed to rule.

No doubt the Duke was fully aware what the Queen's secret wish must be, for we are told that the seats for himself and her Majesty, at the dinner table, were arranged to diminish his own height and to raise the Queen's who sat on his right hand, Prince Albert and the Duchess were opposite.

It was remark'd how extremely solicitous his Grace appear'd to be, in every particular, to render homage and shew the most profound devotion to his little Mistress, and being an adept in all the mysteries of Court Etiquette, he doubtless acquitted himself admirably, but I suppose he had considerable difficulty in drilling the High Sheriff, as to the proper manner of leaving a room, without turning his back to the Sovereign. I can fancy how easily and gracefully the Duke would manage to bow himself out by a side movement but the Sheriff tried to walk backwards, and stumbled, then to hide his confusion and make short work of it turn'd abruptly round and ran from the apartment.

Mrs Stowe said she and some others got very tired of standing all the evening, but no one was seated except the Court party.

Monday, January 20th

The Queen left Stowe on Saturday morning (18th).

The Marquis of Breadalbane followed her Majesty down the steps, and drove off directly. I therefore fear his visit has been only one of Ceremony, and that there will be no reconciliation or reunion between the Brother and sister.

We have heard a few other particulars of the Royal Departure, her Majesty was seen to kiss Lady Anna very affectionately, and in bidding her Adieu she clasp'd a diamond bracelet round her arm.

For distribution amongst the Servants, the Queen left £100, and, as is often the case the distribution of the money so as to give satisfaction proved a very difficult affair.

On Friday, the 17th her Majesty and the Prince each planted two trees (a Cedar & an Oak) near the Concord and Victory; many people collected outside the palisades in the park to witness the proceedings.

The Duke held the Queen's gloves and she said something to him several times; but in so low a voice that nobody could hear what it was. Her Majesty knew very well without doubt that every audible word spoken by her would be repeated in all the newspapers in a day or two.

After hearing many details of the Royal visit, I cannot help thinking it was not quite satisfactory either to the Duke or his Guest.

The Duke had been at great expense and had given himself unbounded trouble to receive her Majesty with the greatest magnificence.

Every part of his noble and vast mansion had been, in part, newly furnish'd and decorated, even articles that are generally made of cheap materials, and for the commonest every day wear — were of gold or *silver* if intended for the Queen's use.

Perhaps the Duke thought to surprise and gratify her Majesty by such delicate flattery, if so, he could hardly have been pleased when she said 'I am sure *I* have no such splendid apartments in either of my palaces' — considering who was the Speaker such an observation must be regarded as a very equivocal compliment.

The expensive and elaborate preparations were so evident that the very idea of having caused so serious an outlay must have been oppressive and unpleasant to her Majesty.

We were told that the Queen would have been far better pleased had her bedroom and dressing room been more simply furnished.

The head housemaid conducted the Royal pair to the apartments especially set apart for their private use, and she reported that the moment the Queen enter'd the bedroom she turn'd to the Prince and said 'O Albert, I know this carpet I have seen it before — it was offered to me, but I did not like to spend so much money on one carpet.' Then she told Mrs Bennett to bring a drugget and lay over the carpet before she came to bed — adding 'I shall feel quite uncomfortable if it is not cover'd.'

Perhaps none of these remarks reach'd the ears of the noble Host and Hostess else one would think they would have considered them rather an ungracious return for their loyal hospitality.

January 22nd

We have entertained the Duke and a large party at lunch today. It is very cold quite a deep snow on the ground.

I knew in the morning that we should be visited by his Grace and fellow sportsmen, towards 2 o'clock, and I expected they would as usual, remain until candle light. We happened to be pretty well provided with cooked provisions but I sent for my sister during the morning, and we made such additions as we judged necessary. Uncle met with the shooting party as they were passing by in their way to three Parks wood — whether *he* first made the proposal or the Duke I dont know. What makes the affair much more trouble to we womenkind is, that our master cannot be satisfied with entertaining the Duke and the Gentlemen of his party — but must also have all the keepers, servants, and even the beaters — so we have Grandees in the parlour, keepers and servants in the best kitchen and beaters in the wood barn.

To these last Uncle attends personally, and I verily believe would not sit down at his ease with the Duke, had he not first attended to the rough set in the out house — but he makes no demand upon *our* services for them, takes a large cream tin, holding between 7 & 8 gallons — down into the cellar, this he fills with ale and delivers himself to the beaters, returning again for 2 bottles of gin — then sends one of the party up to the village shop for 2 loaves and a piece of cheese. At no other place would they or the keepers get any refreshment at all, but they know by former experience what is in store for them here, and take care to come and present themselves.

We always set out a large table in the kitchen for the keepers and servants with a good joint of meat — pork pies & bread and cheese with plenty of ale. I do not believe the Duke has the least idea what a tribe Uncle is feeding and Uncle never says a word to him about it. I expect if his Grace knew he would go out and send them all off.

In connection with this custom, rather a laughable faux pas was made today by an Underkeeper named William Humphris.

This keeper resides very near to us in the Village, and is usually a sober man; but the Gentlemen had given the remaining contents of their spirit flasks to the keepers before they left the woods, and Humphris has no objection to strong drink, when it is to be had out free, so he took rather too much I suppose and hardly knew what he did afterwards, at least I should think so. Lord Hotham happen'd to be a little behind the rest, and was just coming in at the Court Gate, when Humphris met him, and gave him a rough slap on the back, saying very freely — 'Be you a beater, or be you a Sarvant? because if you be a *Sarvant* go into the kitchen, and you'll get plenty to eat and drink, but if you be a beater *you* go into the Hod-barn, and Master Benjamin will bring you some grub.' Lord Hotham turn'd round and said very haughtily — 'What does the fellow mean?' I hope the Duke may not be told of *this* because when he came here with a party to lunch just before Xmas and was speaking of his annual gifts to the poor, he ask'd me to tell him whom I thought were the most deserving. I declined to particularize on the plea that I did not know all the people well enough to do them justice, but he named Humphris himself. I then said I believed *he* was a steady man, I was sure there could not be a cleaner or more industrious woman than his Wife.

His Grace directly requested I would send for her — and when she came, and followed me into the room (dressed in her tidy working garb, and curtsying very low) he took 2 sovereigns from his purse and gave them to her saying, 'Miss George tells me that you are very clean and industrious — here is a little reward for you' — Ann, of course was highly delighted with the Duke's gift — but in the first place she turn'd round to curtsey and thank me — I said — 'You should thank his Grace, not me.' When she was gone the Duke said she was a very nice, respectable woman.

The report of this occurrence was soon spread amongst the villagers and O, what envy and jealousy! — all of them saying — 'why could not Miss George speak of *me* as well as for her?' —

But this is a digression.

The preserves on our farm were not disturbed when the Prince was here, so there has been an immense quantity of game shot today. The Duke asked me to go out and look at it. I found the Courtyard completely cover'd with dead Pheasants, Hares and Rabbits.

Our own labourers had just before brought in the milk, and then stood gazing with folded arms at the game. They said to me 'O Miss, no wonder that you get no corn — all these nasty things have been kept on your Farm, they eat up all the crops, and now Master is feasting all the set, as if the game did him good.' I saw they grudged the Beaters who sat drinking in the Wood Barn. The Duke had ordered a brace of pheasants and 4 hares to be brought into the house for us and told Uncle he should leave him some pheasants and hares.

Uncle replied very bluntly 'Thank you I dont want them: I have had quite enough game.'

I think his Grace took it as a sort of notice that he not only had enough, but too much, for he seemed rather at a loss for an answer; but turning to Anne said 'Miss George, your Uncle will not have the game that I offer him. Will you accept the Pheasants?'

'Thank your Grace I will' said Anne.

After lunch the party took wine and dessert; it had been candle-light more than two hours when they broke up — Anne and I sat in the sitting room when the Duke and his friends pass'd thro' — there was a deal of shaking hands with them all.

His Grace stood behind the rest, some time, talking to us, thanking us repeatedly for our 'kind and hospitable entertainment'. He enquired whether we saw the Queen plant the Trees etc. and ended by asking if we should like to see the Queen's apartments, which he said remained exactly as she had left them — he told us many applications had been made to him for a view of the rooms; and he had refused all but would give *us* an order with pleasure adding — 'You may also bring 6 of your friends if you like. I shall not be at home tomorrow because I have invited a Party to meet me at Wotton. I shall tell the housekeeper you are coming, and you will find the rooms warm and well air'd.' Anne assur'd the Duke we should be much gratified with the view, and would be careful who we invited to go with us. So, tomorrow, we shall, if nothing unforseen happens, see all those splendid things that have been so much talk'd of. Before Anne left, we fix'd upon the party we should ask to accompany us, these were Aaron, Helen Bennett, Anne Scott, Miss Lines and Miss Hadland, and Uncle was to have been the 6th, but he did not care about going, so there will only be 5 besides my sister and I.

— Wednesday night — January 22nd 1845.

Thursday afternoon, January 23rd

My sister and I drove thro' the snow up to Stowe to view the Royal suite of apartments — it was a bitter cold day. Aaron & the rest of the party met us at the house. Mrs Grenuba conducted us thro the rooms — I like Mrs Bennett the head housemaid much better — (C. Grenuba is the Duke's Valet and his wife has lately acted as Housekeeper)

Everything was splendid — magnificent — yet somehow did not excite pleasurable feelings.

The special reporter to the 'Illustrated News' wrote in last week's paper — 'The profusion of rich and costly objects of Art and decoration at first astonishes but soon absolutely wearies and perplexes the senses.'

I think we had all that kind of impression on our minds, as we passed successively, not only thro 3 or 4, but 15 or 16 magnificent saloons and Drawing rooms.

Everything in the way of furniture seemed to be carved and inlaid gilded wood — rich, figured genoa velvet, embroidered satin and gold and silver brocade.

The house was splendidly furnish'd before preparations were made for the Royal visit, and in my humble opinion all these costly additions are de trop and have so crowded the apartments as to give them the appearance of a large furniture warehouse — and no space being left vacant on the floors — you do not appreciate the noble proportions of the rooms. I never liked the house so well as during the last few years of the late Duke's life — he had put the house in complete repair, and had added a great many beautiful artistic things to the former old family collection — not merely rich furniture which money can buy at any time but things unique in themselves, and having, so to speak, a genealogy and a history.

What could be nobler or more appropriate furniture or ornament for the South Portico and the Marble Saloon than the antique statues of heroic size brought by the late Duke from Italy.

The middle of the rooms at that time were not crowded with furniture — one or two very curious or rich tables perhaps, with a few rich chairs stood ready for use, but the greater proportion of furniture was ranged out of the way along the walls — you walk'd freely about, at liberty to gaze on the valuable and rare paintings, sculpture etc.

Now the furniture is arranged in the modern style viz — grouped — Marqueterie tables, each surrounded by seats of different kinds — sofas, ottomans and chairs.

The floors are all completely cover'd with carpets, even the North Hall and passages — also a considerable portion of the beautiful white, marble pavements of the grand saloon — *That* is a change I do not like, nor yet the long trailing curtains to each of the 4 doors (although they are of richest crimson silk velvet) formerly there were only crimson festoons with rich fringe over the door ways — and no other furniture except the crimson cushions to the fix'd seats in the walls, between the 16 columns of sicilian Jasper — the splendid antique lamps suspended from the arches of the niches in which stood the valuable antique marble statues.

In my humble opinion any addition in the way of furniture is as much out of place *here* as it would be in a Grecian Temple.

The two apartments opening from the saloon, viz the state Drawing room on one hand, and the music room opposite had formerly no carpets on the floor in general — tho' carpets were laid down occasionally if required.

These floors were bare and of highly polish'd oak — which in summer had a delightfully cool appearance and made a pleasing variety, without imparting a sombre or gloomy look — for the rooms were a full southern aspect, very light and the walls gay with the finest paintings and gilding.

I think the Venetian blinds have been recently put up, at least they were not closed formerly — if, they were there — and the blinds were not drawn down far but afforded a clear view of the beautifully kept, and extensive lawn — and the well stock'd gay parterres immediately under the windows — the scent of the flowers in summer was perceptible everywhere, and even in Winter, I remember as a child, being charm'd with the rich spring perfume that pervaded the whole range of apartments, and always greatly admired the large oriental china scent jars; some of them 4 or 5 feet high. But now, the perfume is quite overpower'd by a very strong smell of paint, varnish and new furniture.

The apartments prepared for the especial use of the Queen and Prince Consort are at the Eastern end of the House and contiguous to each other. The Green or Summer Dining room was fitted up as her Majesty's Dressing room — the Bedroom was the one formerly called the 'Rembrandt Room' — the State bed had been renovated and modernized. From the bedroom a small winding staircase (very private and well contrived) led down to the Queen's Boudoir — in which was the shower bath, W.C. etc. all fitted up with great elegance and convenience — the closet itself looked like a large mirror occupying one side of the room, in 3 panels — the middle panel being the door.

Besides a beautiful carpet, the floor had several Tiger skins round the bath. The Bath room for the Prince was very near — in that was a large bath of white marble.

The furnace for heating the water if required was hidden in a receptacle in the passage — from these 2 apartments a flight of steps leads to a suite of rooms call'd the 'Buckingham Rooms' — these were appropriated to the Prince as Dressing room, sitting rooms — most beautifully furnish'd and replete with articles of taste and vesture befitting a Gentleman of such intellectual and refined pursuits — and finally 'the Grenville Drawing room' (a fine spacious apartment adorned with all the old Family Extracts) was prepared as a *private* Drawing room for the Royal couple during their visit.

I understood they took breakfast alone there, every morning.

Nothing could be more luxurious than the furniture — the only fault being too much and too many of every kind of thing; so many splendid marqueteries, marble and buhl tables — sofas filled with air and covered with the richest velvet or satin embroidered in colours — window curtains to match.

Quite a variety of Fauteuils & easy chairs — splendid Turkey carpet as soft as moss to tread on.

Magnificent candalabra — All the hangings and furniture look'd quite fresh and new — the fine collection of oriental and other antique china, of course was what we had seen and admired before, also the Paintings (but these had all new frames or at least newly gilt) and the white Marble Statuary.

There was a new horizontal Grand Piano, provided especially for her Majesty, on the top of the Instrument a small Tambourine and castenets were placed — indicating that the Prince accompanied the Queen in her musical recreation.

I had always taken more interest in the 'Grenville Drawing Room' than in any other apartment. The fine and large collection of Family portraits (many of them quite historical) never lost their attraction.

I saw, when passing round to look at them yesterday that they had been newly arranged — the place of Honour was assigned to the Great Grandmother of the present Duke — Elizabeth Wyndham Daughter to the Lord Chancellor, Sir W. Wyndham, niece to the Earl of Egremont, Grand-daughter to the 'Pround Duke' of Somerset, and lastly wife to the eminent statesman — George Grenville of Wotton. This Lady had always been consider'd '*the Beauty*' of the Family — there were two others, quite equal to her in regularity of features, and brilliancy of complexion (I mean Penelope Grenville and Penelope Temple) but I fancy the *Gentlemen* found a charm in Elizabeth Wyndham that they did not see in the other beauties.

I had often gone over the house with parties, and I always noticed that Gentlemen, especially the young ones, would step back again and again to gaze on the portrait of Elizth. Wyndham. I suppose her large dark eyes, (in which there is an expression of languishing softness) pleased them.

When I look'd at Sir Thomas Temple and saw by the date that he was Master of Stowe in the year 1604 — I thought of my own old Farmer Ancestor who lived in this house and farm at the same time — 'John George' who as the Duke once told us — till that period was owner of the farm but sold it to Sir T. Temple when he came to reside at Stowe and bought up all the adjoining lands. The Duke said there were no rent rolls at Stowe farther back than 1604 — the old Parish register and the Churchwarden's books that remain, began about the same date and with the names of John George of Dadford and Thomas George of 'Hoghole' (as 'Brick Kiln Farm' was then call'd) as Overseer, and churchwarden — there have been several 'Moseses' in the family but no Aaron before Grandfather, then my Father and now my dear Brother who is Aaron the 3rd. But this is all a digression, or I could add some laughable items revealed by those old records — the Lady of Stowe was then *Dame* Temple' and the style was 'Farmer George and his wife Mary' and for the labouring class, it was 'Gaffer' and 'Goody'.

Amongst the Family pictures at Stowe of course the two William Pitts are remarkable, the first Earl Chatham having married Hester Grenville — Great aunt to the late Duke.

There was also *the Hester* Temple who conveyed the Stowe estates to the Grenvilles, and her brother — field-Marshal Lord Cobham.

The finest figure amongst the Ladies is that of the Duke's Grandmother Mary Nugent — Marchioness of Buckingham, herself Daughter and Heiress to Earl Nugent whose portrait hangs near — a fine, hearty fatherly looking old Gentleman, with his foot laid upon his knee.

I have heard *my* Grandfather relate surprising tales of the madcap pranks played at Stowe by this Irish nobleman, when he used to visit his daughter — who was not far behind him in that respect — altho' so grand a looking Lady, and withal very highly accomplished, for she painted like an artist (having been a pupil to Sir Joshua Reynolds) and excelled in sculpture, music, needlework & even in spinning flax for fine linen — yet she delighted in playing practical jokes upon all around her — was no way particular into whose house, or at what time, she made her visits — never miss'd a week when at Stowe, without coming to see my Grandmother and would go upstairs to talk to Father and Uncle Thomas in bed, when they were little boys — such a contrast in demeanour to that of her stately, haughty husband, the Marquis of Buckingham. Yet, they were a very happy and attached Pair — and had been called at the time of their marriage 'the finest couple in England'. But, I must not linger any longer in this grand Picture Gallery — I suppose the full length portrait of the present Duke is at Avington (his Mother's fine seat in Hampshire) and also that of his Mother, and the rest of the Chandos race — I should like to see them at Stowe — especially the portrait of the Late Duchess, Anna Eliza Brydges, only daughter and heiress of James, last Duke of Chandos and lineally descended from Henry the 7th.

In the Royal bedchamber, the first thing to attract notice was, of course the state Bed very rich and gorgeous I must allow, but we all agreed that we should not like to sleep on it; there is no look of comfort or repose belonging to it — and even as an item of State furniture I do not admire it (alter'd and modernized), so much as I used to do when placed at the other end of the House (in the apartment *now* called the Duchess' drawing room) when there, the bed stood on a raised Dais in an alcove recess enclosed by gilt railing — on one hand, the Jewel closet on the other, the State Bath ditto.

The bedstead was very spacious and lofty — grand and imposing in appearance — the hangings were of the richest figured crimson velvet lined with satin — the festoons and draperies finished with an elegant tasselled fringe — a beautiful white satin Quilt embroider'd with gold seem'd to relieve and enliven the crimson velvet curtains etc.

Then, it was not the fashion for Great people to sleep on Mattresses — a full down or feather bed look'd much better and more comfortable than the flat and untidy couches do now. The present state bed is hung with yellow silk damask lined with bright crimson satin — the bedstead profusely gilt — with an embroider'd coat of arms at the Head — altogether looks much more glaring and gaudy that it did in its old dress, and when standing on the Dais in the snug recess. Many Royal Personages have reposed on this bed, beginning with the Great Grandfather and Grandmother of Queen Victoria viz Frederic, Prince of Wales and Augusta of Sax Gotha. There is a bed that I like much better in the Japan bedroom, it was provided new for Queen Adelaide when she visited the Duke in 1840.

For Queen Victoria and the Prince a new mattress in a white satin cover, had been provided, sheets of the finest cambric trimmed with costly lace — and the furniture was altogether of the richest and rarest description — a great portion of it being merely for show, and serving to crowd the room and make it inconvenient and uncomfortable, at least for a bed room.

There were no fewer than 20 tables in this and the adjoining apartments five or six large sofas, no end of luxurious easy chairs and fauteuils cover'd in embroider'd silk and velvet carved and gilt frames — window curtains to match the hangings of the bed. Several stately clocks and time pieces, 4 or 5 cabinets of the most elaborate marqueterie and embellish'd with precious stones — noble mirrors in rich, carved frames one being of solid silver, and a small hand glass the size of a cheese plate, with a jewell'd handle, had a gold frame, it was new, and they said cost 250 guineas.

Then there is a large and varied collection of the rarest old china — large bowls and vases, and many cups incrusted with diamonds, emeralds and rubies.

One article of Furniture we all admired, and it was also an useful and necessary thing — I mean the noble Wardrobe that had been appropriated to the Queen. It was formerly call'd an Armoire but had been fitted up and converted into a Wardrobe lately. It is of Ebony, tortoiseshell and buhl — profusely inlaid and carved, with gold hinges etc. the folding doors are richly inlaid inside and the interior is lined throughout with wadded silk, I think the colour is peach blossom. Gilt Brackets and hooks, on which to hang the dresses — altogether quite a fitting receptacle for Royal robes.

In the Dressing room, the hangings, covers of sofas & window curtains are of rich chinese silk, yellow and silver — but how shall I describe the Toilet table, all cover'd with point lace, and the splendid gold toilette service?

I fancy it would puzzle the cleverest dressing maid to brush out the Queen's long hair, without catching some of the numerous little jewelled articles with which the toilet table was set out — there is of course a splendid Cheval glass and all manner of rich things both useful and ornamental — the only fault being that there are too many. The paintings in these two apartments are some of the most valuable in the house being chiefly by Rembrandt, Wouvermans Teniers etc.

I liked Prince Albert's dressing room and sitting room much better — the furniture was equally splendid but had a lighter appearance and they were not so crowded.

I could not pretend to describe or even name half the curious and valuable things that we saw — it would fully employ a long [day] to examine them in detail. We were quite tired in less than two hours and much as I appreciated the Duke's kindness in having invited us to go I felt quite a relief when we got back to our own homely but snug and comfortable home.

November 14th 1846

We have had the Duke to lunch today, with a large party — the Marquis of Chandos being one.

The Duke, Colonel Hall & Captain Johnson stayed till 7 o'clock, turning back after seeing the rest out of the door — saying they should enjoy drawing up to the fire for a snug chat with Uncle and Aaron.

During the London Season of 1846 — The Duke's only daughter, Lady Anna Grenville caused quite a sensation in the fashionable world by her marriage with Mr W. H. Gore Langton, grandson and heir to Colonel Gore Langton of Newton Park near Bath. The young gentleman was 4 years younger than Lady Anna — had been to Eton and Oxford with the Marquis of Chandos and was a frequent Visitor at Stowe.

This intimacy led to a mutual attachment between them, which was strenuously opposed by the Duke and Duchess after the same was discover'd.

Mr Langton however persevered in his suit (being aided in the matter by the Marquis) and Lady Anne having attained her 26th year, the match could not be prevented.

Most people concluded, that the real cause for the Duke's opposition was the £40,000 left to Lady Anne by her Grandfather, the interest of which ought to have been paid to her yearly after she was 21 years of age.

V

Reading all the foregoing memoranda 25 years afterwards, I feel induced by way of sequel to add a brief account of the many surprising changes that have taken place at [Stowe].

I may as well say, that Lady Anna eventually got married to Mr Gore Langton and, it has proved a most happy match — She has now, (in 1871) 5 children — 3 boys and 2 girls — the eldest son, is, I believe about 25 and has recently been married — to a daughter of Sir Graham Montgomery — this young gentleman will be Earl Temple in the future — owner of Stowe, should the present Duke die without male Heirs of which there is little prospect; he has three daughters — the youngest in her 15th year.

During the shooting season of 1846–47 the Duke came 4 times to Lunch at our house. We had heard vague rumours of his Grace being very much in debt — but little imagined to how great an amount — we fancied that a general fall of Timber that could be well spared in the Park and Gardens would raise sufficient to clear off all incumbrances.

We saw no signs of depression of spirits in the Duke — 'au contraire' he talked more and seemed gayer than usual, but I have no doubt it was only assumed to hide inward anxiety and he, as long as possible still kept adding to his debts by sending all manner of expensive furniture to Stowe from London — tho' the apartments were already much too full and he must know *all* would very soon come to the hammer. In May 1847, the Yeomanry went out as usual and for several days the Duke was present in the Park as Commander.

Suddenly the news came that he had been obliged to leave and had travelled all night in his carriage. Some said one thing was the cause others another cause.

Parker the Keeper told Uncle that the real cause was an execution had been put upon all the Duke's property, and he did not believe he would have a dish or spoon of his own left.

The Chandos Property could not be sold; but of course the rents would be all confiscated. People in this neighbourhood could scarcely believe that matters were so bad — for the Tradesmen and work people had been regularly paid.

It was to the great money lending firms that the Duke was chiefly indebted — to them he had mortgaged his estates to such an extent

121

that the interest swallowed up the Rents. This system of mortgaging commenced when he was a young man at college — money then being almost forced upon him by few money-lenders at a high rate, which they did not want him to repay then [knowing] they had all the great landed property as security — so the debt went on at compound interest till it finally doubled itself. It was publicly stated in many newspapers after the execution had been served that the Duke of Buckingham enjoyed the unenviable distinction of being the greatest Debtor in the World, for he owed fifteen hundred thousand pounds (£1,500,000).

It was proved that he was upwards of £1,000,000 involved at the time of the Queen's visit. Of course he was deeply condemned by some, and pitied by others. Those who were most inveterate against him being parties who had been raised from a low estate by his bounty and had gotten a fortune under him.

If all had been known, most people would have felt sorry for the Duke — no doubt he had long suffered the deepest anxiety knowing that an exposure was inevitable.

We were told that his black hair and beard turned quite white in 2 or 3 days after he left the Park so suddenly —

PERSONAL REMINISCENCES
OF THE
BUCKINGHAMSHIRE VOLUNTEERS
BY
OWEN PEEL WETHERED

Officers of the 1st Bucks Administrative Battalion in camp at Wakefield Lawn, Northamptonshire, June 1867.

Standing left to right: Captain Thomas O. Wethered, Captain William Forder (Adjutant), Surgeon Shone, Lieutenant Owen Peel Wethered, Sir Harry Verney, M.P., Captain the Hon. Thomas F. Fremantle, Captain Alfred Selfe, Lieutenant T. R. Hearne, Lieutenant L. A. Way.

Seated left to right: Lieutenant Egerton Hubbard, Lieutenant Thomas Horwood, Lieutenant-Colonel the Hon. Percy Barrington, Quartermaster John Kersley Fowler, Ensign Francis Wheeler, Lieutenant Thomas Marshall.

PERSONAL REMINISCENCES OF THE BUCKINGHAMSHIRE VOLUNTEERS BY OWEN PEEL WETHERED

Introduction

Published memoirs of the Rifle Volunteer Movement of 1859 to 1908 are rare, the best known perhaps being Sir John Macdonald's *Fifty Years of It: The Experiences and Struggles of a Volunteer of 1859*, published in 1909, and William Lamont's *Volunteer Memories*, published two years later.[1] Both, as it happens, are reminiscences by Scottish Volunteers. Additional memoirs in manuscript are just as rare, which makes that by Owen Wethered particularly valuable, especially as he wrote it primarily for regimental use and, therefore, tended on occasions to be more candid than might otherwise have been the case.

Owen Peel Wethered (1837-1908) was of the Marlow brewing family and, with his brother, T. O. Wethered, was one of the original members of the 1st Bucks (Marlow) Rifle Volunteer Corps. Wethered succeeded his brother in command of the Marlow Corps in 1868, having temporarily commanded the 5th Bucks (Slough) RVC from 1864–65. He was promoted to Major in the lst Bucks Administrative Battalion, to which the individual Bucks Corps were affiliated, in 1871 and subsequently commanded the battalion (consolidated as the 1st Bucks Rifle Volunteers in 1875) from 1872–91. His recollections, covering the period from 1859 to 1879, were compiled in 1901 but with minor additions in 1902 and, again, in 1908 at which time the Volunteer Force was absorbed into the new Territorial Force with the lst Bucks Rifle Volunteers being reconstituted as the Buckinghamshire Battalion, which explains Wethered's occasional reference to this later battalion designation.[2] Wethered's son, Francis Owen Wethered (1864–1922) was to command the Bucks Battalion from 1911 to 1915

---

1 J. H. A. Macdonald, *Fifty Years of It: The Experiences and Struggles of a Volunteer of 1859*, Edinburgh and London, 1909; William Lamont, *Volunteer Memories*, Greenock, 1911.

2 For an overview of the development of the volunteers and other auxiliary forces in Buckinghamshire, see Ian F. W. Beckett, *Call to Arms: Buckinghamshire's Citizen Soldiers*, Buckingham, 1985; and for the national context, Ian F. W. Beckett, *The Amateur Military Tradition, 1558–1945*, Manchester, 1991.

while two other sons, Owen Henry Wethered (1867-1931) and Walter Peel Wethered (1869-1917) had also served in the 1st Bucks Rifle Volunteers.

The typescript of his recollections together with a letter book of Wethered, covering the period from 1874 to 1909, were among those documents transferred to the County Record Office by the Bucks County Territorial Association when it was absorbed by the Eastern Wessex Association in 1967.[3] Additionally, also transferred was a memoir — albeit less valuable — by one of Wethered's successors, Alfred Gilbey, who joined the 1st Bucks Rifle Volunteers in 1879 and commanded from 1900 to 1906.[4] While, as will be seen, Wethered considered 1879 a particularly significant year for the battalion, it is not readily apparent why he did not continue his account to the end of his tenure of command in 1891 but Gilbey's account begins in 1879. A further 30 letters between Wethered and the Lord Lieutenant, the Third Duke of Buckingham and Chandos, covering the period between 1868 and 1875 survive in the Stowe MSS at the Huntington Library, San Marino, California.[5]

The five rifle volunteer corps formed in Buckinghamshire between December 1859 and July 1860 — at Marlow, High Wycombe, Buckingham and Winslow, Aylesbury and Slough — were part of the national response to fears of French invasion current in the 1840s and 1850s.[6] More specifically, inflammatory French reactions to the assassination attempt on Emperor Napoleon III in January 1859 by an Italian refugee, Orsini, who had close connections to fellow refugees in England, implied a desire to punish England for harbouring conspirators. Palmerston's attempt to placate the French, with a parliamentary bill making it a felony to plot murder abroad, was regarded as meeting insult with concession and his government fell. The incoming ministry of Lord Derby was far more inclined to review military and naval arrangements in the light of continuing French hostility, particularly given rising tension in Europe which resulted in war between France

3 The typescript of Wethered's memoirs is to be found in Buckinghamshire Record Office, TA Collection, T/A 5/17 and his Letter Book in T/A 5/5. Thomas Wethered had been on a committee to raise volunteers at Marlow in August 1803 — see Buckinghamshire Record Office, Pascoe Grenfell MSS, D86/31/57.

4 *Ibid*, T/A 5/17 for Gilbey memoir.

5 Henry E. Huntington Library, Stowe MSS, Military Correspondence of the Third Duke of Buckingham and Chandos, STG 106.

6 For the background to the establishment of the Volunteers, see Beckett, *Amateur Military Tradition*, pp.163-96 and, for a more detailed account, Ian F. W. Beckett, *Riflemen Form: A Study of the Rifle Volunteer Movement, 1859-1908*, Aldershot, 1982.

and Austria in April 1859. With public demand for additional defensive measures growing through April and May, particularly in terms of the raising of volunteers as articulated by publication of Tennyson's celebrated poem, 'Riflemen Form', in *The Times* on 9 May 1859, a government circular authorized the enrolment of such volunteer corps on 12 May 1859.

The intention as expressed by a second circular on 25 May was 'to induce those classes to come forward as Volunteers who do not, under our present system, enter either the Regular Army or the Militia'. Since the militia, revived during an earlier French invasion scare in 1852, largely drew its rank and file from agricultural labourers and the other home defence force — the mounted yeomanry — largely drew upon the landed and farming community, this left a broad range of the middling elements of society to be drawn to the volunteers. The early volunteer involvement of professional men, tradesmen and of local businessmen such as the Wethereds, therefore, was very typical of the response across the country. Middle class idealism is more than evident in the rules of the new corps with emphasis upon honorary and enrolled members, entrance fees like that at Slough of half a guinea, annual subscriptions such as 10s.0d. at High Wycombe, proposing and seconding of members, and discipline maintained by fines. Volunteers would also provide their own uniforms and equipment at a total cost of £3 at Aylesbury and £2 5s. 0d. at Marlow, where it could be paid off by instalments. Only rifles were provided initially by the government but not until July 1859 and then merely at a rate of 25 per 100 volunteers. To be accepted, a Corps needed a safe rifle range, a place of custody for arms and a uniform approved by the Lord-Lieutenant, establishments being fixed at three officers — Captain, Lieutenant and Ensign — for a Corps of between 60 and 100 men or two officers — Lieutenant and Ensign — for a Subdivision of not less than 30 men.[7]

However, as Wethered notes, the social composition of the volunteer force began to change significantly around 1862-63, as fears of invasion receded, with the disappearance of the middle class and of most of those members of local gentry, who had become involved at least in rural corps. In their place, the volunteer force became dependent upon artisans and, again as Wethered describes, the Bucks Volunteers became increasingly reliant from the 1870s onwards upon employees of the London and North Western Railway Company at Wolverton, where a company was formed by Wethered in 1877, and upon the

7 See Ian F. W. Beckett, 'The Local Community and the Amateur Military Tradition: A Case Study of Victorian Buckinghamshire', *Journal of the Society for Army Historical Research*, LIX, 238/9, 1981, pp.95-110, 161-70.

chairmakers of High Wycombe, where a company was reformed in 1875 after the original had been disbanded in controversial circumstances four years earlier. Wethered entirely approved of such a transformation since he believed that those in regular employment — as opposed to agricultural and day labourers — should be the natural recruiting ground of the volunteer force. He also made the point, however, that officers should remain gentlemen, although this was a theme of his private correspondence rather than of his memoirs and there were perennial difficulties in finding suitable candidates for commission.[8] The special treatment afforded the boys of Eton College serving in the 8th Bucks (Eton College) RVC by Wethered is particularly interesting in this context. Yet, despite their changing social composition, the volunteers remained far more representative of society as a whole than the regular army or militia. Moreover, while national membership was far from constant, there were rarely less than a quarter of a million volunteers under arms for much of the second half of the nineteenth century.[9]

Since volunteers were civilians first, civil employment was of the utmost importance and conditioned all else, as is apparent from the careful arrangement of annual camps, which appear almost the most frequent activity of the volunteers in Wethered's text. It should be noted, however, that volunteers were also required to attain efficiency standards in order to qualify for the annual government capitation grant of 20s. 0d. introduced in 1863. Initially, these standards were satisfied by attendance at nine drills and an official inspection during the course of the year but, in practice, volunteers did far more and, in any case, efficiency requirements were progressively tightened as the basic grant increased to 30s. 0d. in 1869 and to 35s. 0d. in 1887.

Whether attending drill, annual camp, or special national or county events, however, the volunteers were far more visible to society than regular soldiers and, therefore, were projecting military values within society in ways which contributed to the perceived growth of militarism in Britain by the end of the nineteenth century. However, in being more visible, the volunteers were also likely to attract anti-militarism either in the form of physical confrontation or popular ridicule and Wethered's memoir is valuable in recounting two particular examples of such dangers in terms of the Administrative Battalion's first annual camp at Marlow in 1865 and its courting near disaster in

8 Buckinghamshire Record Office, T/A 5/5, Wethered to Baynes, 21 August, 1883 and Wethered to Buckingham and Chandos, 12 November, 1883. The latter is duplicated in HEHL, Stowe MSS, STG 106, which also contains Wethered to Buckingham and Chandos, 11 August, 1882 on this theme.

9 Ian F. W. Beckett, *Riflemen Form*, pp.85, 104.

public relations terms at the review at Stowe in 1875. By contrast, and further illustrating the inter-relationship between volunteers and society, the prestige of the community could also become linked with its local units. Again, this is apparent in the difficulties recounted by Wethered with respect to the volunteer corps in both High Wycombe and Slough, although the parochialism engendered by a lack of ready means of communication within the county should not be discounted. Wethered makes it clear that the volunteers in Buckinghamshire — and this is also true of the country as a whole — could hardly have existed without the earlier development of the railway but, equally, the distribution of lines in the county was not conducive to establishing uniformity of purpose between corps. Inevitably, an element of local politics was also involved in such difficulties, particularly as the Lord-Lieutenant had the right of nomination of all officers until 1871 and Wethered's account throws some further light on the political and other rivalries of the Grenvilles of Stowe with the Carringtons of Wycombe Abbey.

Wethered himself writes well enough although his punctuation and capitalization — no changes have been made by this editor — are erratic. As indicated in the footnotes, too, he does make the occasional error and, in at least one case, he chose to ignore one long-running dispute between himself and another officer in 1874. Nevertheless, it is a very valuable and often entertaining account of a much neglected phenomenon in Victorian England.

I am grateful to Anthony Wethered Esq. for his kind permission to reproduce the memoirs of his great-grandfather. Thanks are also due for permission to consult and quote from archives in their possession to Hugh Hanley and the staff of the Buckinghamshire Record Office (TA Collection, Lieutenancy MSS, Fremantle MSS, Carrington MSS, Morgan-Grenville MSS, Pascoe Grenfell MSS), Devon Record Office (Seymour of Berry Pomeroy MSS), Bodleian Library, Oxford (Hughenden MSS, Lincolnshire MSS), and to Mary Robertson and the staff of the Huntington Library, San Marino (Stowe MSS).

Ian Beckett

PERSONAL REMINISCENCES
OF THE
BUCKINGHAMSHIRE VOLUNTEERS
BY OWEN PEEL WETHERED

It has often been represented to me that my personal recollections of the Bucks Volunteers, of whom I was one of the very first, and with whom I have served continuously ever since — in every rank possible from full Private up to Honorary Colonel (including that of Sergeant Major) would prove interesting to later generations of Volunteers, the vast majority of whom were not born when I was sworn in on December 8th, 1859. I have realised that there is certainly no one living who has so intimate a knowledge as I have of all the facts connected with the rise and development of the Volunteer Movement in Bucks: but I have hitherto been unwilling to commit my recollections to writing, partly because my record must necessarily consist largely of a narrative of my own doings, and partly because I have no longer the opportunity of verifying my dates etc. by referring to such regimental records as exist in the Orderly Room at Marlow. For at the end of 1891 my health compelled me to resign the active command of the Battalion, and to retire to the "otium cum dignitate" of its Honorary Colonelcy; and since then I have had to spend the greater part of every year in the island of Tenerife — 1500 miles from Head Quarters, and it is in Tenerife that I write these recollections.

I am inclined to waive my objections to doing this mainly by the consideration that owing to the War in S. Africa the Commissioned ranks of the Corps have been increased by no fewer than 15 Officers since Oct. 10th 1899,[1] while the ordinary recruits number several hundreds; and that none of these new members can ever otherwise learn anything of the early history of their Corps. Every day, moreover, that passes, adds to the difficulty of the task and to the improbability of its ever being carried out, while it also adds to the interest attaching to by-gone events. I am also greatly influenced by

1 In the absence of the bulk of the Regular Army abroad during the South African War (1899–1902), there was renewed official and public interest in the Volunteers. In Buckinghamshire a Home Defence Committee was established to raise three new companies and it is to this expansion that Wethered refers. See Buckinghamshire Record Office, Fremantle MSS, D/FR/169.

the wishes of the present Adjutant, Capt. W. Owen (Oxfordshire L.I.) who has shewn great interest in the subject, and who will doubtless be able to verify many of my recollections and to correct some errors of dates by reference to Orderly Room archives. I have used above the expression "such regimental records *as exist* in the Orderly Room at Marlow"; and I inserted that limitation advisedly, because these records are necessarily imperfect. In fact for the first few years they are conspicuous by their absence, for in those early days the five widely scattered embryos of the future Bucks Battalion had no cohesion — no connection with each other — no Adjutant — no Commanding Officer. We at Marlow knew far more of what was going on at Maidenhead and Henley (in Berks & Oxon respectively) than in the north of our own County, which was practically "terra incognita" to us, as the quickest way of reaching it was, and still is, via London. Some 20 years ago I collected all the records then extant at the Head Quarters of the several Companies, original attestation rolls, Company Order Books, etc. and, with infinite labour, I compiled a list — as complete as was then possible — of every man who had ever served as a Bucks Volunteer, with dates of promotion to and in the Commissioned and Non-commissioned ranks, but 40 years ago Company Orderly Room work was performed in a very perfunctory manner and my list is consequently imperfect, but it contains many facts which I rescued from oblivion, and, as it is in the Orderly Room at Marlow, it can easily be referred to.

And now, after this somewhat lengthy preamble and explanation I will set to work at my "Recollections".

On December 8th, 1859, the first body of the Bucks Volunteers was sworn in, in the boys' schoolroom at Marlow, by my father, the late Owen Wethered, J.P.[2]

It consisted only of 33 members — a bare subdivision — but it formed the lst Bucks (Great Marlow) R.V. Corps — a military Unit theoretically complete in itself, but lamentably incomplete in practice. It was commanded by (the late) G. H. Vansittart, of Bisham Abbey, and my elder brother — T. O. Wethered (to whose exertions its formation was mainly due), was Ensign.

---

2 The process of raising a volunteer corps was lengthy with initial public meetings, the formation of a steering committee, enrolling of members and then an application to the Lord-Lieutenant. The official formation date was that on which the offer of service forwarded by the Lord-Lieutenant was accepted by the Secretary of State for War, usually coinciding with date of commission of the first officers as given in the Army List. The official date for the acceptance of the 1st Bucks (Marlow) RVC appears to be 16 December 1859. See Buckinghamshire Record Office, T/A, 5/3 for Marlow Corps material. In each case, official acceptance dates are taken from Ray Westlake, *The Rifle Volunteers*, Chippenham, 1982, pp.13–14.

At Wycombe also a Corps was being raised, but as our arrangements at Marlow were more advanced, several leading Wycombe men joined the Marlow Sub-division at the start — among them (the late) Thos. Wheeler, John Parker, T. J. Reynolds, Thos. Marshall, Hammford (?) and one or two more. These men were subsequently transferred to the 2nd Bucks (High Wycombe) R.V. Corps on its formation in February 1860.

This Corps also was at first only a subdivision, but, by Oct. 1860 the enrolment of an outlying squad of recruits at Beaconsfield raised it to a Company. The Corps however fell to pieces soon afterwards. Its first Commanding Officer was Lieut. H. H. Williams, who was not a Wycombe man — though I fancy he had some remote connection with the town. However this may be, great friction arose very early between him and a great number of the Volunteers of the Corps, and in order to put an end to the demoralisation caused by the quarrels, the Corps was disbanded. It was however reformed in the Autumn of 1861, when Thos. Marshall was appointed Ensign, and subsequently Lieut. Lieut-Col. W. Caulfield Pratt, second-in-command, of the Royal Bucks (Kings Own) Militia (which Lord Carrington commanded) was gazetted Captain of the reformed Company early in 1862, and about July 1862 Francis Wheeler became Ensign.[3]

In February 1860, the 3rd Bucks (Buckingham & Winslow) R.V. Corps was enrolled — a subdivision at each place. The Hon. Percy Barrington — afterwards our first Lieut. Colonel, and now Viscount Barrington, was Lieut. Comdg. the Buckingham Subdivision with Robert FitzGerald (the Secretary of the Marylebone Club) as Ensign. The Hon. T. F. Fremantle (now Lord Cottesloe) commanded the Winslow Subdivision as Lieutenant. I don't think that we in the south of the County, ever saw the 3rd Bucks till its two subdivisions had been amalgamated into one Company in 1863. In the meantime Ensign FitzGerald had resigned (Dec. 17th, 1862) and was succeeded by

3 The first public meeting in High Wycombe was on 13 December 1859 (*The Times*, 16 December, 1859) but the official date of acceptance of the 2nd Bucks (High Wycombe) RVC was 4 February 1860 (See Bodleian Library, Lincolnshire MSS, MSS Film. 1145, War Office to Carrington, 4 Feb., 1860) and that of its reconstitution on 22 November 1861 following disbandment sometime in August or September 1861. While Wethered emphasizes the unpopularity of Williams, there was also conceivably some political manoeuvring involved. Robert, Second Lord Carrington (1796–1868) of Wycombe Abbey, Lord-Lieutenant from 1839 to 1868, certainly intended his son, Charles, to command the Wycombe corps, Buckinghamshire Record Office, Carrington MSS, D/CN/C1 (d) Carrington to son, 13 Oct., 1860. The emergence of Walter Caulfield Pratt of Oving House as Commanding Officer may well reflect a compromise. Of the others mentioned by Wethered, Parker and Reynolds were solicitors. For some early Wycombe Corps material, see Buckinghamshire Record Office, T/A, 5/1 (t) and 5/2 (c).

Henry Hearn, who afterwards commanded the Company from 1871 to 1890. Lieut. Barrington had also resigned (June 1862) so we never saw him till he rejoined as Lieut. Colonel in May 1864. Lieutenant Fremantle became Captain of the combined (Buckingham and Winslow) Company in August 1863, and Ensign Hearn became Lieutenant, and in the following November, E. Hubbard (now Lord Addington) who afterwards — 1891 to 1900 — succeeded me in command of the Battalion, was gazetted Ensign.[4]

On March 25th, 1860, the 4th Bucks R.V. Corps was formed at Aylesbury with the Hon. F. G. Irby (afterwards Lord Boston) as Captain, Acton Tindal, Clerk to the Lieutenancy of Bucks, also Clerk of the Peace, as Lieut., and H. A. P. Cooper as Ensign. These officers, however, resigned in 1861, when Alf. Selfe and Thos. Horwood, became Lieutenant and Ensign, and in 1862 were promoted to Captain and Lieutenant respectively.[5]

The 5th Bucks (Slough) R. V. Corps was also formed in the Spring of 1860, and was commanded by R. Bateson Harvey (afterwards M.P. for Bucks, and later still, Sir Robert B. Harvey, Bart.) as Captain, with L. A. Way as Lieutenant. Captain Harvey was also Capt. in the Bucks Yeomanry, and (with the exception of Lieut. Barrington, Buckingham Subdivision, who had been Lieut. in the Scots Guards) was the only officer of the Bucks Volunteers who had any previous military experience, and we in the South of the County naturally looked upon him as an authority in such matters.[6]

4 The date of the first commissions in the 3rd Bucks (Buckingham) RVC was 11 May 1860 but the first public meeting had been as early as 26 November 1859 (*The Times*, 29 Nov., 1859). Thomas F. Fremantle(1830–1918) succeeded as Second Lord Cottesloe in 1890. In turn, his son, also Thomas F. Fremantle, Third Lord Cottesloe (1862 to 1956) and Lord-Lieutenant from 1923 to 1954, commanded the 1st Bucks RV and its successor, the Bucks Battalion from 1906 to 1911. Egerton Hubbard, Second Lord Addington (1842–1915) commanded the 1st Bucks RV from 1891 to 1900. For the Winslow Subdivision, see note 8 below.

5 The official date of acceptance of the 4th Bucks (Aylesbury) RVC was 11 May 1860 but, again, activity had begun far earlier with the first public meeting on 22 December 1859 and the first Corps rules printed on 14 January 1860. See Buckinghamshire Record Office, T/A, 5/1 (m) and (n). Alfred Selfe was a bank manager and Horwood a solicitor.

6 The official date of acceptance for the 5th Bucks (Slough) RVC was 20 July 1860 but it had been first mooted in June 1859 (*The Times*, 30 Jun., 1859) and its rules had been printed on 18 January 1860, Buckinghamshire Record Office, T/A, 5/1, (p). In fact, Harvey did not take command until August 1861 for the original Captain was Lord Seymour, see Slough Corps material in Devon Record Office, Seymour of Berry Pomeroy MSS, 1392M/Box 18/1, 1 and 14. However, Seymour went off to fight in Italy for Garibaldi under the pseudonym of Captain Sarsfield; see Buckinghamshire Record Office, Carrington MSS, D/CN/C1 (d), Carrington to son, 4 Nov., 1860.

A 6th Bucks. Corps was also formed at Newport Pagnell under Captain Tyringham (Praed) and Lieut. S. Newman. I believe it was very smart and well drilled during its short existence, and it lived long enough to take part in a review at Warwick on July 24th, 1861 where it formed a Company with the Buckingham Subdivision. By that time Capt. Tyringham had resigned, and shortly afterwards the Corps came to an untimely end, owing to the lack of sufficient local support, so I had no personal knowledge of it.[7]

I believe that a subdivision was also started as the 7th at Princes Risborough, but I don't think it ever attained to official recognition as the 7th Bucks R.V. C. The Lord Lieutenant refused to give a commission to (I think) the Rev. G. Gray, on the ground of his being a Clergyman, and, as he was the only available candidate, the Princes Risborough Corps fell to the ground.[8]

Such being the composition of our widely scattered force, Marlow, Wycombe, Buckingham and Winslow, Aylesbury and Slough — under 200 in all — we all set to work to do the best we could under such very unpromising conditions.

I can, of course, only speak of the earliest details of my own Corps at Marlow, for it was not till we were brought together at our first camp in 1865 that we got to know anything of the interior economy of the other Corps in the County.

It is almost impossible nowadays to realise the absolute ignorance which prevailed in 1859, especially in country districts, about everything military. The word "Discipline" was of course known to us, but its meaning — its application — in a military sense was a "sealed book" to us all. We had no Staff Sergeants, no Adjutant, to enlighten us; and we amateurs had to grope our way by the sole aid of common sense, from the lowest depths of simmerian darkness towards the faintest glimmerings of light. The Officers were mortally afraid of offending their men — many of whom were of equal social standing with themselves, and

7 A 6th Bucks (Newport Pagnell) RVC was officially accepted on 14 September 1860 and remained in the Army List until June 1864 but no papers relating to it have survived.

8 As Wethered surmised, there is no evidence that a 7th Bucks (Princes Risborough) RVC was ever officially sanctioned but there was a 7th Bucks (Winslow) RVC accepted on 17 May 1861, having been formed on 17 December 1860. This sub-division was then absorbed into the Buckingham Corps to form the 3rd Bucks (Buckingham and Winslow) RVC in 1863. The Order Book of the Winslow Corps is in Buckinghamshire Record Office, T/A, 5/14. One further Corps was attempted at Amersham and Chesham but failed through lack of support and of a safe rifle range; see Buckinghamshire Record Office, T/A, 5/15 and Ian F. W. Beckett, *Riflemen Form: A Study of the Rifle Volunteer Movement, 1859-1908*, Aldershot, 1982, pp.29-31.

whose ignorance of all things military was certainly not more profound than their own.

I well remember that soon after we commenced our nightly drills, my brother came to my home one evening on his way to drill and said "Look here, Owen: I notice that, when I give the word 'Fall in' many of the men fall in with their pipes in their mouths. Now I'm sure that *can't* be right, so I want you to fall in tonight with *your* pipe in your mouth. I shall then pitch into you, and after that I can blow up anyone else who does it." I was a Corporal at that time, and my height made me right-hand man of the line. The above "ruse" was duly carried out. I was roundly pitched into — and after that evening pipes were duly pocketed at the "Fall in".

Soon after we started we secured the services from Wycombe of one of the Staff Sergeants of the Bucks Militia, Sergeant Shortland by name, who came over once or twice a week to superintend our drill. But we had no Staff Sergeant of our own till more than 20 years later, for early in 1860 we enrolled an ex-sergeant of the Grenadier Guards, who was living at Marlow as Cottage Agent of the Lord of the Manor. His name was James Columbine, but he was by no means Columbine-like in form, for he was 6ft. 3in. in height and large in proportion, weighing nearly 20 stone. But he was the best "Recruit-drill" I ever came across, and he continued to act as our Instructor till his death.

In June 1860, the Queen held her first review of the newly formed Volunteers in Hyde Park, the Marlow, Wycombe and Aylesbury Corps being present, and this was their first experience of any larger formation than a single Company.

On Aug. 13th, 1860 there was a Field Day and Sham Fight at Velvet Lawn, organised by the 4th Bucks (Aylesbury) Corps. Most of the Bucks Corps were present, also one or two of the Hertfordshire Companies — the whole force being under the command of Colonel Pratt. It was a case of "trying to run before we could walk" but it brought us prominently before the County, as nearly 3,500 people paid the admission to the grounds, and from a spectacular point of view I believe it was a great success, and I don't suppose it entailed a financial loss to the Aylesbury Corps.

Apropos of finance; it should be remembered that at first, and for some considerable time afterwards, the Government did nothing for us beyond lending us rifles. All of our funds were raised from subscriptions from enrolled and Hon. Members, and donations from the public. As a rule enrolled members had to provide their own uniforms, though in many instances they were helped to do this out of the donations to the Corps Fund, and in other cases gentlemen, who were unable to serve personally, paid the expenses of a suitable substitute, for at first we had many gentlemen in our ranks — men of social position equal, and in many cases superior to that of their Officers. These men gradually "dropped out" and it became the fashion about 1863-4 to deplore the deterioration of the class of recruits. Personally I never shared these laments. It seemed to me unreasonable to suppose that men who might be willing under the stress or supposed stress, of a national emergency to give up their late dinners, go out to night drills, frequently many miles away, in all weathers, in order to shoulder a rifle and stand in the ranks between (say) their own Gardeners and their Grocers' Assistants, would continue to do this indefinitely in cold blood after the emergency had passed away. Personally I rather welcomed the change because I had always considered the artisan chap to be the backbone of the Volunteer Force, and our natural recruiting ground, as the agricultural (and other) day-labourers are for the regular army and militia. I consider that if we enrol members of the latter class we do positive harm to the Senior Services by poaching on their natural preserves, to ourselves because the limited amount of soldiering which is all that they can learn with us is not sufficient to make them smart Volunteers, whereas the superior intelligence of the Artisan enables him to profit to the utmost. I hold that our proper function is to give the maximum instruction compatible with our civilian duties to those classes, and those classes alone, which, in 99 cases out of 100, would otherwise have no opportunity of getting any military instruction at all. As soon as I was in a position to do so, I acted on those views, and laid down strict rules for the guidance of the various Companies' recruiting Committees throughout the County as to the classes from which the 1st Bucks R.V.C. should be recruited.[9]

But this is a long digression and I must "hark back" to 1860. From the first we at Marlow looked up to the Berkshire Volunteers — and especially to the Maidenhead Company — with intense respect as a model for all corps. Berkshire of course had (and has) many advantages over Buckinghamshire. Intersected by 8 branches of railway,

9 Wethered's concern to recruit artisans is also apparent in his surviving correspondence, for example, Wethered to Buckingham and Chandos, 12 November, 1883 in Buckinghamshire Record Office, T/A, 5/5, Wethered Letter Book, 1874–1909 and also in Henry E. Huntington Library, Stowe MSS, STG 106. An example of one of Wethered's Instructions to his Recruiting Committee dated 6 August, 1885 is to be found in Buckinghamshire Record Office, T/A, 5/6, Order and Scrap Book, 1888–97: 'Inasmuch as the class of Agricultural and day labourers is the natural recruiting ground for the Regular Forces and the Militia, members of that class *will not be admitted* into the 1st Bucks RVC. In a purely agricultural county like Bucks an agricultural or day labourer may be defined as one who not being a clerk, tradesman's assistant, artisan or apprentice does not earn at least 18s. 0d a week regular wage.'

communication between its many considerable towns — Reading, Windsor, Maidenhead, Newbury, Wallingford, Wokingham, Hungerford, Abingdon, Wantage, etc., etc. was easy. The vast number of gentlemen's residences in the "Royal County" provided an ample supply of Officers; while — more important than all — the Berks Volunteers had the inestimable advantage of an ideal Commanding Officer from the first in Colonel Loyd Lindsay V.C. (now Lord Wantage) and formerly Lt. Col. Scots Fusiliers who duly retired from the Command of the Corps in 1895, when he also resigned the Command of the Home Counties Brigade, which he had held from its formation in 1888.[10] (Since this was written I am (June 28, 1902) grieved to see that Lord Wantage died on June 10th. No one did more, or worked harder to make the Volunteer movement a success than he did, and he will always be remembered as one of the ablest and wisest of its promoters).

The Maidenhead Company was also commanded by an old Guardsman, Colonel Vansittart, a cousin of our Lieutenant-commanding and it was probably this relationship which led to our being asked to keep the ground for them on the occasion of their first inspection in the summer of 1860. I had never before seen an inspection, and I recall the admiration which I felt at the precision of their drill, and especially of their skirmishing.

A little later, in July 1860, the Marlow Subdivision underwent its first inspection at the hands of Colonel Higginson (Grenadier Guards — now General Sir George Higginson, K.C.B.) who was probably selected for duty owing to his being one of our leading residents in Marlow.[11] It is interesting to note here that the same Officer, when Major-General commanding the Home District, again inspected the lst. Bucks R.V. Corps at our 1883 camp in Temple Park, when we had developed a strong Battalion. In 1860 we mustered under 40 of all ranks, and I have no recollection of being so much pleased with our performance as I had been with that of the Maidenhead Company. The Wycombe Corps kept the ground for us, and several Maidenhead Volunteers were also present and attended the inevitable dinner after-

10 Robert Loyd-Lindsay, Lord Wantage (1832–1902) won the Victoria Cross with the Scots Fusilier Guards in the Crimea. Conservative M.P. for Berkshire, 1865–85; Financial Secretary to the War Office, 1877–78; founder of the British Red Cross. He received the KCB for his services to the Volunteers in 1881 and was created a peer in 1885. See *Lord Wantage, V.C., K.C.B.: A Memoir by His Wife*, London, 1908.

11 General Sir George Higginson (1826–1927) was one of the few regular officers to take the Volunteer Force seriously, particularly while GOC Home District from 1878–85. He inspected the Bucks Battalion at Marlow in August 1926 when aged 100.

wards. One of them who happened to be Mayor of Maidenhead at the time, made a very energetic speech after the dinner on the importance of the Volunteer Movement, which (he said) "would safeguard our liberty and make Despots shake, and Tyrants tremble".

On Oct. 18th and 19th, 1860, the Lord Lieutenant (Lord Carrington) gave prizes for competition among the Volunteers, in his Park at Wycombe Abbey. The first prize — a handsome silver cup — was won by a Marlow Volunteer, Private Jas. Columbine (the son of our Drill Instructor), while the 2nd and 3rd prizes were won by Aylesbury men (Ward and Kirby).

Curiously enough I learnt accidentally in 1891, shortly before I resigned the active command of the Battalion, that Priv. Columbine's Prize Cup (he had died in the meantime) was being exposed for sale in a Silversmith's Shop window in an out-of-the-way part of London. As I didn't like the idea of its passing into strange hands, bought it, and it is now at Marlow waiting some object connected with the 1st. Bucks R.V. Corps to which I may give it as a Challenge Cup. I mention this here in order that this cup should not be allocated to any regimental object before my death, my Executors may be informed of my intentions and wishes respecting it.

The disbandment of the Wycombe Corps late in 1860, and its reformation in Nov. 1861, have already been mentioned, and I can't recall any other striking event until Nov. 26th, 1862 when the first step was taken to form a connecting link between the various Bucks Corps by the appointment of an Adjutant, William Forder (who had for many years been Sergeant Major of the Bucks Militia) with the rank of Captain in the Army. We always supposed that Lord Carrington wished to get a more up-to-date Sergeant Major for his Militia, and was glad to give the old one the berth of Adjutant to us. He was a most estimable person and doubtless a good non-commissioned officer, but he was hardly an ideal Adjutant of Volunteers in a County like ours, and I cannot honestly say that his appointment had much effect in welding together our scattered Corps.

Those of us who looked beyond our own detachments realised that the "welding" process could only be begun by bringing our Units together for continuous instruction — no easy matter in our case.

In 1862 or 1863 the Berkshire Battalion adopted the system of Regimental Camps — I think they were the first Corps to do this — and I remember being much struck by what I saw at their Camp at Cookham — I think in 1862. But Regimental Camps pre-suppose a Commanding Officer and a good deal of money, and we had neither — certainly no Colonel Loyd-Lindsay, both able and willing to provide the sinews of war. It was therefore necessary, before we could start a Regimental Camp, to get a Commanding Officer appointed, and to secure pecuniary support from the Community at large, in other words — to form a County Rifle Association.

We accordingly took advantage of the opportunity afforded by our first Battalion inspection at Aylesbury[12] on Oct. 28th, 1863. Col. Ibbetson was our Inspecting Officer and Col. Pratt — then Captain of the reformed Wycombe Corps — commanded the Battalion pro-tem.

I have a very vivid recollection of the way in which the Inspecting Officer succeeded in "rubbing us all up the wrong way". By 1863 the "hot wave" of approval with which the Volunteer Movement was greeted in 1859–60 had been succeeded by a "cold wave" of official indifference, and I think that regular Officers as a rule, General McMurdo being the most conspicuous exception, regarded us, at the very best as harmless lunatics, and at worst, as utterly valueless as a military force, and in any case, as a great nuisance. At all events Colonel Ibbetson on this occasion left us in no doubt as to his sentiments towards us and conspicuously failed to gain our affections.[13]

After the Inspection the Officers dined together at the "George", Aylesbury. (By this time I held a Commission, as in the Spring of 1863 the Marlow Sub-Division had become a Company). But it was a very hurried gathering as most of us had to catch trains to take us and our men back to our respective Headquarters. Nevertheless we managed to get a considerable amount of work done, even if it was in a somewhat informal manner.

First — as to the Commanding Officer. We were unanimous in wishing that Captain Harvey, commanding the Slough Corps, should be appointed. He had long held a Commission in the Bucks Yeomanry and he was universally popular throughout the County — but he was Conservative Candidate for Bucks (he was elected in March 1864) and he was brother-in-law to the Duke of Buckingham. At this time, and until early in 1872, all commissions in the Auxiliary Forces were given by the Lord Lieutenant direct, and it was suggested that we should memorialise Lord Carrington to give us a Commanding Officer without further delay, and that Captain Harvey should be appointed. Colonel Pratt, however, pointed out that anything in the nature of a "round robin" would be a breach of military discipline,

12 Pratt had previously encountered Ibbetson during an inspection of the Wycombe Corps in 1862 and adjudged him the worst kind of regular to inspect volunteers, Buckinghamshire Record Office, D/CN/Box 28 (C), Bundle 27, Pratt to Carrington, 25 February, 1862.

13 General Sir William Scott McMurdo (1819–94) was the first Inspector-General of the Volunteer Force, 1860–65, having previously commanded the Land Transport Corps in the Crimea.

and we had to be content with asking him to represent our views to his Chief — Lord Carrington.[14]

After this it was almost impossible to fix the attention of the meeting on the subject of a County Rifle Association, which was new to most present. Eventually, however, we succeeded in getting some formal resolutions passed to the effect:-

1. That it is desirable to form a Bucks County Rifle Association for the encouraging of rifle shooting, and for the formation of Volunteer Camps.

2. That the Lord Lieutenant be asked to accept the office of President.

3. That the Duke of Buckingham and all other Peers resident in or owning property in the County, be asked to become patrons.

4. That the Members for the County (and all other County Magnates) be asked to become Vice-Patrons.

5. That Capt. T. F. Fremantle (3rd Bucks) and Lieut. O. P. Wethered (1st Bucks) be appointed Honorary Secretaries.

Armed with these resolutions, Capt. Fremantle and I got to work at once. Between us we sent out over 300 circulars to "all and sundry", taking the County Directory parish by parish,[15] and by the Spring of 1864 we had nearly £300 promised in donations and more than £300 in annual subscriptions. We had hoped to hold our first camp in 1864, but alas! May came and we were still without a Commanding Officer — nearly four and a half years after our formation. At last, on May 24th, 1864, not Captain Harvey, but the Hon. Percy Barrington was gazetted Lieut-Col. It was, however, then too late to begin making arrangements for a Camp during that summer.

On June 22nd, 1864 a large review of the Metropolitan and Midland County Volunteers was held at Stowe, at which General McMurdo was (I think) in command. The Bucks Corps were all present

14 Carrington had previously objected to a round robin from the Slough Corps requesting Harvey's appointment to command that Corps on the grounds that it infringed his right as Lord-Lieutenant to appoint whom he thought proper, see Devon Record Office, Seymour of Berry Pomeroy MSS, 1392M/Box 18/14, Brown to Seymour, 26 July 1861 and 1 Aug., 1861. Wethered habitually refers to the Duke of Buckingham but, of course, he means Richard Grenville, Third Duke of Buckingham and Chandos (1823–89). Harvey's election to the County parliamentary seat vacant through the Hon. W. G. Cavendish's succession to the peerage as Second Lord Chesham was in December 1863 rather than March 1864 as Wethered suggests.

15 Examples of the circular are to be found in Henry E. Huntington Library, Stowe MSS, STG Military Box 8 (2) and Devon Record Office, Seymour of Berry Pomeroy MSS, 1392M/Box 18/1.

under Lt-Col. Barrington, who appeared at our head for the first time. Colonel Barrington's appointment was the cause of serious trouble with the Slough Corps. Colonel Barrington himself had nothing to do with this directly; he had simply been offered the command of the Battalion and he had accepted it. But it was perhaps natural that Capt. Harvey should feel aggrieved at being passed over by the Lord Lieutenant, and it was also natural that his men should sympathise with him. At any rate Captain Harvey sent in his resignation, and unfortunately he ventilated his grievance in the County papers. Naturally this did not mend matters, and considerable "friction" ensued. Captain Harvey considered that his recent election as M.P. for the County and his relationship to the Duke of Buckingham — between whom and the Lord Lieutenant no love was lost — were the cause of his having been passed over.[16] However this may be, he resigned and the command of the Slough Corps was offered to Lieut. Way but he was unwilling to undertake the responsibility and expense of the position. No one else in the neighbourhood would accept the command and the result was that (I think) on the day before or the very morning of our second Battalion Inspection, Nov. 2nd, 1864, we received a Regimental Order saying that, as there was no one responsible for the Government arms at Slough, the War Office had ordered them to be returned into Government Stores at once, and that the 5th Bucks Corps was to be disbanded. If this decision had been carried out, it must have proved the death blow to our newly formed County Association, for it would have left us with only 4 weak Corps, for whom it would have been absurd to incur the heavy expenses of a regimental camp. Accordingly, when I saw Col. Barrington at our Inspection I told him if he approved, I was willing to undertake the command of the Slough Corps as a temporary measure. He consented and procured the withdrawal of the sentence of disbandment, and I at once took over the command, though my Commission as Captain was not gazetted till Jan. 20th, 1865. Lieut. Way withdrew his resignation, and continued to act as subaltern for some years longer.

I wish here to bear my testimony to the excellence of the non-commissioned officers of the Slough Corps, not only at that time, but

16 The rivalry between the Grenvilles of Stowe and Carrington was not just political for the latter was also regarded as a parvenu by the former. As Thomas Grenville had once expressed it to the Third Duke, then Marquess of Chandos, Carrington was the son of a man who 'thirty years ago was a stranger to the County without an acre in it' (Buckinghamshire Record Office, Morgan-Grenville MSS, D55 AR 40/63, Grenville to Chandos, 22 January, 1839). Harvey's own dissatisfaction and his concern that his resignation from the Volunteers might affect the Conservative cause in the County is expressed in Bodleian Library, Hughenden MSS, B/XXI/H/275-8, Harvey to Disraeli, 9 October and 14 October 1863 and 11 May 1864.

as far as I know, up to now — certainly up to the time when I resigned the active command of the Battalion. Had it not been for the excellent spirit which prevailed among them, and their continued influence for good, I feel convinced that the Corps must have fallen to pieces under the adverse circumstances which threatened its existence in 1864, and in equally difficult times which were still to come — as will be shown hereafter. I retained my command until June 14th, 1865 when Mr A. Sylvester, a personal friend of Capt. Selfe (Aylesbury Corps) was gazetted as Captain — a position which he held till July 1868.

On Easter Monday — April 17th, 1865, I took a combined Company of Slough and Marlow Volunteers to the Brighton review, and repeated the experience on Easter Monday April 2nd, 1868 — but I came to the conclusion that the game was not worth the candle — at any rate for Country Corps so far from the scene of action. It may have been different in the case of Metropolitan Corps — though I much doubt their "Discipline" being permanently improved thereby, for a vast number of their members made it an excuse for spending 3 or 4 days at the sea-side — in a semi-military capacity — but under no effective military control, and when their Corps reached Brighton on the Monday morning, these men fell in with them, or didn't fall in, preferring to be spectators than actors in the day's proceedings. For us at Marlow the programme consisted of (1) Parading at Headquarters at 4 a.m., (2) a march of 4 miles to our nearest station, (3) a railway journey of several hours, (4) arrival at Brighton much overdue, (5) a hustled march to the heights above the town, (6) much marching and counter-marching to get us into position where we could see nothing — generally in Reserve, (7) standing (or lying) "easy" for an hour or two, (8) a march past on the Race Course, (9) a march to the station and a scramble for a train, (10) another long railway journey, and (11) another 4 miles at the end of it — reaching our Headquarters about 24 hours after we had left there — and, next day, we had the satisfaction of saying that we had been to the Brighton review, and of reading in the morning papers a glowing account of what had happened there, for we didn't know, excepting as to our own part in it, and I doubt whether anyone under the rank of a Staff-Officer knew much more about it! To sum up, in my opinion these Brighton reviews afforded a minimum of instruction out of all proportion to the cost in money and vital energy involved, and I discouraged attendance at them in the future.

And now I come to the first of our long series of camps. This was fixed for Monday, July 31st to Thursday, August 3rd., 1865 — only 2 clear days, as it was thought that our men could not give more than that from their civil occupations. None of us, from the Colonel downwards had had any previous experience of the kind, and we made the initial mistake of attempting too much in the time.

As I was acting Secretary of the County Association which provided the necessary funds, it was decided to form the camp at Marlow, where all the preliminary arrangements could be made under my personal supervision. I accordingly obtained the sanction of the Marlow Vestry for our exclusive use for the time of a field containing about 4 acres, which had been assigned by the Inclosure Commissioners to the Parish as a Public Recreation Ground, but which was practically never used for that purpose. It was situated near the outskirts of the Town, and 500 or 600 yards from our Marlow Rifle Range, from which, however, it was separated by the river Thames.

The Duke of Buckingham had made it a condition of his support to the Association that we should offer prizes to be competed for by the Bucks Yeomanry, whom he commanded. Apart from this, however, we had always intended that they should be included in the scope of our Association, and some even hoped that in time it might be possible to hold our Camps jointly with them; but this was not to be.

Our Prize Programme was very comprehensive — County Challenge Cup, Company Challenge Cup, a Series of lst Class Shots, 2nd Class Shots, 3rd Class Shots, Recruits, Honorary Members, Yeomanry etc. I think there were nearly a dozen distinct competitions. Of course additional Range accommodation was necessary, but the Quarry Woods afforded ample background for the 6 sets of targets which we provided. The expense of these, with necessary Markers Butts, Militia Staff — Sergeants for the firing points and as markers, a constant service of Ferry-boats to and from the ranges, etc., proved a heavy drain on our finance.

At last all the arrangements were complete, and by mid-day on July 31st, most of the Corps had marched into Camp — from Bourne End — drenched to the skin — for this was our first, but by no means our last — experience of a soaking wet Camp. I don't think that any of us got dry again until after Camp, for in those early days we had no second uniform of any kind. A few of the Shooting Sergeants had invested, each for himself, various forms of Norfolk Jacket; and I had invented a Patrol Jacket and Forage Cap for my own wear (and this the Colonel approved as the Regimental pattern), but most of us only had the uniforms we stood up in and even among these no two Corps were alike, for each local tailor put a different interpretation on the details of the "Sealed Pattern" and it was not till several years had passed that absolute uniformity was attained.

Our Marching-in State shewed 17 Officers, 18 Sergeants, 188 Rank and File — 223 of all ranks, and this was a very high percentage of our "total enrolled strength" especially for a first experiment of camp life. We improved upon this in succeeding camps, for it became an axiom with us that all enrolled members must spend at least 3 nights in camp, unless absolutely prevented by illness or otherwise; and I was told some years later by the A.A.G. for Auxiliary Forces that our Camp returns shewed a higher percentage of attendance than those of any other Corps in the Kingdom. I remember indeed that on one occasion (I think at one of our Temple Camps), we actually had more men present at Inspection than we returned as efficient at the end of the Volunteer Year.

On Monday afternoon we had a Battalion Drill, when our ranks were fuller than at any subsequent drill during that Camp; for the great number of our men engaged at the Rifle Range, together with the necessary "Camp Duties" left a mere skeleton battalion for parades. But it was absolutely necessary that our Prize Programme should be carried through, and carried through it was, but I have never ceased to marvel at that result being obtained; for all 6 targets had to be kept continuously occupied — otherwise time would have failed — and the incessant rain was not conducive to rapidity of tabulating results, re-squadding competitors, many of whom were engaged in several competitions at the same time, to say nothing of the initial difficulty of deciphering the original target registers, all blurred as they were by rain. I know that it took 2 or 3 of us all day, and the greater part of each night, to get through the mere clerical work; but the last shot was fired about 11 a.m. on the Thursday morning, the Prizes were distributed about noon — I think by the Lord Lieutenant — and the Camp was broken up that afternoon.

But a rather exciting incident had happened overnight. It will be remembered that our camping ground belonged to the parish, and all parishioners had consequently a prima-facie right of access to it. In 1865 (and possibly even in later years) Marlow numbered among its inhabitants some specimens of a class which was generally ready for a "row". Although the parish had, through its Vestry, given up all its rights to us, for the time, these men weren't going to be bound by that. Anyhow, they resented being excluded from the field, when the Camp was cleared at night, and we received hints that a "storm was brewing" for the last night in Camp, so the guards were doubled. A "Camp Fire" had been arranged for that night. A real "Camp Fire" — (a large bonfire) — Punch — Songs — Speeches. I was much too busy with target registers, etc. to join in the fun, but in the middle of it all I was summoned to go to the entrance gate — a common field gate — to exert my local influence in pacifying an infuriated mob of indignant "Parishioners" — I forbear to call them "Roughs". I found them on the point of breaking down the gate — so I formed up the Guard in line in front with fixed bayonets at the "Charge". Fortunately the fences round the ground were in good order and when the leaders realised that, if they broke down the field-gate, they would have to impale themselves on our fence of cold steel before they could attain their object, my representations had effect on them and the mob gradually melted away.

Not to camp on public land — *Not* to hold an overcrowded Prize Meeting during Camp, were two negative lessons which our first Camp taught us! It also brought out in strong relief innumerable differences in the organisation, discipline, and interior economy of our several Units, and we all set to work to remedy our special defects. Hitherto Company Officers had thought only of their own Companies. Now we began to realise that our credit was bound up with that of the Bucks Battalion as a whole — in short, the seed of a very healthy Regimental "Esprit de Corps" had been sown, and it soon bore fruit. Some of the Corps were far ahead of the others in the matter of drill — others in uniformity of equipment and general "smartness". With the object of bringing up the laggards to the standard of the best, the Colonel gave an Annual Prize for the "Best equipped Company", and my brother, then Capt. Wethered, gave a Challenge Cup (and the Association added £10) to be adjudged to the "best drilled" Company by the Inspecting Officer. These Competitions had an excellent effect, and, after a few years, there was little to choose between the different Corps, so that it became very difficult to adjudge the prizes, and the Competitions were given up. I remember that before the last competition for the "best equipped" prize, my brother, hoping to score a point for his old Company, provided each of the Marlow men with a pair of white gloves, in which they were paraded for the first Comdg. Officer's parade in camp, but alas! the Colonel promptly ordered them to be hidden away as contrary to Regulations.

Our 2nd Camp was fixed for Monday, July 23rd – Thursday, July 26th 1866 (again only 2 clear days) at Halton, in a small field just outside Sir Anthony de Rothschild's Park at Aston Clinton, in which we drilled, but all our arrangements were very nearly upset by a Regimental Order, dated June 30th, informing us that the Slough Corps was (again) to be disbanded — that the Battalion was too weak without them to form a Camp — and that consequently there would be no Camp. We at once represented to the Colonel that — whatever the offence of the Slough Corps might be, it was very hard that we should all be punished for it, and our remonstrances resulted in another order on July 4th, withdrawing the former one. On enquiry we ascertained that the cause of the Colonel's anger with the Slough Corps arose in the following way:- By arrangement with the Officers Commanding the several Corps he made a Spring Inspection of each at its own Headquarters. I say "by arrangement" because we were, till 1875, an "Administrative Battalion", and not a "*Consolidated* battalion": and the position of a C.O. of an Administrative Battalion presented many anomalies, which I am not surprised that Colonel Barrington had not, at that time, fully grasped.[17] For instance, his authority over each component Corps of his Battalion only began when two or more of them came together under him, and only lasted as long as they remained together under him. At its own Headquarters each Corps was absolutely independent of him, and solely under its own Captain. The Colonel could suggest, recommend or advise, but he could not *order*. He could *order his Adjutant* to pay monthly visits to each Corps, but he could *not order the Corps* to parade for the Adjutant (or anyone else). As a rule this did not lead to serious difficulty — partly because the Colonels were careful not to ignore the strict rights of Officers Commanding Corps — partly because the latters' good sense taught them that the Colonel's recommendations or wishes were for the good of their Corps. On this occasion, however, the result was lamentable.

The evening arrived on which it was arranged that the Colonel should inspect the Slough Corps — the Corps paraded in full strength but no Colonel appeared. He had simply missed his train, as most of us have done at some time or other. But he *ordered* the Corps to parade again for his inspection on a later day, which happened to be a most inconvenient one for the Corps, and which would not have been chosen if the Captain had been consulted.

No doubt the Corps hadn't got over its "soreness" at Capt. Harvey's supervision, and illogically "had a grudge against Colonel Barrington" on that account. No doubt some of them looked upon the missed train as an additional slight — no doubt the second day was inconvenient. Anyhow the result was that, when the Colonel arrived on parade the 5th Bucks R.V. Corps was represented by about a dozen men — most of whom were Officers or Non-commissioned Officers. The Colonel was very angry, and the order of June 30th was the result. The revocation of this order on July 4th. enabled the camp arrangements to go on, and on July 23rd. the Battn assembled at Halton.

N.B. I place what follows within brackets (1) because I do not know what may be done hereafter with the "personal recollections" — a decision which I am content to leave to my successors in Command of the Corps for the time being. I write them primarily *for the Corps* and

---

17 Wethered's description of the differences between an Administrative and a Consolidated Battalion is admirably clear, the varied organization of each type of battalion being authorized by government circular on 24 March 1860. The 1st Bucks Administrative Battalion came into existence in July 1862 and the 1st Bucks Rifle Volunteer Corps in April 1875.

the incidents I am about to relate are so personal to Colonel Barrington and myself, that I do not wish them to be given to the *Public at large*. I leave my successors to decide whether these special incidents should be issued for "*private circulation* only" — i.e., among the members of the lst Bucks R.V. Corps. To me they have always remained one of the most interesting of my Volunteer reminiscences; and their effect upon me — the fact that the Colonel took the remonstrances of a Subaltern as he did — was to give me a respect and affection for him far greater than I should have felt if he had never made a mistake at all. They also had a lasting effect on the Battalion, for his tact and consideration were never again at fault. The memory of these incidents led me, in 1880 (when our 1879 Camp had proved that the Honorary Colonelcy of the Regiment would be no empty honour), to ask Colonel Barrington to accept the position, and renew his connection with the Corps, which he had been obliged by ill-health to sever in 1870.

(I was prevented by business from joining the Camp before the next morning, when I arrived in time for the first C.O's Parade. Before dismissing us the Colonel harangued us, taking as his text the delinquencies of the Slough Corps. But he included us all in his condemnation. He told us that "it was no pleasure to him to command us" — and so on — and so on. I was furious, and told Capt. Fremantle immediately after parade that I should send in my resignation. Very wisely, he advised me to think it over. When I was cooler I did so, and decided to "have it out" with the Colonel. For some reason or other our Annual Inspection was made that afternoon (Tuesday), and although there had been only two preliminary drills, the Inspecting Officer (Col. Deshon) was well satisfied with our work. After it was all over I saw Colonel Barrington, and told him exactly what I felt, and that others also resented what he had said that morning: that I knew he could pull me up for insubordination in speaking to him as I was doing, but that I did it in the interest of the Battalion as a whole: that, whatever fault he might have to find with the Slough Corps — and pointed out to him the extenuating circumstances above referred to — it was unjust to abuse us all as we had done all we could to make the movement a success, and our men good and efficient Volunteers, etc., etc. The Colonel listened to me most patiently, and then asked "What do you wish me to do? Do you want me to eat my words?" I replied "No Sir — certainly not, but I think you might take advantage of the Inspection having passed off well to issue an Order in terms which will take the sting out of your words, and remove the bitter taste which they left in our mouths!" That night he brought me an Order which he had drafted & asked "Will this do?" It was exactly the right thing: its issue next morning had the effect I anticipated, and from that time onward no "friction" ever arose between Colonel

Barrington and the Bucks Volunteers.[18] He was an excellent Commanding Officer — knew his work thoroughly, and sowed the seeds of discipline in the Bucks Battalion, which have since developed into a healthy plant: and his successors in the Command have only had to continue his work on the lines which he originated.)

The Prize Shooting during the Halton Camp was limited to the County Cup, and the Company Cup Competitions, and as these only took a few men at a time from the ranks, our Battalion Drills were more satisfactory than at Marlow. After 1866, however, we had no Prize Shooting at camp. Except the Inspection, which (as I have said before) passed off satisfactorily on the Tuesday, I cannot recall any later incident worth mentioning, and the Camp ended on the Thursday.

In 1867 the Duke of Grafton, who commanded the Northamptonshire Volunteers, invited the Bucks Battalion to join his Corps in a Camp at his park — Wakefield Lawn — from Monday June 17th till Saturday June 22nd. As this gave us four clear days in Camp with no Prize Shooting to be got through, the improvement from the drill point of view was very great, and the fact that we were with another Battalion did much to develop our "Esprit de Corps" and to pull our own Corps together. Again (for the second time in 3 years) we marched into Camp drenched to the skin. We detrained at Wolverton and had 7 or 8 miles to march. Both at Wolverton and at Stony Stratford (where we halted for lunch) I made enquiries as to the possibility of forming Corps — but the time for that was not yet, though it came 10 years later. At Stony Stratford I found that a Squad of 15 to 20 men had joined one of the Northamptonshire Companies, so the ground was already occupied by invaders. At Wolverton — the great carriage building works of the L.N.W. Railway Compy., there was an abundant supply of splendid raw material for a Corps, but I had then neither the time nor the necessary authority for conducting long negotiations with the authorities.

18 In fact, Barrington was clearly increasingly frustrated by the anomalous position of the Lieutenant-Colonel arising from an administrative rather than a consolidated battalion. There was another incident concerning the Slough Corps in January 1869 when its Band defied regulations to play in uniform at a reception for the Liberal M.P. for Windsor, Roger Eykyn, and accepted financial contributions from the public for Corps funds (See Henry E. Huntington Library, Stowe MSS, STG 103, War Office Note, 24 Jan., 1869). Reflecting on this, Barrington wrote to the Third Duke, 'Personally I hate volunteering and should be most happy to resign if you can find anyone to take my place' (*Ibid.*, STG 98, Barrington to Duke, 18 January, 1869). Subsequently, he wrote that he would have resigned long before if he had not thought the movement would collapse in the county (*Ibid.*, Barrington to Duke, 23 January, 1869). Eykyn was a Cornet in the Taplow Troop (South Bucks Yeomanry Cavalry).

In order to shorten our route to Camp, our Quartermaster had got permission for the Battalion to march by private cart track through an apparently interminable forest. This would doubtless have been delightful under a blazing sun; but under the actual conditions we didn't bless our guide. Previous rains had converted the deeply rutted track into a quagmire, and torrents fell during the whole of our march. I doubt whether any Unit of the troops in South Africa has presented a more miserable appearance during the last 18 months, than did the Bucks Battalion — bedraggled with mud, and soaked through and through — on our first appearance before our Northamptonshire comrades.

There was not much "fraternisation" between the two Battalions. The Northamptonshire men were principally shoe-makers and straw-plaiters, and consequently of a very different class from our men. On the occasions of our parading together as a Brigade, the Duke of Grafton and Colonel Barrington commanded alternately. On the Friday there was a review (in which the Duke of Manchester's Light Horse[19] took part) and our Inspection; and on the Saturday we broke up.

On Jan. 20th, 1868, I succeeded my brother as Captain of the Marlow Corps. One of my first acts was to abolish our Drum and Fife Band. From the first it had always been assumed that each Corps — even if only a sub-division — must have a band, either brass or drum and fife — sometimes both — "in order to make the Corps popular". It was a constant expense, and an actual *hindrance* to efficiency. In those days we had monthly or quarterly "compulsory drills", when every member had to be present, under penalty of a fine, and on these occasions of the largest musters it seemed a pity not to utilise the Band, so it became the custom to have a "march out" to some neighbouring village, and then to march home again. This seemed to me a deliberate waste of good opportunities for *drill*; so I decided to do away with the band. Some of my N.C. Officers told me that it would break up the Corps; but I replied that, if so, it would show that the Corps was not worth keeping up, and I was amply justified by the results; for I have always considered that the comparatively high state of efficiency which the Marlow Corps attained was largely due to that act.

The Battalion entered on a new era in June 1868, when Capt. Clement, who had recently retired from the 68th Regt. was gazetted Adjutant, vice Forder — resigned. Capt. Clement was pre-eminently a "smart"

19 While the majority of Volunteer units were infantry or Rifle Volunteers, there were some artillery and engineer corps and; very occasionally, mounted units, one such being the 1st Hunts (Kimbolton) Mounted Rifle Volunteers, also known as the Duke of Manchester's Light Horse.

Officer — thoroughly "up to date" in all details of "drill", and not afraid of initiating reforms in our antiquated procedure. He soon became "persona grata" to us all, and every man who served with him, or under him, still regards him as a personal friend. For myself I don't think that I should have accepted the Command of the Battalion in 1872 if I had not known that I should have the able assistance and loyal co-operation of Capt. Clement. But I am anticipating.

10 days after Captain Clement had been gazetted, a Royal Review (I think in honour of the Sultan) was held in Windsor Park, on June 20th, 1868. On this occasion I was placed, much against my will, in a very prominent but most unenviable position. The published "Detail" had said that the Bucks Battalion and 3 Companies of (I think) Wiltshire Volunteers were to form a Provisional battalion under the command of Colonel Barrington. It seemed, however, that Colonel Barrington had never intended to go; and he wrote to the Senior Captain telling him to take Command. I don't know whether the Senior Captain had intended to accompany his Corps to the review, at any rate he didn't go; and sent me a telegram (which reached me just before I started from Marlow with my Company) telling me that I had to Command the Provisional battalion. I, the junior Captain of only 5 months standing, who had never been out in front of a battalion in my life; and on the occasion of a Royal Review, with a scratch Battalion which I had to command on foot.

What was I to do? I had no charger — my hunter was out to graze, and it was too late to borrow a mount locally. I determined to trust to luck. On reaching Windsor I hurried to the Cavalry Barracks and implored the loan of a Trooper's Charger, but every horse was on duty on such an occasion. I even appealed to Sir Richard Mayne (who was then Chief Commissioner of Police, and in that capacity on duty at Windsor) to let me have one of his men's horses, but it was of no avail, and I had to accept the inevitable. I don't know that I ever felt greater trepidation than when I took my position in front of the Battalion for the Royal Salute — the sole dismounted Officer in a long line of Commanding Officers.

When our Band — part Bucks and part Wilts — moved out for the March Past, as we were moving on to the Saluting Base, a Staff Officer galloped up to them and hustled out a luckless individual in plain clothes — probably a Volunteer whose uniform hadn't come in time — and then pitched into me, as the real culprit. Poor me — who had no more to do with the composition of the Band than he had. With that exception everything passed off well. After the March Past there was a long Field Day, towards the end of which we found ourselves — very hot and very *thirsty* (for in those days we had no water bottles) in reserve in the welcome shade of the "Long Walk" and in close proximity to a huge refreshment tent. I remember debating within myself what I should do if any men broke their ranks in pursuit of drinks. I don't suppose that my temporary Colonel's Command gave me the power of dismissal from the Corps, even over the Bucks Companies — certainly not over the Wiltshire men. Nevertheless I decided to dismiss the first offenders, but happily there was no necessity. 2 men per Company were told off to fetch beer, and the Column remained perfectly steady. But my anxiety on the subject was not unnatural, for in 1868 Volunteer Discipline had not reached a very high point, as was shewn that very evening when several other Battalions, who had to entrain for their return journey at Datchet Station, got completely out of hand, and the next day's papers told us that there had been gross insubordination.[20]

Our 1868 Camp was held at Ashridge, on the borders of Bucks and Herts. It began on Tuesday July 26th, and ended on Saturday August 1st. We were inspected on Friday morning by Colonel Elliott, and that afternoon was devoted to Camp Sports. The summer of 1868 was one of the hottest on record, and while I was superintending the sports, I was knocked over by the sun. It was this, followed by very hard work during the general Election in October,[21] which led to my being ordered, later in the Autumn, to give up all work and go abroad for at least a year. I cannot, therefore, speak from personal knowledge of the Volunteer events of 1869, and have always regretted this break of continuity in my recollection, though of course I know, from other sources much of what occurred.

The Brighton Review — March 29th, 1869 — very nearly proved a fiasco. It was a bitterly cold day — a hurricane blowing — hail and rain falling in torrents — and the troops were soaked through before leaving their several rendezvous in Brighton. Although the Duke of Cambridge (Commander in Chief) had not yet arrived from London, the Senior Officer at Brighton ordered the Review to be abandoned and the troops dismissed. But when the Duke arrived later he didn't at all approve of this, and at once ordered the Parades to be reformed and the Review to be carried out. By this time, of course, the men were scattered all over Brighton, and it was no easy matter to get them together again. However, it was accomplished more or less, though many hundreds never knew of the fresh orders till it was too late for

20 Two units, the 9th Essex (Silvertown) RVC and 2nd Herts (Watford) RVC were disbanded as a result of the disturbances at Datchet railway station when trains were delayed in June 1868; see Ian F. W. Beckett, *Riflemen Form*, p.177.

21 Wethered was obviously working for his brother, T. O. Wethered, who was successfully elected as Conservative M.P. for Marlow in November 1868 by just 31 votes ahead of Edmund Hope Verney. Wethered retained the seat until 1880 when he did not contest it.

them to fall in with their Corps. The original programme was carried out, and I believe that the Duke's surprise "Assembly" had a very beneficial effect on the Volunteer Force.[22]

On July 26th, 1869, the Bucks Volunteers joined the Berkshire Corps in their Camp at Abingdon — on the Berkshire banks of the Thames, just opposite Nuneham. Not long before the Camp, Colonel Barrington was taken seriously ill, and lay at death's door for several months. As we had no Major, the Command during the Camp devolved on Capt. Selfe (Aylesbury Corps), the senior Captain, and of course a vast amount of extra work and responsibility fell to the Adjutant, who proved himself quite equal to the occasion and I believe the Battalion did at least as well as could be expected in the very difficult circumstance in which it was placed. General Lindsay inspected both Battalions on Friday, July 30th, when Prince and Princess Christian were present (the Prince having been gazetted to the Hon: Colonelcy of the Berkshire Corps on the preceding day) and the Camp ended on the Saturday.[23]

In March 1870 I returned to England, and in July we again camped with the Northamptonshires at Wakefield Lawn. Colonel Barrington who was supposed to be a confirmed invalid for the rest of his life, had resigned the Command on March 26th, and was succeeded by Colonel C. M. Chester of Chicheley Hall, Newport Pagnell, who now saw the Battalion on parade for the first time. I cannot remember any incident of special interest during our 2nd Camp at Wakefield Lawn. We marched into Camp on Tuesday, July 5th and broke up on the Saturday. We were to be inspected by Companies later on in the month at our respective Headquarters, so there was no inspection of the Battalion in Camp.

In 1870 Certificates of Proficiency were instituted, and the first Schools of Instruction for Militia and Volunteer Officers were held in October of that year. As I thought that the Schools would not get into good working order at the start, I decided to wait until the second School began, on Nov. 1st, when I went to Aldershot for the month's training, at the end of which I obtained a Field Officer's Certificate. It was entirely owing to this fact that I was promoted to be Major in 1871, and to the Command of the Battalion in 1872.

Our 1871 Camp was formed at Halton (as in 1866) on Monday July

---

22 Wethered is at error for the Easter Review of March 1869 was held at Dover and not Brighton. George, Duke of Cambridge (1819–1904) was Commander-in-Chief of the British Army from 1856 to 1895 although formally he was General Commanding-in-Chief until 1887 and only thereafter Commander-in-Chief.

23 Major-General the Hon. James Lindsay was Inspector-General of Reserve Forces from 1868 to 1874.

3rd, and lasted till Saturday July 8th. On the Friday we were inspected by Colonel Danbury, and (fortunately for me) the 4 days previous shouting on parade had made both Colonel Chester and the Adjutant absolutely voiceless — neither could speak above a whisper — and on the Inspecting Officer asking if any Captain held a F.O's Certificate, I was called to the front. Later in the day Colonel Chester offered me the Majority, and, as he told me that the Captains who were senior to me were willing that I should be promoted over their heads, I accepted, and was duly gazetted Major on August 12th.

I should have mentioned earlier that, in Feb. 1867, the Eton College Corps became the 8th Bucks (Eton College) R.V. Corps — the numbers 6 and 7 having been assigned in 1860 to the short-lived Corps at Newport Pagnell and Princes Risborough respectively. From the time when the Rev. E. Warre, now Headmaster of Eton (who had been the first Commanding Officer of the Oxford University Corps), went to Eton as a Master, there had been a Cadet Corps in the School, mainly composed of boys under 17 years of age, who could not consequently be "enrolled". In 1866 the number of boys over 17 years had increased, and application was made to the War Office to sanction the formation of an enrolled Company. As Eton is close to Windsor, its relations with Berkshire are much closer than with Buckinghamshire; and the school authorities naturally wished the Corps to form part of the Berkshire Battalion, but the War Office would not sanction this departure from the County organisation of the Volunteer Force. Somewhat unwillingly, therefore, the Eton College Corps became the 8th Bucks, but we saw practically nothing of them before 1871.[24] Our Colonel was their Colonel, and inspected them once a year at Eton. Our Adjutant was their Adjutant, and paid them periodical visits, but as far as the rest of us were concerned, they might as well have been a Yorkshire Corps. As an old Etonian myself, and a personal friend of several of their Officers, I was naturally anxious to draw closer the relations between the Eton Corps and the rest of the Battalion, and soon after I became Major, I obtained the Colonel's consent to my organising two Field Days, the Eton College Corps on one side and our other Southern Corps on the other, on October 18th, and Nov. 9th at Burnham Beeches and Hughenden respectively.

On Oct. 18th, the Marlow and Wycombe Corps drove to and from

---

24 The 8th Bucks (Eton College) RVC officially came into existence in May 1867 with a Cadet Corps being officially attached to it from August 1868. See Buckinghamshire Record Office, Lieutenancy MSS, L/P 14 Carrington to War Office, 4 March, 1867 and 23 April, 1867; *Ibid.*, Pakington to Carrington, 17 April, 1867. Some returns for the 8th Bucks are preserved in Henry E. Huntington Library, Stowe MSS, STG Military Box 8 (4) and (5).

Burnham Beeches in vans, and the Slough Corps marched. Unfortunately, neither of the Wycombe Officers were able to be present, and that Corps was commanded by its Sergeant-Instructor. The Field Day was very satisfactory, and at its close I, of course, ordered all surplus ammunition to be collected, but it subsequently turned out that, in the case of the Wycombe Company, this order was not thoroughly carried out, for, as Capt. Clement and I rode homewards, we noticed an empty cartridge case by the side of the road, and then others further on, and on our enquiry at a wayside public house, on the way to Wycombe we learned that the occupants of one of the Wycombe vans had amused themselves by firing off the ammunition which they had secreted. Of course I felt bound, in my report to Colonel Chester of the day's proceedings to mention this breach of discipline by a few men, and I don't think that I was unreasonable in supposing that I should hear more on the subject before any final decision was taken. I was therefore greatly astonished to receiving on Nov. 3rd, a Regimental Order stating that the 2nd Bucks (High Wycombe) R.V. Corps was to be disbanded, but that the Officers would be allowed to resign their commissions. I thought then, and I think still, that this, the severest punishment of the whole Corps for the fault of a few only, was a grievous mistake, and I telegraphed to Colonel Chester that I was starting at once to see him at Chicheley that night. I couldn't reach that out-of-the-way corner of the county — many miles from a railway station, — till nearly midnight, and my reception was far from cordial. I learnt afterwards that Colonel Chester had a great friend high on the staff of the War Office, whom he invariably consulted on all points of difficulty, but this friend had recently died, and this question was the first which Colonel Chester had to decide "proprio mori". He was inexorable, and turned a deaf ear to all my representations, and I left Chicheley next morning, having effected absolutely nothing by my visit. The sentence of disbandment was carried out, and for 4 years there were no Volunteers at Wycombe, for it was not till 1875 that the "soreness" caused by what all Wycombe considered harsh and unjust treatment had sufficiently worn off to allow of any steps being taken towards raising a new Company there — and even then very few of the old members rejoined.[25]

25 Correspondence on the disbandment of the 2nd Bucks is to be found in Henry E. Huntington Library, Stowe MSS, STG 101 between Chester and the Duke of Buckingham and Chandos as Lord-Lieutenant. An additional factor was Chester's view that the officers of the Wycombe Corps were inefficient, having so far failed to pass for the certificates of proficiency (Chester to Duke, 2 November, 1871) and he clearly found Wethered's night visit irksome (Chester to Duke, 4 November, 1871).

I think that Colonel Chester must have very soon realised that he had made a mistake, which had impaired his influence with the Battalion, for he sent in his resignation early in 1872. Just at this time, fresh regulations were issued as to the Commissions of Officers of the Auxiliary Forces, which in future were to be signed by the Crown, on the nomination of the Sec. of State for War, instead of by the Lord Lieutenant as heretofore, but of course Lords Lieutenant retained the right of recommending candidates. The Duke of Buckingham, who, on the death of Lord Carrington in 1868, had succeeded him as Lord Lieutenant of Bucks, invited the Officers Commanding Companies to Stowe, to consult with him as to the future Command of the Bucks Volunteers. We accordingly assembled there on March 26th and as it appeared to be the general wish that I should succeed Colonel Chester, the Duke forwarded my name to the Sec. of State; and I was gazetted to the Command on April 10th, 1872. I was thus, I believe, the first Commanding Officer of Volunteers whose Commission was signed by Queen Victoria.

I confess that my appointment was a great surprise to me, for I was only 34 — younger than any of the Captains and than several of the Subalterns. Both Col. Barrington and Col. Chester were County Magnates and had previously held Commissions in the Army. I had neither of these advantages, and my sole recommendation was my "keenness" as a Volunteer, but this alone would not have justified me in accepting the responsibilities of the Command if I had not been assured at Stowe of the hearty support of the other Officers Commanding Corps — assurances which were loyally fulfilled, and if I had not known that Capt. Clement would remain to be my right-hand man.

I have said above "the *other* Officers Commanding Corps" because, although I was Major of the Battalion, I was also Captain of the Marlow Corps — a position which I retained when Lieut-Colonel up to 1875, when the Battalion was "consolidated".

Up to 1872 Aylesbury — the County Town — was the official Head Quarters of the Bucks Battalion. But Capt. Clement had permission from the War Office to live at Loudwater — 16 miles from Aylesbury and about 5 miles from Marlow, and all Orderly-room work was practically conducted at Loudwater.[26]

26 Clement's residence had provoked some discussion between Barrington and the Duke of Buckingham and Chandos when the latter became Lord-Lieutenant in 1868, see Henry E. Huntington Library, Stowe MSS, STG 98, Barrington to Duke, 21 June, 1868, 13 August, 1868 and 28 August, 1868. There was similar discussion between the Duke and Chester (*Ibid.*, STG 101, Chester to Duke, 16 April, 1870) after the Secretary of State for War, Cardwell, had raised the matter of Clement's travelling expenses officially with the Lord-Lieutenant (*Ibid.*, STG 100, Cardwell to Duke, 9 April, 1870). However, Cardwell formally approved Clement's residence subsequently (*Ibid.*, Cardwell to Duke, 17 May, 1870).

Owing to its very indifferent railway service, Aylesbury was not a good centre. Capt Clement's tenancy of his Loudwater house happened to be drawing to a close, and, as it would obviously be more convenient for me to have him to live at Marlow, I applied for and obtained War Office sanction to make Marlow the Regimental Head Quarters instead of Aylesbury. I thus had my Orderly Room and Adjutant at hand. From an Adjutant's point of view also, Marlow was at least as convenient as Aylesbury for his visits, to the outlying Companies, while, situated as it is close to the Thames, in the midst of some of its prettiest scenery, it is certainly not less pleasant as a place of residence than Aylesbury.

On the invitation of the Duke of Buckingham our 1872 Camp was arranged to be held at Stowe, close to the private grounds of Stowe Place, and with his sanction we invited the Northamptonshire Corps to join us. The Duke took the closest personal interest in all our arrangements and I was at least as anxious as he was to make this — my first Camp in Command of the Bucks — a success, as it proved to be.

I have always felt the keenest satisfaction at the fact that it was owing to my initiative that the Eton College Corps came to camp with us for the first time at Stowe, and have continued to camp with us with rare intermissions ever since. During May 1872 I made my first Inspection of the Bucks Companies at their own Head Quarters, and on May 26th, I went to Eton to stay the night with Capt. the Rev. E. Warre, to be ready for my inspection of the 8th Bucks early on the following morning. Overnight I told Capt. Warre that I wanted him to bring the boys to camp at Stowe, but he held no hopes at all — "it was impossible". In the first place the Governing Body wouldn't hear of it, next the parents wouldn't allow it, and lastly the boys wouldn't like it.

This was not encouraging, but I have always held that "difficulties are made to be overcome" and I didn't despair. Next morning, while the boys were forming up in the Schoolyard, I strolled on to the playing fields where I was to inspect them (N.B. Those sacred precincts may not be polluted by horse hoofs, so I was of course dismounted). There I found, amongst others waiting to see the Inspection, Dr Goodford — the Provost of Eton — who had been my Tutor during my Eton days, and who was now of course the Provost, the presiding genius of the Governing Body. I told him what I wanted, and what Capt. Warre had replied. To my delight he said "I am not so sure about the Governing Body objecting. Personally I shall be very glad for the boys to go". This was indeed very encouraging. So after the Inspection, and after my comments on their Drill, etc., I told them what had passed overnight with Capt. Warre, and that morning with the Provost, and I ended by saying "and now it rests with you boys. If you want to come — get your mothers to back you up, and then your *fathers* will consent and we shall have you at Stowe this summer". In the result between 90 and 100 came, and added greatly to the attractions of the Camp, as well as to the strength of the Battalion.

Of course it was necessary to make several modifications of our previous camp arrangements. Hitherto we had never spent a Sunday in Camp. We had always marched in on a Monday or Tuesday and had never broken up later than the following Saturday. But the Eton boys were tied to a definite day, their summer holidays always begin on the Friday before the August Bank Holiday, and if they were to come at all, they must come direct from Eton on the Friday. So we arranged for the Camp to begin on Thursday, August 1st., when the Bucks and Northamptonshire Battalions marched in, and the Eton Corps joined us on the following day. Thenceforth, the Thursday before the Bank Holiday was our regular day for marching into Camp.[27]

During our march from Buckingham to Stowe we were all greatly pleased to find our old Colonel Barrington, waiting for us at the entrance to Stowe Park. I hadn't seen him since our 1868 Camp, and when he resigned in 1870 it was not considered possible that he could ever ride again; but there he was, and apparently as well as ever. Lord Barrington came out here (Tenerife) a few years ago, and we had many talks about old Volunteer days. I never saw him again, and it was with the deepest regret that I read a few days ago in the "Times" that he died on April 29th, 1901.

As the Eton boys were, of course, both in station and age entirely different from the ordinary Volunteers, it would hardly do for them to mess with the others; so we made them honorary members of the Officers Mess, but I was unwilling to make any distinction between them and other Volunteers of the same rank, so I issued an order that any member of the Battalion might mess with us, if introduced by the Captain of his Company, and in uniform. Practically none but the Eton boys ever took advantage of this, but their inclusion brought our members up to about 120 — the largest Regimental "Officers' Mess", I imagine, in the service.

Many amusing incidents occurred at this Camp. The average Private couldn't understand Noblemen doing "Sentry go", fatigue duties, etc., and I overheard one of them saying to another (a party of Eton boys was passing carrying blankets, palliasses, etc.) "I say Bill, that there Private's a *Herl*". But "Herls" or Commoners the boys worked exactly the same as the other Companies, with whom however, we took care not to mix them up off parade more than

27 The Volunteer Movement as a whole and especially those M.P.s who were Volunteers supported agitation for Early Closing, Bank Holidays and Saturday Half-Holidays but, ironically, the Bank Holiday Act of 1871 actually worked to their disadvantage in opening up more attractive recreational opportunities for potential recruits. See Beckett, *Riflemen Form,* pp.98, 101–2, 147.

necessary. For instance, each Company in turn furnished all the Camp "duties" on successive days, and they were never so "smartly" performed as when they were taken by the Eton boys.

A story is told of the (great) Duke of Wellington that, on one occasion, when hunting some few miles from Strathfield Saye, he came to a gate guarded by a yokel with a dung fork, and the yokel barred his passage. On the Duke saying who he was, the yokel replied — "I don't care who you be. Master says as no one's to come through here, and you bain't coming". The Duke was so pleased with the man's obedience to orders that he gave him half a crown, and went round by another way. Whether true or not, this incident was exactly reproduced (except as to the half crown) between the Duke of Grafton and an Eton Sentry. Our camping ground was separated from the private grounds of Stowe by a deep haw-haw 18 or 20 feet wide, which was temporarily spanned by a plank bridge, near which our rear-guard was posted. The Duke of Grafton who had commanded the Northamptonshires from the first, was of course senior to me, but he didn't come into camp until the Saturday, when the Eton boys happened to be taking the duties, and until he came I was in command of the Camp. I had issued an Order that no one was to be allowed to leave Camp by this bridge, except Volunteers "properly dressed" in uniform. The Duke of Grafton came into Camp just before luncheon on Saturday, and, as soon as I knew of his arrival, I notified the fact in Camp Orders, and that he took over the Command.

Immediately after luncheon — before my order had reached the Guard — the Duke of Grafton started to call on his brother Duke at Stowe. But he had arrived in mufti, and had snatched up a forage cap in a hurry, and this was the only article of uniform he was wearing. On reaching the plank bridge, the Sentry barred his progress, and when the Duke told him who he was, and that he was in Command of the Camp, replied "Very sorry Sir, but my orders are to let *No-one* pass unless properly dressed in uniform". So the Duke had to return to his tent and get "properly dressed". By the time that he had returned to the bridge, my Order had reached the Guard, and they then "turned out" and presented arms to him with all due ceremony.

The "Establishment" of the Eton Corps was one enrolled Company and one Cadet Company, and, as almost all their Officers came to Camp, while they only formed one Company on parade, their surplus officers supplied some of the gaps in our Commissioned ranks. Although Capt. Warre was always the real Commanding Officer of the whole Corps, his actual Commission at this time was that of Honorary Captain of the Cadet Corps; Captain S. Evans being Captain of the Enrolled Company, and as both of them couldn't Command the Company I "mounted" Capt. Evans as Acting-Major. But extemporised chargers are apt to "charge" at the wrong time and in the wrong direction, and although Capt. Evans knew his work well, his horse didn't and frequent differences of opinion between them as to where they ought to be at the given moment resulted in their making joint excursions to distant regions of the park — much to the amusement of the onlookers, but far more to the annoyance of the principal actor, who took it terribly to heart.

The Archdeacon of Buckingham, Dr. Bickersteth (soon afterwards Dean of Lichfield) conducted our Camp Service on Sunday morning, which was attended by the Duke's many guests at Stowe, and a large gathering from the neighbourhood. I know of no more impressive service than these open air church parades in camp. At the same time I know few things more trying to the rank and file, than to stand motionless in close order during the 30 or 35 minutes (to which I used to limit our Chaplains) especially if the sun be powerful. It is, however, extraordinary how its rays lose their apparent effect upon the men, if the situation is properly grasped by the *Medical Staff*. I remember that, on one occasion, a stiff dose of brandy and water was administered to the first man who fell out, and this had the instantaneous effect of intensifying the sun's powers, and man after man succumbed, but when the Dr. changed his treatment, and gave a nauseous mixture instead of the more palatable restorative, the epidemic was promptly arrested.

On Sunday afternoon the Duke of Buckingham threw open his house and private grounds, and this was highly appreciated by the Volunteers.

The Eton College Corps had been previously inspected at Eton, but the rest of the Battalion was inspected by Colonel Daubeny on the Tuesday morning, and immediately afterwards the then Duchess of Buckingham presented the County Prizes (which had been shot for before Camp) from the top of the broad flight of marble steps in front of Stowe Place. This "function" was temporarily interrupted by what might have proved a very serious accident to an Eton boy. I had given my charger, a very nervous but not vicious mare, somewhat "light-of-heel" to my Orderly, an Eton boy, with strict injunctions to let no one come near her. Another Eton boy, however, got too near and received a severe kick between the shoulders, fortunately on the front of his cross belt, so no great damage was done, but thenceforth every Charger I had was treated with becoming respect.

For many years the last afternoon in Camp was devoted to camp sports — races, etc., confined of course to the Volunteers, in Camp, and this was done at Stowe Camp, and for several years afterwards. Later on, however, these Sports had to be abandoned owing to the definition of an "amateur" laid down by the Amateur Athletic Association.

We marched out of Camp on Wednesday August 7th, after a most successful week, and I have always looked back upon our Stowe Camp as a very satisfactory inauguration of my 20 years Command of the Battalion. Alas! on the next occasion of our marching from Stowe to Buckingham my feelings were very different. But this will be explained later on.

I think that the only other events in 1872 which are worthy of record are 2 Field Days at Burnham Beeches and Hedsor, on July 4th. and October 18th. respectively.

On June 12th. 1873 we had a Field Day and Battalion Drill at Addington, and on June 24th. we took part in the great Volunteer Review held in Windsor Park by the Queen, in honour of the Shah of Persia.

Our 1873 Camp was held at Medmenham — close to the old Abbey — July 31st. - Aug. 6th. As our Camping ground was on the banks of the Thames, the Eton boys had ample opportunity of demonstrating their amphibious nature. Their early morning "bathing parades" afforded much amusement. All their movements were done by word of command, taking the water in line by simultaneous "headers" as only Eton boys can take "headers". They would form fours, front form, wheel into column of sections, deploy, in fact do all movements usually done on land. On one or two occasions they swam the river with their rifles and ammunition, and their "Scouts" fired from mid-stream at the imaginary enemy on the opposite bank, and when they gained the bank, it was amusing to see the main body, stark naked, save for their waistbelts, extend in skirmishing order as at an ordinary field day. At this, and at all our many river-side camps, a flotilla of boats was provided from Eton, and the more serious camp work was pleasantly diversified by boat races, water polo, etc. We passed an excellent inspection on the Tuesday, the first Commanding Officer of the newly formed Brigade Depot at Oxford being our Inspecting Officer, we marched out of camp on the following day.

1874 was not an eventful year, at any rate as far as the Bucks Volunteers were concerned.[28] We camped at Bourne End, another riverside camp

28 Wethered is somewhat disingenuous here for August to November 1874 was a troubled period for him in terms of his relationship with Captain W. H. Cutler of (perhaps significantly) the Slough Corps, who resented being passed over for the vacant majority following Wethered's own elevation to Lieutenant-Colonel. The point at issue according to Cutler was his perceived lack of County standing. Correspondence on the matter can be found in Wethered's Letter Book, Buckinghamshire Record Office, T/A, 5/5. The dispute which resulted in the resignation of Cutler, who lived at Salthill House, was sufficiently acrimonious to be noted in the nationally circulated *Volunteer Service Gazette* on 12 December, 1874 (Volume XVI, 1875-75, p.79), reproducing the long correspondence between Wethered and Cutler, which had already appeared in the *Windsor and Eton Express*.

— July 31st. – Aug. 6th. For some reason which I can't remember, changing our day for marching in from Thursday to Friday, and for marching out from Wednesday to Thursday.

In 1875 many important events occurred. Early in the year the Officers Commanding the separate Corps in the "Administrative Battalion" consented to the Battalion being "Consolidated", and the War Office authority for our "Consolidation" was dated March 15th, 1875. By this step the Captains of the Companies gave up their exclusive control of their "Corps", but the elasticity of the Battalion was enormously increased. For instance — as an "Administrative Battalion" each "Corps" composing it was bound to maintain its strength within the limits of its "Establishment" which, in the case of a Company Corps was a minimum of 60 of all ranks, and a maximum of 100. In a "Consolidated Battalion" on the other hand, it doesn't signify what is the strength of each Unit. So long as the "Total Enrolled" strength does not fall below or exceed the "Establishment" of the Battalion as a whole. In anticipation, therefore, of our "Consolidation", I took steps, during the Winter of 1874–5, to resuscitate the Volunteer spirit in Wycombe, which had been dormant since the disbandment of the Wycombe Corps in 1871. By this time — 1874–5, the "soreness" engendered by that event had somewhat worn off, and, although no leading Wycombe man was then willing to accept a Commission, it was generally felt that, as the most populous town in Bucks, it was not creditable that it should not be represented in the County Battalion. As a preliminary step therefore, to remedy this state of things, I enrolled, on Feb. 8th. 1875 between 30 and 40 Wycombe Volunteers as members of the *Marlow Company*, and on Feb. 24th. I presided at a Public Meeting in the Wycombe Town Hall, at which a Committee was appointed to collect funds and to take all other steps for forming a Wycombe Company. We had hoped that the old rifle range in Wycombe Abbey Park might still be available, but Lord Carrington[29] made it a condition of his support of the new Company that we should find a range elsewhere, and this, and the want of Officers, caused considerable delay, so that it was not till April 29th. 1876 — when Mr. Alfred Gilbey Junr. — the present Commanding Officer of the Battalion — was gazetted — that the Wycombe Company had an independent existence; and as the new range at Wycombe Marsh was not completed till October 1877, the Wycombe men had still to go to Marlow for class-firing.

29 This Carrington, of course, was now Charles, Third Lord Carrington, later First Marquess of Lincolnshire (1843–1928), who was to be Lord-Lieutenant from 1915 to 1928. For the reformation of the Wycombe Company, see Wethered to Duke of Buckingham and Chandos, 27 January, 1875 in Henry E. Huntington Library, Stowe MSS, STG 106.

After camping in consecutive years in the South of the County, we went in 1875 to Claydon Park, near Winslow, which Sir Harry Verney kindly placed at our disposal. Sir Harry took the keenest personal interest in all our arrangements, and it was a sight to see him — he was 74 then, and lived to the age of 93 — leading the Eton boys "headers" into the lake at their accustomed matutinal bathing parades. Sir Harry was one of the very long lived trio of leading men, living in that part of the County, the others being Lord Cottesloe, who lived to 92, and Lord Addington, who was nearly 85 at his death.[30]

Owing to the extreme weakness of the Battalion at our early camps, and our consequent unwillingness to weaken the Companies still more by detailing men to act as Cooks, we had from the first entrusted out commissariat in Camp to a Contractor, who supplied the men's meals at a fixed price in an enormous marquee. Up to 1875 some Hotel Keepers in the neighbourhood of our camp had always held the contract, but we could get no one near Claydon to undertake it, and our camp was too far off from all our former Contractors for any of them to be willing to do it. It was not until about a fortnight before camp that we realised that we must find our own commissariat but it was too late then to strike out an entirely new line by adopting the Army cooking arrangements, so we became our own Contractors. As far as the men were concerned the arrangement was a success, but the financial results were appalling.

We marched into camp on Friday July 30th — were inspected by Colonel Sergeant, the new Brigadier at Oxford, on August 4th, and marched out on Thursday, August 5th.

And now I have to record the most anxious, and the only really miserable time that I ever passed as a Volunteer. Anxious I have often been, lest the Corps should not acquit themselves as well as I expected them to do, whether as Volunteers or as respectable men off parade, and never, except on this one occasion, did they disappoint me. Miserable I was when I addressed them in 1891 for the last time as their Commanding Officer, but I then had the satisfaction of knowing that I left them as a strong Battalion, which anyone might feel proud to command, not only for their smartness on parade, but even more for individual good conduct as citizens. But on Oct. 6th, 1875, I could find no redeeming feature in the situation, which I thought then must inevitably result in the break-up of the Corps in well-merited disgrace.

The facts are as follows:- The Duke of Buckingham had recently

30 Sir Harry Verney, Bt., (1801–94) was successively Whig and Liberal M.P. for Buckingham from 1832–41, 1857–74 and from 1880–85. A photograph reproduced in this volume shows Verney (in top hat) with the officers of the 1st Bucks AB during the camp at Wakefield Lawn in Northamptonshire in June 1867. See Ian F. W. Beckett, *Call to Arms: Buckinghamshire's Citizen Soldiers*, Buckingham, 1985, p.54.

been appointed Governor of Madras, and before leaving England to take over the appointment, he invited the Bucks Yeomanry (which he commanded), and the Bucks Volunteers to a field day and farewell entertainment in Stowe Park, on Oct. 6th. In order to reach Stowe in good time it was necessary for Southern Companies to leave their Headquarters very early in the morning, and, of course, to get their breakfasts still earlier. Our Special Train was timed to reach Buckingham soon after 10 a.m., and I had arranged to halt there for half an hour, and for men to have a second breakfast before marching the 4 miles from Buckingham to Stowe Park. But our "Special" was more than half an hour late, and, on reaching Buckingham we found a Staff Officer awaiting us — specially sent to hurry us on — who told us that the Yeomanry were ready in position, and that we had kept everybody waiting a long time. As we still had more than an hour's march before reaching the scene of operations, we hurried off, and, immediately after our arrival, the field day began. It was 4 o'clock before the operations were over, and we found ourselves very hot and tired, with empty stomachs and a consuming thirst, at the large tent in which a sumptuous repast was provided.

Naturally the men, almost before they had taken their seats, poured out tumblers full of the first liquid handy, and drank them off at a draught. It was not till they had emptied their tumblers that they realised that they had been drinking — not light Claret, as they supposed, but neat Port. I did not learn this till 48 hours afterwards, for, inside the tent there were no signs of anything being wrong. The usual Toasts were given — the usual complimentary speeches made and responded to, and, as far as those at the "High Tables" could judge, the entertainment had been most successful . . . But directly the Battalion fell in outside preparatory to marching back to Buckingham, I noticed one man "unfit for duty" and promptly ordered him under arrest, thinking it an isolated case of misconduct, but before the column was told off several other men showed signs of unsteadiness, and I moved off the Battalion as soon as possible, as I foresaw that we should have difficulties in catching our Special Train. But the movement and the fresh air had precisely the opposite effect to what I hoped.

I shall never forget the march down the long Stowe Avenue, and I trust that I shall never see such a sight again. Man after man staggered to the road-side, where they lay like logs — and for these we impressed farm wagons in which they were conveyed to the station like corpses. Many others could just keep their feet, and for these we detailed men to help them along. At least half the Battalion were out of the ranks, either incapable or helping along "incapables", so that our march through the streets of Buckingham was the reverse of "Triumphal". I remember saying to the Adjutant during our journey home that I would have far sooner been disgraced in my own person than that the Battalion as a whole should have so disgraced itself. We couldn't understand it. It was absolutely inexplicable to us till 2 days later, when we learnt the key to the enigma. The Duke had given the purveyor "carte blanche" as to the drinkables to be provided. The latter, possibly thinking that beer and shandy-gaff, which the men would much have preferred to anything else, were too plebeian for so august an occasion, (or possibly because there wasn't so much profit to be got out of them) provided nothing but wine, including a large quantity of port and champagne. For men who have not tasted food for 9 or 10 hours, tumblers full of 66 port are not a good preparation for a great feast and few realised that those men who, without knowing what they were drinking, slaked their thirst in that way, were more "sinned against than sinning". Still, whatever were the "extenuating circumstances" the fact remained that we had made a public exhibition of ourselves of a very disreputable character, and of course this was known throughout the County, so it was necessary to let the whole facts become known. Accordingly, in the following week, I went round to special parades of every Company, and it speaks volumes for the general good sense and kindly feeling of Buckinghamshire that the fiasco of Oct. 6th, 1875, has never once been thrown in our teeth, and, as it occurred more than a quarter of a century ago, it is not likely now that it ever will be. My "recollections" however would be incomplete without a full account of this episode, and I have therefore stated the whole facts.

Early in 1876 the Rev. Walter F. Short, Warden of St. Paul's College, Stony Stratford, started a Company in connection with the school, and applied to be attached to the 1st Bucks R.V.C. Very few of the boys of course were old enough to be enrolled, the great majority of them belonging to the Cadet Corps. The Warden and another Master were gazetted Officers of the Company on Apr. 29th, 1876, and one of the older boys became Hon. Lieutenant of the Cadet Corps.[31] I had never forgotten my tentative efforts in 1867 to start companies at Wolverton and Stony Stratford, and, on the occasions of my visits to St. Paul's College in 1876 and 1877, I resumed them, with eventual success. Our 1876 Camp was again at Medmenham — Thursday Aug. 3rd. - Wednesday Aug. 9th., when the St Paul's College Company joined us for the first time.

31 There is considerable correspondence on the formation of the Cadet Corps at St. Paul's College in Buckinghamshire Record Office, Fremantle MSS, D/FR 135/14 since the First Lord Cottesloe was acting as Lord-Lieutenant during the Duke's absence in Madras. Some is duplicated in Buckinghamshire Record Office, Lieutenancy MSS, L/P 14 Lieutenancy Order Book, 1862–1907. The Corps was accepted by the Secretary of State for War on 9 February, 1876 but appears to have disappeared about 1883.

It was not until 1876 that the Brigade Depot at Oxford became more than a name. In 1871 Lord Cardwell's "Army Regulations Act" had transferred the control of the Auxiliary Forces from the Lords Lieutenant to the Crown. His "Localisation of the Forces Act" had assigned every Infantry Regiment, Regulars, Militia, and Volunteers, to one of the newly created Regimental Sub-Districts. Greatly to the disgust of our County, Buckinghamshire was merged into Oxfordshire — the old Buckinghamshire Regiment (the 14th) was assigned to Yorkshire. The Royal Bucks (Kings Own) Militia was transferred into the 3rd. Battalion, Oxfordshire Light Infantry. The War Office wished the 1st Bucks R.V. Corps to become the 3rd Volunteer Battalion, Oxfordshire Light Infantry, and to change our uniform from our old dark grey to the more showy but less serviceable scarlet, but I resisted both innovations — the first because we were the only Battalion retaining the name of the historic County of Bucks — the second because of the enormous cost of the change, and of the subsequent "up-keep", for I had found by experience that the average life of a private's dark grey uniform was not less than 6 years — much longer than the scarlet of the Oxfordshire and Berkshire Corps.

The University Authorities had, from the first, bitterly opposed Oxford being made a Military Centre, and this caused great delay in carrying out the War Office scheme. Then land had to be acquired, and the Barracks built, and it was not till the Autumn of 1876 that these were ready for occupation. Hitherto the O.C. the Sub-District had lived in Oxford with no staff or office, other than that of the Oxfordshire Militia, and we had seen nothing of him, except at our Annual Inspections. I had hoped that, as soon as the Depot came into existence, it would become a real centre for all the Auxiliary Forces in the Sub-District, and I tried to persuade the Brigadier to organise a Brigade Camp near the Barracks, but this was not to be. We had, however, an annual Brigade Drill at Oxford, and the first of these was ordered for May 28th, 1877.

In order to use the opportunity to the utmost, we reached Oxford early in the day, and had a Battalion Drill in the Parks in the forenoon, and then dismissed for dinners. By the time we fell in again to march to Port Meadow — 3 miles outside Oxford, where the Brigade was ordered to assemble, it was raining heavily, and we expected every minute to receive counter orders. However, none came, so off we marched, and reached the rendezvous at the appointed hour. Not a soul was there except ourselves. Port Meadow may be a pleasant place under some conditions, but in such a "blizzard" as we experienced on this occasion, we didn't appreciate its advantages. A bitterly easterly gale chilled us to the bones. Deluges of rain and hail drenched us to the skin, not a particle of shelter to be found, and after more than an hour of this an Orderly Sergeant appeared in a hanson cab to tell us that the Brigade Drill was abandoned. The authorities at Cowley Barracks had forgotten all about us. Brigade Drills at Oxford were not popular with us after this, but we attended 3 more in full strength — in 1878, 1879 and 1880, at one of which the University Corps paraded with 6 companies of 8 files each — just enough to form half-companies and sections. After 1880 the Brigade Drill was held during our camp week, the Oxfordshire (County) Corps joining us for the day — until they came to camp with us regularly (I think 1885 was their first camp), and then, of course, the procedure was simplified.

Our 1877 Camp was again held at Medmenham, Aug. 2nd - 8th for the third and last time, for by 1878 our numbers had outgrown our camping ground. On Sept. 8th, 1877 we had a Field Day at Wooburn — I think only the Marlow and Wycombe Companies took part in it, and Mr Gilbey — the father of Colonel Gilbey (who joined as a Subaltern in 1876) entertained us most hospitably in an enormous barn close to Wooburn House. I mention this particularly, because (as will appear when I come to our 1879 Camp) it had an important bearing on our 1879 doings.

On Nov. 26th, 1877 No 6 (Wolverton) Company came into existence. On that evening I attended an enthusiastic meeting of the L.&N.W.R. Comp's employees at their Carriage Works, and enrolled a strong Company, which very soon became one of the smartest in the Battalion.[32] On Dec. 15th, 1877, the late Queen paid her memorable visit to Lord Beaconsfield at Hughenden; and the 1st Bucks furnished a Guard of Honour at the Station, and lined the streets of Wycombe on her passage to and from Hughenden.

In 1877, Capt. Clement had a serious illness, and, under medical advice gave up his house at Marlow, and moved to Clewer. The state of his health made his frequent journeys to and from the outlying Companies, in all weathers, most undesirable, and it became evident that he ought not to remain Adjutant of the 1st Bucks. In the spring of 1878 the Volunteer spirit among the Eton boys received a great impetus, and Capt. Warre obtained the War Office sanction to the former No. 8 Compy, lst Bucks R.V.C. having a separate organisation as a 4 Company

---

32 The first public meeting to form a Wolverton Company was actually held at the town's Science and Art Institute on 22 October 1877, presided over by Wethered; the Rev. Short from St. Paul's College; G. W. Wilkinson, a local farmer; T. G. V. F. Johnson of Wolverton Mill; and three prominent men from the London and North Western's works (Buckinghamshire Record Office, Fremantle MSS, D/FR 135/13). Sir Frank Markham has suggested that there was an attempt to form a company from the LNWR in 1861 but there appears no substantial evidence for this, see Markham, *The History of Milton Keynes and District,* vol. 2, Luton, 1975, p.256.

Battalion, with an Adjutant of its own, under the name of the 2nd Bucks (Eton College) R.V.C.[33]

The strongest proof of the high estimation in which Capt. Clement was held at Eton (as also throughout the County) is the fact that so exclusive a Corps should have applied for him — a non-Etonian — as its first Adjutant. Grieved as we were to lose him from the 1st Bucks, we rejoiced that his services were still retained in the County, and, as his new duties involved no long journeys or night drills, his health rapidly improved.

Of course, Capt. Clement's impending resignation of the Adjutancy of the 1st Bucks made it necessary to find a new Adjutant; and the conditions had been entirely changed since his appointment in 1868. The abolition of Purchase in the Army — which had been effected in 1871 by a somewhat arbitrary exercise of the Royal prerogative, had made it necessary to provide other means to secure a flow of promotion in the Regular Services. Hitherto Adjutants of Auxiliary Forces had been appointed from retired Officers, and there was no time limit to the tenure of their appointment. Soon after 1871, however, orders came out that Adjutants of Auxiliary Forces were to be selected from Captains still serving with the Colours of the Territorial Regiment — that they were to be "seconded" during their tenure of the appointment, which was treated like other "Staff appointments" and limited to 5 years. This, of course, enabled a certain number of Lieutenants to become Captains, to take the place of the "seconded Adjutants", but this was only a temporary measure, as the Adjutants had to be provided for on the termination of their 5 years appointments. It was further claimed for the new arrangement that it gave us men who were thoroughly up-to-date in matters of drill, etc., and this was no doubt true. But from the point of view of the C.O. of a Volunteer Battalion it had its disadvantages. Finance plays a very large part in Volunteer Corps, and very few Captains of Regulars are "born accountants". It takes some time for a Captain fresh from the strict discipline of his regiment, to realise the difference between Volunteers and Regulars — and still longer to learn the right way of dealing with them. Practically, I found by experience, that it takes 2 years before a 5 years Adjutant becomes "part and parcel" of the Corps to which he is attached, and that, long before his 5 years are expired, both he and his (temporary) Commanding Officer are looking forward — the Adjutant possibly

33 The 1st Bucks RV having been consolidated in 1875, the 2nd Bucks (Eton College) RV had its first officers officially gazetted on 15 June 1878. The Battalion was redesignated 4th (Eton) Volunteer Battalion, Oxfordshire Light Infantry in December 1887 but once again designated the 2nd Bucks (Eton College) Volunteer Rifle Corps in 1902.

with pleasure ; but (as far as I was concerned) the Commanding Officer invariably with regret — to the time when the 5 years would expire. I don't know whether the 1st Bucks has been exceptionally fortunate in its Adjutants. I do know, however, that, during my 20 years in Command, each Adjutant in turn became one of my intimate personal friends, and gained the respect and affection of all ranks.

Theoretically, then, Capt. Clement's successor as Adjutant was to be a Captain in the Oxfordshire L.I., and I was to have no voice in his selection. Practically, however, no such Captain was available at the time, and I was told to make my own selection. I was fortunate in securing the services of Capt. Philip C. Yorke, of the 4th King's Own Lancashire Regiment, who took over the duties just before our 1878 Camp. I think that his first appearance on parade was on July 31st, when a great "Reception" was given at Wycombe to Lord and Lady Carrington after their marriage.

On the following day, Aug. 1st, we went into Camp in the grounds of St Paul's College, Stony Stratford — our Officers Mess being held in the College Hall. Stony Stratford was selected principally out of compliment to the newly formed Company at Wolverton — 2 miles distant — which we wished to encourage; but my first act in Camp was a decided "snub" to the only Officer of that Company, for on marching into Camp I noticed a very pretty flower garden on either side of his tent, à la Wimbledon.[34] This was so marked a departure from the severe simplicity which had always characterised our Regimental Camps that I felt constrained, much against my will, to order the immediate removal of the flower decorations. That night, also, one of the leading Sergeants of the Wolverton Company — who had taken a very prominent part in its formation — came into Camp "unfit for duty" and I well remember the anxiety this caused me. Had he belonged to another Company I should have dismissed him from the Corps, but the Wolverton Company differs from all others in the Battalion in that the men are all in the same employ, and that dismissal from the Corps, would almost certainly mean dismissal from their civil employment. I had, also, of course, to consider the effect of a very severe punishment on the new Company, having their first taste of strict military discipline; but this would not have inclined me to leniency, if I had felt it wrong on other grounds. In the result I reduced him to the ranks and it speaks well for the man's

---

34 Wethered refers to the annual meetings of the National Rifle Association, designed to promote musketry among the Volunteers, the first of which had taken place at Wimbledon on 2 July 1860. The annual meetings continued to be held at Wimbledon until moved to Bisley in 1890. The Third Lord Cottesloe was particularly prominent in the affairs of the NRA, see Buckinghamshire Record Office, Fremantle MSS, D/FR 165, 168, 169, 177.

right feeling that he remained in the Corps for some more years, and (I think) was eventually re-promoted to Corporal and later on to Sergeant.

With the exception of these two incidents, the Stony Stratford Camp passed off satisfactorily in every way. We passed an excellent inspection (by Col. Baynes, the new Brigadier at Oxford) and marched out of Camp the following day. The lesson in discipline learnt by the Wolverton Company bore excellent fruit, and it was rarely, if ever, that I had occasion to find fault with any of its members.

I mentioned on an earlier page that in 1867 there was a squad of Volunteers in the town of Stony Stratford, belonging to one of the Northamptonshire Companies. By 1878 this squad had dwindled away, and our 1878 camp paved the way for the formation, a few years later on, of a Stony Stratford Company of the 1st Bucks. This Company has, however, since I retired from Command, ceased to exist as an independent Company. It was never very strong, and my successor Lord Addington, amalgamated it with the Wolverton Detachment, which now consisted of 2 strong Companies.

I have always considered that 1879, with its flooded out camp at Bourne End, was the making of the 1st Bucks. Before that we may have *thought* we were a good Corps; after that we *knew* it. It may appear to outsiders, reading this 22 years after the event, to be a small matter — not worth the space which I am about to devote to it, but all who were partakers in those events will realise that the "welding" process was completed during those few days, and that, from that time all ranks had complete confidence in each other, and in the Corps as a whole.

The Camp began on Thursday morning July 31st., and was to last till Thursday August 7th — the longest time for which it was supposed that most of the men could leave their civil employment, and our Inspection was fixed for Wednesday August 6th. The site was the same as our 1874 camp — close to the river, the bank of which was a few inches above the level of our actual camping ground. All went well till "Last Post" on Saturday night, Aug. 2nd., when a terrible thunderstorm came on with torrents of rain. We had had 3 days hard work, and were all dead tired and looking forward to our Sunday rest. I turned in soon after and slept soundly till I was waked, about 2 a.m. by Qr. Mr. Sergt. Hedges (he became Quartermaster in 1883, and is still I am happy to say serving in that capacity) — he shouted "Colonel, Colonel, we're washed out". I expressed doubts, and he rejoined "put your hand down Sir, and you'll find I'm right". I did so, and sure enough the water was several inches deep in my tent. He wanted my permission for the large Canteen Tent, which happened to stand on the highest part of the field, to be opened, so that the men might take refuge there.

Of course I gave authority — but there was nothing more to be done at the moment; for it was pitch dark and it wanted one and a half hours to daybreak. So I turned over again in bed and thought out the problem — "What is to be done?" With the first streak of light I went up to the Canteen Tent, and I shall never forget the anxiety as to the line I should take which was depicted on the sea of upturned faces on my entrance, nor the round upon round of cheers when I said "If 150 men will stand by me, we will see this thing out". On my return to my tent, I found Mr Alfred Gilbey Snr., who had ridden over in the grey dawn, and who asked if he could help us. I replied "Yes you can. Take us all in at Wooburn. That large barn of yours in which you fed us 2 years ago, will take one-half Battalion, and there's another barn at the other end of the Village and the Schoolroom, which will take the other half Battalion". This was no slight request to be made at 5 a.m. on a Sunday morning, for we were more than 500 strong. But Mr Gilbey assented without a moment's hesitation — so I ordered my Charger and an impromptu parade, at which the men fell in shoeless and stockingless (for the ground was more than ankle deep in liquid mud) — I told them what I intended to do — gave orders to rouse up the various paper mills in the neighbourhood and ask them to put their drying rooms at our disposal — gave permission to go home to all men who might wish to do so (between 20 & 30 of the less robust men availed themselves of this permission, but with one or two exceptions — men who were really ill — they all came back before the Wednesday) — I ordered a "marching out" parade for 7 a.m. — & then rode away with Mr Gilbey to Wooburn two and a half miles distant, to make the necessary arrangements there. We roused up the Malsters, Bakers, etc. — everybody who had a kiln or an oven, and got them to light their fires — got permission from the Vicar to use his schoolroom, and from the owner of the second barn to use that. We met with no refusals — everyone in the Village was imbued with the one idea — to do everything possible to help us. I then rode back to camp to complete the arrangements there, and to "march out" with the Battalion. I found to my regret that Major Warre had already marched the Eton boys out, the responsibility of the Eton Officers to the boys' parents being too great to justify them in taking any unnecessary risks. They marched from Bourne End, to Eton, and were distributed thence to their respective homes for the holidays.

The sodden straw was being emptied out from our palliasses and bolsters, and they and the blankets were being rung out preparatory to sending them to the various drying rooms at the paper mills. The men got such breakfasts as were available under the circumstances and by 7.30 a.m. we were en route to Wooburn having left strong fatigue parties to continue the work with the stores. The question of transport was a difficult one, for 6 horses were required to move each wagon through the slush, whereas 2 had sufficed to bring it on to the ground before the Camp. I sent a telegram to the Brigadier at Oxford, reporting the facts and asking for orders, but as it was Sunday, I felt sure that I shouldn't get a reply till too late to influence our actions; so it turned out. When his answer came early on Monday morning "See no alternative to breaking-up Camp" — I had already arranged to move the camp to another ground. After assigning the Companies to their respective quarters and arranging for their rations, the Adjutant and I rode back to camp to select a new site. We found a suitable field not far off, on higher ground, routed out the tenant and got permission to use it — arranged for a fresh supply of straw for the palliasses, etc., and then rode back to Wooburn, expecting that our Chaplain the Archdeacon of Buckingham (now Dean of York) had arrived for our customary Sunday Camp Service. But he had been unable to get to us owing to the storm having washed away part of the railway between Aylesbury and Wooburn. He drove over, however, later, and we had our Church Parade in the afternoon on the lawn of Wooburn House. Mr & Mrs Gilbey placed all the resources of their large establishment at our disposal, and nothing was too much trouble for them or their employees. The Officers' Mess was established in the Coach House, and every available bed in the house was got ready for us. We preferred, however, to share our men's straw — and the rats! — in the barns etc., and we didn't get much sleep in consequence. One of the Companies had overflowed into a Cowshed, and, on paying my last visit to the various detachments, I was much amused to see that the Captain of this Company had taken up his quarters for the night in the manger.

On the following morning, after an early breakfast, we all marched back to Bourne End for a day's fatigue duty. At the usual mid-march halt, I told the Battalion that I didn't like the storm robbing us of two days regular camp work, and that if 250 men would remain till Saturday, I would apply for permission to continue the Camp till that day, instead of breaking up on the Thursday. Almost every man present consented to stay on so I sent in my application, which the War Office granted.

OSCAR BLOUNT'S NOTES ON BULSTRODE

BULSTRODE

OSCAR BLOUNT'S NOTES ON BULSTRODE

Introduction

For most of the nineteenth century the Bulstrode estate, centred on Gerrards Cross in the parish of Hedgerley, formed part of the extensive possessions of the historic family of Seymour, dukes of Somerset. It was purchased in 1810 by Edward Adolphus (1775-1855), 11th Duke, scholar and amateur scientist, who appears to have made use of the existing mansion as a residence until around 1840, after which it was let to tenants on long leases until 1860.[1] The 11th Duke was succeeded by his son — also called Edward Adolphus (1804-85) — by his first marriage to Lady Charlotte Hamilton, a daughter of the 9th Duke of Hamilton. Unlike his father, the 12th Duke took an active part in public affairs. He was First Lord of the Admiralty from 1859 to 1866 and was also a trustee of the British Museum and a commissioner of Greenwich Hospital.[2] Between 1861 and 1870 he rebuilt the house[3] which became one of the family's two principal residences (the other being Maiden Bradley in Somerset) and the scene of much entertaining by the Duke.

On the death of the 12th Duke without surviving male offspring in 1885 his estates were divided and Bulstrode descended to his youngest daughter, Lady Helen Guendolen (d. 1910), who married Sir John William Ramsden (1831-1914), baronet, in 1865. Their son, Sir John Frecheville Ramsden, baronet (1877-1958), inherited. The estate has since been broken up and the house is now occupied by the Worldwide Evangelization Campaign, who acquired it in 1967.[4]

Oscar Blount, the author of these historical notes and personal recollections of Bulstrode, was the 12th Duke's agent at Bulstrode. He

---

1 For the use of the house as a residence at this period see text; for leases see n.25.

2 Unless otherwise indicated, biographical information given in the introduction and footnotes is taken from the *DNB*, *The Complete Peerage* and other standard biographical and genealogical reference works.

3 Nikolaus Pevsner and Elizabeth Williamson, *The Buildings of England: Buckinghamshire*, 2nd edn., London, 1994, p.203.

4 Buckinghamshire Record Office, catalogue of Ramsden Papers; Pevsner and Williamson, *op. cit.*, p.204.

was born around 1842, the second son of William Blount (1799–1885) of Orleton Manor, Herefordshire, and his second wife, Lady Charlotte Jane Seymour (1803–89), whom he married in 1839. Lady Charlotte was the eldest child of the 11th Duke by his first marriage and Oscar was thus a close relation of the ducal family. His early life appears to have been spent at Orchard, or Orche Hill, House in Gerrards Cross, which Lady Charlotte purchased from the estate around 1842. He was joint master, together with Leicester Hibbert of Chalfont Lodge, of the Old Berkeley Hunt from 1869 until 1875 and some letters of his about the Hunt and its history have been preserved. In 1878 he married Mary Frances, daughter of Sir Frederick and the Honourable Lady Smythe, of Acton Burnell Park, Shrewsbury. At the time the notes were written in 1913 Blount was no longer living at Gerrards Cross having moved by 1903 to Windsor, where he died in April 1933 in his ninety-second year.[5]

The manuscript consists of a small, bound notebook with lined pages now among the Ramsden (Bulstrode) Papers in the County Record Office.[6] The cover is endorsed 'Notes and recollections on the history of Bulstrode' in an unknown hand. In the transcription capitalization has been modernized and the punctuation, which is somewhat erratic with many superfluous stops and dashes, has also been standardized.

Hugh Hanley

5 O. P. Serocold, 'The Old Berkeley Hunt', in J. Page, ed., *The Victoria History of the Counties of England: Buckinghamshire* (*VCH*), London, 1905–28, ii, p.225; Buckinghamshire Record Office, D/X 831/3, letters from Oscar Blount, 1909–25; *Kelly's Directories* of Bucks and Berks; short obituary of Blount in *The Times* of 11 April 1933.

6 Buckinghamshire Record Office, D/RA/A/5/18. The Ramsden Papers include, in addition to extensive estate records of Bulstrode, personal and other correspondence of the 11th and 12th dukes.

Notes on Bulstrode. 1913

by

Oscar Blount. 2nd son of

Mr. and Lady Charlotte Blount

of

Orleton Manor Herefordshire, and

Orchard or Orche Hill

Gerrards Cross Bucks

Lady Charlotte[7] was my Grandfather's sister
daughter of the 11th Duke by his Hamilton Duchess.
She was born in the Swiss Cottage.
In my boyhood Oscar had all the prestige
of 'the oldest inhabitant'—
He acted as agent for my Grandfather at
Bulstrode

J[ohn] F[rechville] R[amsden] 17/10/53

---

7 The following paragraph is in a different handwriting from that of the rest of the
text. The Swiss Cottage referred to was a house on the estate (see text). Lady
Charlotte was born some years prior to the purchase of the estate.

The Legend of The Shobington Family
from
Sir Bernard Burke's Vi[ci]ssitudes of Families[8]

When William the Conqueror had conquered the Kingdom 1066 he bestowed the lands since called Bulstrode on one of his Norman lords. The Shobingtons (the Saxon owners of these lands) got knowledge of this, prepared for resistance, and threw up entrenchments in what is now the park. Whether they wanted horses is uncertain but having collected many bulls, they mounted them and sallying out, gave battle to the Normans, over came, and dispersed them. The Norman King then sent for Shobbington, and asked him why he dared resist. The Shobington answered, that if the King would allow him to keep his estates he would be·faithful to him. The King then granted to him his royal word and gave him his estates. From that time he was called Shobington Bullstrode. In process of time the first name was discontinued, and that of Bullstrode spelt with one L only. "Bulstrode" remained.

Extract from the Inventory of Historical Monuments Commission appointed on the "twenty-seventh day of October 1908" by command of His Majesty King Edward the 7th[9]

Of Gerrards Cross. Prehistoric Bulstrode Park. The Plateau Camp stands on level ground. It is remarkable as an important example of its class and as the largest defensive earth work in the county.. The Camp is roughly oval in shape, and encloses about 22 acres. The defences consist of an inner and outer rampart and ditch except on the west and north west sides, where the outer ditch is obliterated. Of a flint wall added on the inner rampart on the north west the foundations remain, in the middle of the east side of the Camp and on the south and north east sides are gaps, some of which may be original entrances. Condition — fairly good. Oak trees planted on the ramparts.

8 Sir John Bernard Burke (1814–92), Irish genealogist and publisher of *Burke's Peerage*. His *Vicissitudes of Families* was published 1859–63. The relevant passage is reproduced in. J. J. Sheahan, *History and Topography of the County of Buckingham,* London, 1862.

9 Royal Commission on Historical Monuments (England), *Inventory of the Historical Monuments in Buckinghamshire*, London, 1912–13, i, p.160.

The owners of Bulstrode since the Conquest A.D. 1066. The Bulstrodes[10]

1265 — The manorial estate granted to the Abbess and Convent of Burnham.

1500 — Agnes Bulstrode marr[ie]d William Brudenell, and took the lands called the manor of Brudenell since called Chalfont Park from Bulstrode.

1534 — The suppression of lesser monasteries and of Burnham Abbey and grant of Bulstrode by King Henry VIII to Bisham Abbey.[11]

1539 — Dissolution of the monasteries. Up to this time the Bulstrodes seemed to have lived on their estates, in a castle or fortified building.

1645 — The Park impaled and Lodge built about this time. The Bulstrodes sold the property. The mansion house or castle destroyed by fire; then Robert Drury, Thomas Gower, and Ambrose Bennett Esq[ui]res held Bulstrode for a short time.

1676 — Lord Jeffreys.[12]

1690 about — Earl and Dukes of Portland.

1812 or so — The 11th Duke of Somerset

Notes on Bulstrode giving an account of the foundation of the Abbey of Burnham and the manor of Bulstrode attached to it and recollections of modern times.

The late Sir Bernard Burke Ulster King of Arms about 1869 published a book The Vicissitudes of Families. In it he gave an account of the Bulstrode family residing at Bulstrode from the time of the Norman Conquest 1066 until the out break of the Civil War in England 1642.[13]

10 This summary and the historical notes which follow it contain many inaccuracies. In particular the manor of Temple Bulstrode was not granted to Burnham Abbey until 1329, having earlier been held by the Knights Templar; and it passed to Bisham Priory in, or soon after, 1337. For the descent of the manor see VCH, iii, p.280; a fuller account is given in Michael Rice, ed., A South Bucks Village — The History of Hedgerley, Hedgerley Historical Society, 1980, chapter 5.

11 In Berkshire.

12 See n.21.

13 See n.8.

The foundation of the Abbey of Burnham
in the County of Bucks

On the 18th day of April 1266 there was a notable gathering at the royal manor house of Cippenham[14] in the southern extremity of the county of Bucks opposite the King's castle of Windsor.

In the reign of Henry II it was held as a hunting seat by his brother the famous Richard Earl of Cornwall.[15] The King of England himself was there and his son Prince Edward and the Bishop Giffard of Bath,[16] the Lord Chancellor of England. The bishop of "the diocese" was there from Lincoln, and the Bishop of Coventry and Lichfield and gentlemen of the neighbourhood. The occasion was the endowment of the Abbey which Richard Earl of Cornwall had newly founded.

Richard Earl of Cornwall had fought on his brother's side at the battle of Lewes 1264, been defeated and taken prisoner. In nine months he was able to use his influence for peace and regained his liberty.

The foundation of the house of Augustinian nuns at Burnham was his thanks offering.

At his manor of Cippenham on the date above named "Richard by the Grace of God King of the Romans, ever Augustus["], set his seal to the foundation charter, of which King Henry and the assembled princes prelates and gentlemen were witnesses.

By it he granted to Almighty God and the ever Blessed Mary, the mother of God and to the monastery of Burnham which he caused to be founded, and to the nuns there serving God, and their successors in free and perpetual alms for the health of his soul and the souls of his predecessors the Kings of England the manor of Burnham with its appurtenances and rights and the advowson of the church and also certain portions of the rights and possessions that pertained to his manor of Cippenham to be held by the said nuns freely and entirely without any reservation to himself and his heirs.

The gift was expressly freed from all courts, from royal service, and from other secular demands, all and singular, saving due and customary ward of the castle of Wyndelsore.[17]

The donor reserved to himself a remainder of the manorial rights of Cippenham and the following manors were bestowed upon the Abbey.

---

14 In Burnham parish. For a brief account of Burnham Abbey see *VCH*, i, pp.382-4.

15 Richard, Earl of Cornwall (1209-72). He was elected King of the Romans in 1257.

16 Walter Giffard (d. 1279), Bishop of Bath and Wells, 1265. Following the battle of Evesham (4 August 1265) he was briefly lord chancellor.

17 I.e. Windsor.

Beaconsfield
Holmer
Little Missenden
and Bulstrode all in the county of Bucks
and Silver[s]ton[e] in Northamptonshire.

The 1st great benefactor of the Abbey was Sir John de Molins[18] treasurer to King Edward III, who had obtained the manor of Stokes by his marriage with the heiress Egidia Poges, and bestowed it upon the Abbey in 1338 providing for a priest to serve there, for the good estate of himself and Egidia his wife at the altar of St Catherine.

In 1534 the last abbess but one accepted the King's Supremacy. No fault could be found with the house and favourable terms were allowed. Five years later it was dissolved, the last abbess and nine sisters receiving pensions.

At the time of the Dissolution the dependents were 2 priests 21 hinds and fourteen serving women.

About the year 1500 Agnes Bulstrode marr[ie]d William Brudenell and took the lands since called Chalfont Park from Bulstrode. All documents connected with Chalfont P[ar]k were destroyed by fire in the reign of George III.

In the year 1534 the abbey of Burnham was bestowed on the Benedictine abbey of Bisham[19] near Marlow. The final dissolution took place in 1539.

On the outbreak of the Civil Wars 1642 Colonel Bulstrode[20] raised a regiment of Bucks militia in the park at Bulstrode. He commanded the regiment at the "battle of Edgehill["] 1642 in which action the regiment took a prominent part when fighting was hardest.

On the close of the Civil War the Bulstrode family ceased to hold possession of the estate. The castle or mansion house was burnt down and 1676 the estate was bought by Lord Jeffreys,[21] the infamous judge. He built a fine mansion at Bulstrode bloodstained, as the common people called it. Here according to Clarendon he gave an entertainment

18 Sir John Moly(e)ns (d. c1360), of Stoke Poges. He was treasurer of the King's chamber in the 1330s. In 1338 he founded two chantries in Stoke Poges and for this and other charitable purposes granted land (but not the manor) to Burnham Abbey. See *VCH*, iii, pp.305, 310, 312.

19 See n.10.

20 Thomas Bulstrode (1602–76), Parliamentary soldier. According to Ruth Spalding, *Contemporaries of Bulstrode Whitelock, 1605–1675*, Oxford, 1990, he was the son and heir of Henry Bulstrode of Horton, Bucks. The Bulstrode family never held the Bulstrode estate.

21 George Jeffreys (1648–89), 1st Lord Jeffreys of Wem, judge, lord chancellor to James II; notorious for presiding over the 'Bloody Assize' following the defeat of Monmouth's rebellion in 1685. He purchased the estate from Sir Roger Hill in 1686 (*VCH*, iii, p.280).

to James II and Mary of Modena, Rich and riotous living characterized his sojourn at Bulstrode.

Lord Jeffreys' daughter sold the estate to William Bentinck Ist Earl of Portland[22] and the 4th Duke of Portland sold the estate to the 11th Duke of Somerset.

Lady Charlotte Blount the eldest child of the 11th Duke of Somerset who married in 1839 William Blount Esq. of Orleton Manor Herefordshire says it was the usual thing on a fine morning to walk up to the Lodge Gates at Gerrards Cross to see the mail coaches go up and down the Great Oxford Road. "Outside the Park Gates" was an old elm tree and 7 feet or so from the ground it was studded over with large nails and here the post boys used to fasten up their tired horses and leave them to cool. Lord Algernon St Maur[23] "Lady Charlotte's" youngest brother, was very fond of driving the mail coaches. He used to drive the stage from Wycombe to Gerrards Cross "very often." One afternoon coming down Du Pre's pitch at Wilton Park[24] the off-side wheeler kicked over the traces. The passengers begged him to pull up and put things straight. Not at all said his Lordship the mail is late and I can only reach the Bull Hotel, Gerrards Cross by not stopping. I hope to be in time. He was punctual to a minute. Being in the Blues he often drove the mail on the Bath Road from the Barracks at Windsor.

The following properties have been sold from Bulstrode from time to time Orchard or Orche Hill bought by Lady Charlotte Blount about 1842. Also were sold the Duchess of Portland's school and grass fields on both sides of the Bull Lane the Bull Hotel, and French Horn Inn on Gerrards X Common Piners Farm Langley Lodge and Hatche's Farm.

Some-time after 1830 the Duke of Somerset having taken a long lease of Wimbledon Park from Lord Spencer let Bulstrode to General Reid[25] or as he then was Colonel Reid of the 2nd Life Guards a fine handsome man. In fact George 4th said he was the handsomest man

---

22 William Bentinck (1649-1709), Dutch born soldier and courtier; friend of William III.

23 Algernon Percy Banks (1813-94), third and youngest son of the 11th Duke. He became the 14th Duke in 1891 in succession to his brother Henry Algernon, 13th Duke. He is said to have been one of the best amateur 'whips' of his time. The surname St. Maur (from St. Maur in Normandy), an early form of Seymour, was adopted by the 11th Duke and his children.

24 See below and n.31.

25 Major-General George Alexander Reid, M.P. for Windsor, 1845-50. He was tenant of Bulstrode House and the Swiss Cottage from February 1841 until his death in 1851, and of other estate properties from around 1843 (Buckinghamshire Record Office, D/RA/2/363, 366; 4/139).His sisters erected and endowed St. James's church, Gerrards Cross, as a memorial to him in 1859 (Pevsner and Williamson, *op. cit.*, p.338).

in the army. Being a bachelor, his 2 sisters Miss Jane and Miss Louisa Reid lived with him. They were most kind people, rich, lived in the wing of the old house at Bulstrode (all the rest had been pulled down) and kept a large establishment. They drove grey ponies, with 2 grooms on grey ponies riding behind; like Queen Victoria. Their small phaeton was beautifully turned out. They kept bloodhounds 3 large powerful dogs each chained to his kennel each kennel opposite to the present entrance to the old wing; at night one hound was loose to keep foot-pads off the Park. Poachers and thieves were much afraid of these hounds, and sheep-stealers were much about. Sheep-stealing went on in the neighbourhood until about 1849. Then the parish constable was succeeded by the county police. General Reid died very suddenly in 1851, then Mr Festing[26] the Duke's agent let the house and shooting to Mr Edwards[27] a lawyer and financier from the West of England. The Duke of Somerset died in 1856,[28] and then Mr Edwards removed to The Pickeridge and there he remained a few years.

Lady Charlotte mentions having with her mother visited at Hall Barn the home of the Waller family famous on account of Waller[29] the poet having lived there. On the close of the long war with France, the Waller family had to reduce; a reduction of rents on all landed property became general. They then determined to sell Hall Barn and retire to their other property in Gloucestershire. Hall Barn was then purchased by Sir Gore Ouseley.[30] He entertained largely, and was visited from time to time by the royal Dukes of Cambridge and Gloucester. Sir Gore had been ambassador to Persia.

Wilton Park was inhabited by Mr Du Pre.[31] He began public life 4 years before the death of Pitt and Fox while Lord Nelson had a seat in the Upper House and the Duke of Wellington sat in the House of Commons as The Honourable Arthur Wellesley. Mr Du Pre served as High Sheriff for Bucks in 1825. He represented Gatton Aylesbury and Chichester from 1802 to 1812.

26 Michael John Festing (D/RA/4/143).

27 Of Westbourne Terrace, London and Bradford Manor, Witheridge, Devon; he took a 7-year lease of the house and grounds in October 1853 and another of Pickeridge House in January 1860 (Buckinghamshire Record Office, D/RA/2/369, 372; 4/143).

28 *Recte* 1855.

29 Edmund Waller (1606—87), poet and politician, born at Coleshill near Amersham. Hall Barn is in Beaconsfield.

30 Sir Gore Ouseley, bart. (1770–1844), diplomatist and oriental scholar; purchased the estate in 1832 (*VCH*, iii, p.159).

31 James Du Pre (d. 1870, aged 92); he was the son of Josias Du Pre of Wilton Park, Beaconsfield. See: Robert Gibbs, *A History of Aylesbury*, Aylesbury, 1885, p.250.

He was succeeded by his son Caledon George Du Pre. He sat for his native county of Bucks for more than 30 years his colleague being Mr Disraeli who became Lord Beaconsfield, the Liberal member being the Hon[oura]ble William Cavendish who became the 2nd Lord Chesham.[32]

Lord Grenville[33] resided at Dropmore originally called "one-Tree Hill" which place he transformed from wild heath land to the finest plantation of desiduous trees in England. Lady Grenville survived her husband many years and lived almost entirely at Dropmore; she was succeeded by the Hon[oura]ble George Fortescue, a most accomplished man and well versed in literature. The property has been much curtailed Burnham Beeches and East Burnham commons having been sold away. This was the ancient manor of Allards.

Lord Taunton[34] bought Stoke Park from Mr Penn. He made it a house for political gatherings during the summer. He was a great Whig.

The Ladies Molyneux[35] lived at Stoke Farm. They always had a great gathering for Ascot Races. Lord Sefton brought his coach and the party was generally composed of noblemen and gentlemen of the turf and Mr Greville,[36] who was Clerk of the Council, and has since astonished the world with his book of memoirs, Annals of the Court in the reigns of George IV, William IV and Queen Victoria.

Hedgerley Park was inhabited by Mr Shard[37] a hunting man and sporting celebrity. On his death some-time after 1830 Mr Clayton[38] bought the property. He was a younger brother of Sir William Clayton

32 For the political career of Caledon George Du Pre (d.1886) see Richard W. Davis, *Political Change and Continuity: a Buckinghamshire Study*, Newton Abbot, 1972. William Gordon Cavendish (1815-82) became 2nd Baron Chesham in 1863.

33 William Wyndham Grenville (1759-1834), 1st Baron Grenville, statesman, brother of George Grenville, 1st Marquess of Buckingham, of Stowe; prime minister 1806. According to Pevsner and Williamson, *op. cit.*, he began building Dropmore House (in Taplow parish) in 1792. The Hon. George Matthew Fortescue, who succeeded to the estate in 1864, was his nephew (*VCH*, iii, p.172).

34 Henry Labouchere (1798-1869), 1st Baron Taunton (1859), politician, purchased the estate from Granville Penn in 1848; he sold it in 1863 (*VCH*, iii, p.307).

35 According to Sheahan, *op. cit.*, p.871, Stoke Farm (now Sefton Park) in Stoke Poges was then the residence of Lady Maria Molyneux, daughter of the 2nd Earl of Sefton. She died in 1872.

36 Charles Cavendish Fulke Greville (1794-1865), diarist, clerk of the privy council, 1821-59. His diaries were published 1875-87.

37 Charles Shard was the ratepayer in 1817 and was apparently still resident in 1833. The house, earlier called Hedgerley Grove, was demolished in the 1930s. See Michael Rice, *op. cit.*, pp.50-1.

38 Rice Richard Clayton (1790-1879), 4th son of Sir William Clayton, bart, of Harleyford, Marlow; M.P. for Aylesbury 1842-47 (Gibbs, *op.cit.*, p.294).

of Harleyford who they said had shewn the white feather at Waterloo. Mr Clayton was a good old fashioned Tory and stood for Aylesbury through the influence of her[39] sister Lady Fremantle of Swanbourne. Mrs[40] Clayton had many political gatherings at Hedgerley. There one met Disraeli[41] Mr Du Pre[42] and Lord Nugent[43] the antiquarian who wrote the essay on Hampden the patriot of Great Hampden Bucks.

Cold winters at Bulstrode. 1845 to be noted on account of its long and hard frost. It commenced the middle of January and lasted until Good Friday March 21st. On Easter Monday March 24th intense heat set in for a short time. Mr Davis the royal huntsman brought the royal hounds on that day to Stoke Common. The heat was so great there was no pleasure in hunting.

Also in 1855 the frost and cold was of exceptional severity. It lasted from the beginning of January until March. The park was full of stock — the frost came very suddenly and owners did not or could not remove their animals. Horses remained about the park dead. Snow remained on the ground until early in March.

Oscar Blount's recollections of Bulstrode.
He was the 2nd son of Mr and Lady Charlotte Blount.

About 1849 or 50 being then 8 or 9 years old I was taken to an afternoon party at Bulstrode. My mother drove over in her phaeton and the Miss Reids received us in the wing which then constituted the house. The party met in the biggest room then the drawing room. A large party was given by General Reid and his 2 sisters. A procession was formed and we walked two and two — by the tower (on the left near the pumping tower, only close to the Lime Avenue and Bank was a small conservatory) — and up the Lime Avenue to the big cedar, and then to the head of the Canal to the Swiss Cottage. There we saw a cow fastened to a tree.

39 *Sic* in MS. Louisa Elizabeth (d.1875), Lady Fremantle, wife of Sir Thomas Francis Fremantle (later 1st Baron Cottesloe) of Swanbourne, near Winslow, and Clayton's wife Maria Amelia were sisters, the daughters of Field Marshal Sir George Nugent, bart, of Westhorpe House, Little Marlow.

40 *Sic* in MS.

41 Benjamin Disraeli (1804–81), Earl of Beaconsfield (1876), statesman and novelist, M.P. for Buckinghamshire, 1847–76. He purchased Hughenden Manor in 1847 and remodelled it in 1862–3.

42 See n.31.

43 George Grenville (1789–1851), Baron Nugent, politician, youngest son of George, 1st Marquess of Buckingham; M.P. for Aylesbury, 1818–32, 1847–51. His biography of John Hampden (1594–1643) was published in 1832.

After the cow had been milked and all the company assembled sillybub was made, of which everyone partook, and many compliments. I think the band of General Reid's regiment — the 2nd Life Guards was there. The crowd seemed to me enormous. I think it was about the middle of the summer.

The Duke of Somerset commenced building the present house about 1860. Messrs Cubitt were the builders. Some time elapsed before the foundations of the house could be commenced on account of the difficulty of finding good brick earth. A good vein was discovered on the High Meadows on the hill opposite to the end of the Duke's wood. A kiln was erected near the present block of cottages and the bricks proved good and hard.

The Duke in each year resided at Bulstrode at Easter and Whitsuntide and again from the end of the London season to the middle of September when he departed to Maiden Bradley. During the time the Duke and Duchess stayed at Bulstrode they had many visitors. Those I mention visited most frequently.

Lord Bathurst[44] who had been clerk to the Privy Council for many years, a gay old bachelor.

Maria Marchioness of Ailesbury[45] one of the leaders of society.

Alfred Montgomery a commissioner of Inland Revenue, noted for his kindness, conviviality and amusing gossip.

His brother Sir Henry[46] member of the Indian Council, and Lady Montgomery celebrated for her dogs "Pekinese".

Lord and Lady Bath.[47] She a daughter of Lord de Vesci, and very beautiful.

Lord and Lady Cork.[48] He the speaker in the House of Lords master of the Buck hounds, from time to time. Lady Cork immersed in politics for her side and a great help to the Whig party.

Mr Sheridan[49] brother to the Duchess a very handsome amusing man.

---

44 William Lennox (1791-1878), 5th Lord Bathurst, clerk to the Privy Council for over 30 years; died unmarried.

45 Maria Elizabeth (d. 1893), 2nd wife of Charles Bruce, 2nd Earl and (1821) 1st Marquess of Ailesbury whom she married in 1833.

46 Sir Henry Conyngham Montgomery (1803-78), Indian civil servant, member of the new council of India in London, 1858-76.

47 John Alexander Thynne, 4th Marquess of Bath (1831-96), diplomat, ambassador at Lisbon 1858 and at Vienna 1867. His younger brother married the 12th Duke's second daughter Ulrica in 1858.

48 Richard Edmund St. Lawrence (1829-1904), 9th Earl of Cork; appointed one of the speakers of the House of Lords in 1882. He was master of the Buckhounds in 1866 and again in 1868-74 and 1880-5.

49 See n.84.

Mr Walter,[50] owner of The Times. He was considered rather pompous.

The Speaker Mr Denison[51] such charming manners, and he himself so full of information. His wife Lady Charlotte dau[ghte]r of the Duke of Portland that sold Bulstrode to the Duke of Somerset equally delightful. She was too young — she told me — to remember much of the old "Jeffries cum Bentinck["] house but she said it was bad and the rooms low. They became Lord and Lady Ossington.

Mr Tomline[52] the son "of Mr Tomline of Orwell, Suffolk tutor to Mr Pitt the Prime Minister" He inherited Orwell and the Duke and Lord Archibald St Maur[53] used to go and stay with him. He was quiet and reserved but noted for his wealth and the intense comfort at Orwell.

Lord John Hay.[54] A jovial sailor. Amused himself by always questioning the Duchess's clever stories and putting them right.

Lord Houghton.[55] Poet critic author and his two daughters constant visitors.

Mr Motley.[56] The American ambassador the friend of Bismarck whom he had known all his life. Historian author most agreeable, and his wife. She rather an American accent and their daughter pretty.

Mrs Ives.[57] Very clever and amusing.

Lord Morley.[58] A neighbour of the Duke's in Devonshire. Chairman of committees in the House of Lords, and one of the governing body of Eton College.

His sister Lady Catherine Parker a special favourite of the Duke's.

---

50 John Walter (1818–94), chief proprietor of The Times and grandson of its founder.

51 John Evelyn Denison (1800–73) 1st Viscount Ossington (1872), speaker of the House of Commons, 1857–72.

52 Presumably William Edward Tomline, son of Sir George Pretyman Tomline (1750–1827), tutor of the younger Pitt.

53 Lord Archibald Henry Algernon St. Maur (1810–91), 13th Duke (1885); younger brother of the 12th Duke.

54 Lord John Hay (1827–1916), naval commander, Admiral of the Fleet 1888; of Fulmer Place, Bucks.

55 Richard Monckton Milnes (1809–85), 1st Baron Houghton (1863), author, and politician. A close friend of Tennyson and other eminent literary figures.

56 John Lothrop Motley (1814–77), American historian and diplomat, ambassador at London 1869–70.

57 Untraced.

58 Albert Edmund Parker (1843–1905), 3rd Earl of Morley (1864), under-secretary for war 1880–85.

Clever fond of art spent much of her time painting from nature clever studies from the woodland scenery at Burnham Beeches.

Mr and Lady Anne Blunt.[59] He a traveller in Egypt and the Atlas and Sahara full of Eastern stories. She, the grand-daughter of Byron the poet full of conversation and cleverness.

Sir Richard Burton[60] and "his wife["] a writer of some reputation and met many people "having travelled much in Italy and Levant etc." He most celebrated as being the only Christian disguised as a Dervish that got into Mecca. He was a great linguist quite a mèssofante[61] and knew at least 8 different languages. Tall and handsome dark and in conversation reserved.

Sir Samuel and Lady Baker.[62] She an Arminian and very good looking. He the opponent of the Madhi, and governor of the Nile Provinces, above Khartoum linguist and adviser to the government of the Khedive. Most pleasant and easy to get on with.

Sir Bartle and Lady Frere.[63] Clever and amusing. He the celebrated Indian governor and ruler of Scinde.

"Mr Disraeli[64] Lord Beaconsfield" the life-long friend of the Duchess. Lord B. had the highest opinion of the Duke and he consulted him on many of the appointments that he was about to make and did make.

Caroline Duchess of Montrose.[65] Met every body knew every body. Devoted to racing and used to visit Bulstrode for a little quiet.

Earl Grey.[66] Sec[retary] of State for the Colonies. Being lame from birth, he hobbled about the house, and gardens with a stick. A personal friend of the Duke's. They walked much together.

59 Wilfrid Scawen Blunt (1840–1922), traveller, politician and poet. He married in 1869 Anne Isabella Noel (1837–1917), granddaughter of the poet Byron.

60 Sir Richard Burton (1821–90), explorer, scholar and author; translator of *The Arabian Nights* (1885–88). His wife (née Isabel Arundell, 1831–96) shared in his travels and writing.

61 *Recte* mezzofanti, a person of exceptional linguistic ability. From Guiseppe Mezzofanti (1774–1849), an Italian cardinal who was master of more than fifty languages (*OED*).

62 Sir Samuel White Baker (1821–93), explorer and sportsman. Appointed governor-general of the Sudan by the Khedive of Egypt in 1869.

63 Sir (Henry) Bartle Frere (1815–84), bart, statesman; chief commander of Sind, 1850–59.

64 See n.41.

65 Caroline Agnes (d. 1894), wife (1836) of James Graham (1799–1874), 4th Duke of Montrose. She remarried twice.

66 Henry George Grey (1802–94), 3rd Earl Grey (1845), statesman, colonial secretary 1846–52.

I should mention that it was either during the occupation of the old wing at Bulstrode by General Reid or Mr Edwards that I was taken to Bulstrode to see the moon through a telescope.

About 10 o'clock one evening in the early autumn Sir James South,[67] the Astronomer Royal (who was visiting at Bulstrode) came out in front of the wing and set up an enormous telescope on a tripod. It was called a 40 feet reflector. Through it we all looked at the moon by turns.

The moon was over the Lower Gardens on the right of the Windsor Lodge. The interior of the moon seemed a broken up mass of rocks mountains and valleys very rugged and precipitous every-thing so dry. It is said the moon is waterless and no living thing can exist there.

Earl St Maur[68] the Duke's eldest and only surviving son, died Sep[tember] 30 1869. I used to walk with him. On Tuesday, Sep[tember] 28 we met. He did not complain of being ill. Wednesday he went to London to his father's house 20 Dover Street and on Thursday he passed away suddenly. The Duke died Nov[ember] 1885. I had known him intimately for many years. He was one of the best read men I ever met. It was most instructive to be in his company. He was a most intellectual companion.

The ground plan of Burnham Abbey is taken from The Historical Monuments of the County of Bucks published by command 1911.[69]

Notes on the Sculpture and Pictures at Bulstrode

In Hall. "Bust in marble by Chantrey[70] the celebrated sculptor of Lord Webb Seymour.[71] Lord Webb born 1777 died 1819. I believe of consumption. He lived mostly at Edinburgh among the scientific men of that day and was fond of geology. He corresponded with my

67 Sir James South (1785–1867), astronomer.

68 Edward Adolphus Ferdinand (1835–69), the elder of the 12th Duke's two sons. The title of Earl St. Maur was presumably in right of his father, to whom it was granted in 1863.

69 See n.9. The reference is to a rough copy of the plan which has been inserted in the MS.

70 Sir Francis Legatt Chantrey (1781–1841), English sculptor, famed for his portrait statues and busts.

71 Lord Webb Seymour (1777–1819), younger brother of the 11th Duke. He had a lifelong interest in science.

mother all her early life, until his decease. My mother writes to Lord Webb from Maiden Bradley April 19 1818. "Dear Uncle Webb I fear you will think me very negligent for delaying so long to answer your last letter, but I have been very busy translating an Italian pamphlet for Mr Joseph Banks,[72] which describes the manner of making Parmesan cheese."

My mother also writes ["]1819 April 8th. My father went to Edinburgh, having received indifferent accounts of dear Uncle Webb's health. He died April 19 1819. My father was with him. I was much afflicted at the news of his death; for in him I lost a kind relation and a most valuable and enlightened friend["]. He was buried in the Chapel Royal at Holy Rood Castle.

The picture of the Duke of Hamilton[73] by Lonsdale.[74] Charlotte Duchess of Somerset was a favourite child.

My mother writes ["]1819 February 16th. Grand Papa died at Ashton Hall Lancashire about eleven in the evening. 27th. My father went to Lancaster to attend the funeral["].

The picture of Sir Joseph Banks by Lonsdale. A great friend of the Duchess of Somerset. President of the Royal Society 1778 to 1820.

"Elizabeth of York"[75] with the Roses. The Duke hung it in the dining room over the door. He used to say to me. There. You see. The union of the 2 Roses. After his coronation Henry VII married Elizabeth Wydevile the widow of the Lancastrian Sir John Grey of Groby.[76] Picture originally at Maiden Bradley then at Wimbledon Park.

Lord Nelson by Hoppner[77] I believe. The Duke considered it one of the best of the great admiral. On the Duke showing the picture to a lady "perhaps Lady Sligo" she said. Ah. Yes. Duke you mean "the man that was in the navy".

The Duchess of Somerset[78] wife of Webb 10th Duke. "Miss Bonnell" called in the family the Lincolnshire heiress. Brought into the family

---

72 Sir Joseph Banks (1744–1820), the celebrated botanist. He was president of the Royal Society for 41 years. See also below.

73 Archibald Hamilton (1740–1819), 9th Duke of Hamilton and Brandon.

74 James Lonsdale (177–1839), English portrait painter.

75 Elizabeth of York (1465–1503), consort of Henry VII; she was the eldest daughter of Edward IV and Elizabeth Wydville, or Woodville.

76 Blount is here confusing Elizabeth of York with her mother, whose first husband was Sir John Grey.

77 John Hoppner (c.1758–1810), English portrait painter.

78 Mary Anne Bonnell (d. 1802), daughter and sole heiress of John Bonnell of Stanton Harcourt, Oxon; she married Webb Seymour, 10th Duke in 1769.

the Lincolnshire estates the estates left by the 12th Duke to his daughter Lady Ulrica Thynne.[79] Painter not mentioned.

Portrait of "the proud Duke of Somerset"[80] by Sir Godfrey Kneller. Marr[ie]d Elizabeth Percy heiress of the historic family of Percy. The Duke died 1748 aged 87 having filled high offices at the courts "of James 2nd" William III and Queen Anne.

"Catalines Conspiracy" by Salvator Rosa.[81] Much thought of by my mother. Originally at Maiden Bradley I think.

Landscape by Salvator Rosa formerly at Stover.[82] Left by 12th Duke with Stover and all things in it to Harold St Maur, his natural grand-son, illegitimate son of Earl St Maur.[83] Sold at Christie's on sale of Stover collection of pictures. Purchased by Sir John Ramsden.

Portrait of Miss Linley and her brother.[84] A copy from the original picture by Gainsborough[85] at Knole[86] then belonging to Lady De La Warr. It then passed to Lord Sackville and he has sold the original Gainsborough portrait for 40,000£ to Mr Pierrpoint Morgan[87] the, American millionaire. Elizabeth Anne Miss Linley was the elder daughter of Thomas Linley the musical composer. Born 1754. Sang with her sister Mrs Tickell at concerts at Bath. Married Richard Brinsley Sheridan, the celebrated orator and dramatist at Lisle whither she had travelled with the idea of entering a convent. She was remarkable for

---

79 Lady Ulrica Frederica Jane St. Maur (d. 1916), daughter and co-heir of the 12th Duke; she married Lord Henry Thynne in 1858.

80 Charles Seymour (1662–1748), 6th Duke, known as the 'proud'. He married Elizabeth Percy, Countess Ogle, daughter of the last earl of Northumberland.

81 Salvator Rosa (1615–73), Italian painter and poet famed chiefly for his landscapes.

82 Stover Lodge, Torquay, Devon.

83 Richard Harold St. Maur (b. 1869). See also n.68.

84 Elizabeth Linley (1754–92) one of the gifted daughters of Thomas Linley (1732–95), the composer. She married Richard Brinsley Sheridan (1751–1816), the dramatist, in 1773. Their granddaughter Jane Georgiana (1809–84), youngest of the three beautiful daughters of their only son Thomas, married the 12th Duke in 1830. Her two older sisters were Helen Selina (d. 1867), who married Price Blackwood, 4th Baron Dufferin and Claneboye, in 1825, and Caroline Elizabeth Norton (1808–77), poet and novelist, who is said to have been the model for the heroine of George Meredith's novel *Diana of the Crossways*, (1885).

85 Thomas Gainsborough (1727–88), English landscape and portrait painter.

86 Kent mansion, seat of the Sackville (later Sackville-West) family, formerly dukes of Dorset. Mortimer (1820–88), 1st Lord Sackville, was the son of George John West, younger son of the 5th Earl de la Warr and Elizabeth Sackville.

87 John Pierpont Morgan (1837–1913), American banker, financier and art collector.

her beauty. Macaulay[88] in his essay on the trial of Warren Hastings speaks of her. She died of consumption 1792. Her 3 grand-daughters Lady Dufferin Mrs Norton and the Duchess of Somerset were celebrated for their great beauty. Her brother Thomas Linley composer and violinist born 1756, was drowned 1778.

Portrait of Charles 10th Roi de France.[89] In Madame Recamier's[90] Memoires it is mentioned that she came to England in 1802. She was a beautiful woman, and became a great friend of Charlotte Duchess of Somerset and Douglas who became the 10th Duke of Hamilton.[91] On the rupture of the peace of Amiens 1802 Charles 10th was exiled[92] from France by the Emperor Napoleon. Lord Douglas gave him rooms at Holy rood Palace, and for this after his restoration he presented his picture to the Duchess of Somerset. Madame Recamier mentions her walks in Kensington Gardens, with Douglas and her sister. Crowds of people used to walk in Kensington Gardens and gaze at these two beautiful ladies and this very handsome man. Horatio, Duchess of Somerset[93] wife of 14th Duke told me Douglas was a very handsome man.

Earl St Maur by Swinton.[94] Swinton looked at the picture with me and told me he considered it a success. Ferdinand Lord St Maur,[95] eldest son of 12th Duke of Somerset, was summoned to the House of Peers in his father's barony of Seymour. Accompanied Lord Clyde on his staff during the suppression "of the Indian Mutiny" as a volunteer. Volunteered and accompanied Garibaldi in his campaign, undertaken for the freedom of Italy and suppression of the papal states.

Lord Edward St Maur[96] 2nd son of the 12th Duke of Somerset was educated for the diplomatic service and went to the British embassy at

88 Thomas Babington Macaulay (1800–59), 1st Baron Macaulay, historian and author.

89 Charles X (1757–1836), king of France 1824–30, known as the Comte D'Artois before his accession. He fled abroad at the beginning of the Revolution and later lived at Hartwell, Buckinghamshire, and Holyrood.

90 Madame Jeanne Francoise Recamier (177–1849), French beauty and wit; Parisian hostess of the Restoration period.

91 The 10th Duke was actually Alexander (1767–1852), who succeeded to the title in 1819.

92 Charles X was already in exile in 1802. See n.89.

93 *Recte* Horatia (d. 1915), née Morier. She married Algernon Percy Banks, 14th Duke (1891) in 1845.

94 James Rannie Swinton (1816–88), English portrait painter.

95 See n.68.

96 Lord Edward Percy St. Maur (1841–1865), the 12th Duke's younger son.

Madrid; then joined Sir Bartle Frere[97] the governor at Bombay. Went out bear shooting and was killed by a bear December 1885.[98] Picture painted by Swinton who looked at with me and said he was not quite satisfied with it.

Derivation of the name Gerrards Cross

Prior to the Reformation and the Dissolution of the monasteries 1539, it is said a shrine existed on Gerrards Cross. The shrine was called according to the legend St Jarretts Cross.[99]

At this shrine travellers performed their orisons for having arrived so far in safety on the Great Oxford Road the road being the resort of highwaymen and robbers.

At the shrine there was probably a statuette of the Holy Virgin the Mother of God and also one of the Crucified Redeemer.

97 See n.63.

98 *Recte* 1865.

99 A. Mawer and F. M. Stenton, *The Place-Names of Buckinghamshire*, Cambridge, 1925, cites Jarret (1761) as a colloquial form of Gerard, but states that the origin of the place name is unknown.

BUCKINGHAMSHIRE RECORD SOCIETY

The Society was founded in 1937 to publish transcripts, calendars and lists of the primary sources for the history of Buckinghamshire, and generally to stimulate interest in archives relating to the county. The annual subscription for individual members is £15, which entitles a member to receive one free copy of each volume published during the year. Members also have the privilege of purchasing previous volumes still in print at special prices.

Recent and forthcoming volumes include:

Prices quoted do not include postage. Special rates for members are given in parentheses. Publications and details of membership may be obtained from the Honorary Secretary of the Society, County Record Office, County Hall, Aylesbury, Buckinghamshire HP20 1UA.